THE MEGILLAH:
Majesty
&
Mystery

THE MEGILLAH:
Majesty & Mystery

A Commentary on
Megillat Esther
and the
Ma'ariv Evening
Service for Purim

By

RABBI NORMAN LAMM

Compiled and Edited by
JOEL B. WOLOWELSKY

RIETS
YESHIVA UNIVERSITY PRESS

Copyright © 2012 Orthodox Union
Library of Congress Cataloging-in-Publication Data

ISBN: 978-1-60280-197-4

Jacket design by Daniel Harcsztark
Layout by Marzel A.S. — Jerusalem
Manufactured in the United States of America

Published by
RIETS
Yeshiva University Press
500 West 185th street
New York, NY 10033

OU Press
an imprint of the Orthodox Union
11 Broadway
New York, NY 10004
www.oupress.org
oupress@ou.org

Distributed by
KTAV Publishing House, Inc.
888 Newark Avenue, Suite 119
Jersey City, NJ 07306
Tel. (201) 963-9524
Fax. (201) 963-0102
www.ktav.com
orders@ktav.com

In Honor of

the Bat Mitzvah of our Granddaughter
Tova Aliza Sidlow
טובה עליזה שידלוב

October 29, 2011   שבת פרשת נח

Dedicated by
Mordecai D. and Dr. Monique C. Katz

———•———

In Loving Memory of Our Parents

Joseph and Gwendolyn Straus
יוסף שמואל בן בנימין
גיננדל בת משה יעקב

Roslyn Brickman
שושנה בת נחמן זלמן

Dedicated by
Moshael and Zahava Straus

———•———

In Honor of

Rabbi Dr. Norman and Mindy Lamm

*Mentors, role models and sources of inspiration for
our family and the entire Jewish community*

And In Loving Memory of Our Father

Isadore Gibber
יצחק בן אריה ליב

*With an abiding Faith, he appreciated the beauty of God's
World as he personified a life lived with honesty and integrity.*

Dedicated by

Elliot and Debbie Gibber and Family

In Tribute to

Rabbi Dr. and Mrs. Norman Lamm

Whose warmth, dedication, erudition, and friendship have
been, since the 1960's, a significant part of our lives

and

In Loving Memory of Our Parents

Maurice M. and Golde N. Rothman

משה ב"ר חיים יצחק

גאלדע בת צבי זאב

Meyer A. and Lillian Shatz

מאיר ב"ר שרגא דוד

לאה בת חיים שמחה

Dedicated by
Henry and Golda Reena Rothman

———•———

In Loving Memory of

Our Beloved "Uncle Marty"

Martin Schwarzschild

החבר מרדכי בן אשר

Dedicated by
Jeff Singerman and Ruth Borchardt and Family
Murray and Shifra Singerman and Family

Table of Contents

Preface. 9

Introduction 11

Ma'ariv with Commentary 15

Megillat Esther with Commentary 58

Derashot on Days of Salvation and Thanksgiving

    Hanukkah 144

    Yom ha-Atzma'ut 149

    Yom Yerushalayim 163

    Thanksgiving Day. 184

Preface

It is indeed an exceptional honor for OU PRESS, together with RIETS/ Yeshiva University Press, to publish Rabbi Norman Lamm's commentary on Megillat Esther and Ma'ariv for Purim night and to present the Jewish community with this delightful combination of intellectual rigor and eloquent expression. Rabbi Lamm, a gifted communal and educational leader, has devoted his extraordinary and distinguished career to fostering the widespread acceptance of Torah in the contemporary world.

The Zohar comments that *Yom Kippurim*, the Biblical name for the holiday of Yom Kippur, can be read *Yom k'Purim* — a day which is "similar to Purim." What is the nature of this similarity? Yom Kippur and Purim share a common theme — the centrality of Torah and its transmission through the chain of tradition. Each holiday was a day of *kabbalat haTorah* — the receiving and acceptance of Torah. Yom Kippur is the day Moses descended from Mount Sinai with the second Tablets of the Law. The Beit HaLevi, Rabbi Joseph Soloveitchik's great-grandfather, teaches that on that Yom Kippur, Moses also brought down the *Torah Shebe'al Peh*, the Oral Law, which was accepted by the Jewish people and transmitted from one generation to the next, as it was inculcated in the mind of the Jew and inscribed on his soul. Purim, as well, was a day of acceptance of Torah for all generations. Megillat Esther tells us that *"kiy'mu ve-kiblu haYehudim"* — the Jewish people "confirmed and accepted" the observance of Purim for themselves and their descendants. Our rabbis tell us that *"kiy'mu ve-kiblu"* does not refer only to the observance of Purim, but to the entire Torah, and that Purim was the day that the Jewish people confirmed the acceptance of the Torah that had occurred so many centuries before, and reconsecrated themselves to its transmission throughout the generations.

That the acceptance and transmission of Torah are fundamental themes of Purim is not surprising. In the story of Megillat Esther, the actors are buffeted by quixotic winds of chance, at the mercy of random and unpredictable forces. How is the Jew to make sense of what seems to be an existence governed by happenstance? Emerging from the Megillah is the fundamental truth that only through the prism of Torah can a seemingly senseless series of events be integrated into an intelligible worldview. It is a worldview in which the Jewish people are endowed with a unique mission. Through Torah we achieve the realization that Purim's fortuitous confluence of undirected events is, in reality, God's plan. Purim, the day whose narrative tells of a world of chance and apparent lack of purpose, is also the day which celebrates and commemorates Torah, whose message is that, in truth, all of existence is governed by God's direction. How fitting it is that we can now celebrate Purim, a holiday whose theme is the acceptance of Torah and its transmission, with the penetrating insights of Rabbi Norman Lamm.

The material in the commentary is culled from Rabbi Lamm's writings, most from the sermons he delivered at The Jewish Center in New York City. The community owes thanks to Pearl Berger, Dean of Libraries of Yeshiva University, who had the idea of assembling Rabbi Lamm's sermons on the Lamm Heritage website at Yeshiva University. How fortunate were his congregants to hear such powerful *divrei Torah* week after week, and how fortunate are we to have them available to enrich our Purim holiday.

Dr. Joel B. Wolowelsky, the editor of this volume, selected the material and, working with Rabbi Lamm, edited it into a coherent commentary. Dr. Wolowelsky has been invaluable to our community in disseminating Torah through his role as a yeshiva educator and his editorial work for the Toras Horav Foundation and *Tradition*. We are especially grateful for his continued contributions as a significant advisor for OU Press. Rabbi Simon Posner, Executive Editor of OU Press, collaborated with Dr. Wolowelsky and coordinated all aspects of this edition, and David Olivestone, in charge of graphics at the Orthodox Union, supervised the challenging design elements of the book. We thank Daniel Harcsztark, who designed the cover.

We are also most grateful to the following sponsors who provided the financial support for this project: Elliot and Debbie Gibber, Mordecai and Monique Katz, Henry and Golda Rothman, Jeff Singerman and Ruth Borchardt, Murray and Shifra Singerman, and Moshael and Zahava Straus.

Menachem Genack
General Editor, OU Press

Introduction

Let me begin with a brief explanation of the title of this book: *It was not my choice!* In fact, I was puzzled as to a title, and so consulted my children and grandchildren. In order to stimulate their curiosity and encourage their creativity, I confessed my cognitive aridity and solicited their help. I announced a contest: Whoever of my family produces the title that I am seeking will have his or her name credited in this Introduction and will be my guest in a restaurant of his or her choosing. I insisted that the primary focus of the title be on Purim and be appropriate to the general theme of "Days of Salvation and Thanksgiving," a theme that would include some sermons on Hanukkah, Yom ha-Atzma'ut, and Yom Yerushalayim. My older son Joshua was in general in charge of the "contest," but the choice of the most acceptable title would be mine and mine alone.

I was overwhelmed by their imagination and originality. The two winners were my younger daughter, Sara Lamm Dratch, who proposed *The Megillah: Majesty and Mystery,* and my grandson-in-law, Stuart Halpern, who proposed *The Megillah: Mystery and Majesty.* The two winning titles were almost identical, and I shall happily take both winners to dinner.

The "majesty" part is fairly obvious: the Purim story, as recorded in the *Megillah,* revolves around two "majesties": Ahashverosh, the king of Persia, a man of consummate stupidity; and Esther, the charming Jewess who was chosen by the king to be his queen after winning a national beauty contest. Each of them resorted to others: Ahashverosh, who in an act of characteristic obtuseness listened to Haman, who planned to commit genocide against all the Jews in the one hundred and twenty-seven provinces of his realm; and the heroic Esther, who listened to Mordecai, her wise uncle and guide, who was, in a literary sense, the counterpart of Haman.

11 ⤸

The "mystery" was manifold: how Esther attained her throne by modesty and understatement in a society that spent half the year in drunken orgies, and whose predecessor lost her royal position by defying the king's humiliating order to appear in public unclothed; how Haman was so offended by Mordecai's refusal to bow to him, a rapacious official whose vaunting ambition and concupiscence could not be satisfied as long as a single "unofficial" Jew would not subscribe to the apotheosis and fulsome adulation he demanded of his subjects. And so on.

But the mystery aspect of the *Megillah* is far more than this strange story of foolish kings, evil officials, beautiful princesses, and wise relatives. A more profound and puzzling phenomenon is negative, namely, the total "blackout" of any mention of the Deity: the only book in the entire Hebrew Bible in which there is no direct mention of God! How does a volume of this sort find its way into the Tanakh? We shall discuss this problem later in the text.

We must first confront the problem of what we may call the "double face" of the *Megillah*. On the one hand, the narrative is deadly serious — the threatened genocide of all the Jews in the land of the Persians and the Medes, probably the heaviest concentration of Jews in the ancient world. On the other, the story takes a radical turn and the pro-active Mordecai stirs his niece — the beautiful but apparently passive queen, Esther — into action. The quiet, modest Esther now shows her leadership ability by tricking the archenemy Haman to the palace and getting the king to turn the tables against him and his cohorts.

The results of the two halves of the tale are celebrated by the Jews, the intended victims, by remembering the awful horrors that were intended for them, by fasting and praying; and then the utter joy at their deliverance, a rescue engineered by clever ploys — first by Mordecai, then by Esther. The dread and terror followed by deliverance calls for an expression of gratitude for the salvation. The Halakhah is clear in legislating our expected conduct, and an entire tractate of the Talmud is dedicated to Purim, and especially to the writing and reading of *Megillat Esther*, the sacred scroll which tells the story of Purim, the timing of the reading, who is required to attend the reading, and several mitzvot attendant upon the acts of remembrance and the gratitude expressed by exchange of gifts, special prayers, and acts of charity. The Halakhah is as specific and intellectually challenging in the celebration of Purim as it is in any of the Biblical commandments — even though the laws of Purim are of rabbinical, not scriptural provenance.

And yet, despite the seriousness with which the Halakhah takes Purim and the *Megillah*, there is an overlay of levity and joy which is inescapable. Even the most solemn yeshivas have evening celebrations of dancing and what today would be called "clean fun" — students would choose one of their own to act as the "Purim Rebbe," dressing up in their teacher's rabbinic uniform, imitating the teacher's speech patterns, and giving a *she'ur* which is usually a form of brilliant nonsense — as is the so-called *Kiddush,* which is a string of verses that can be hilarious (since there is no formal *Kiddush* prescribed for this day). Students often use this as an opportunity to say things they would not dare to say to or about their rabbis — but Purim is an exception! I recall reading a serious, even profound halakhic discourse that tried to find halakhic justification for such infractions as ridiculing one's teacher, playful "stealing," cross-dressing, and other carrying-on which would ordinarily be frowned upon as bordering on sexual misconduct. This redemption called for a special kind of jubilation, one that comes close to what we of later centuries might call "fun."

All this, and other such borderline phenomena, are probably related to or derived from the remarkable exception concerning excessive indulgence in alcohol. Thus, the Talmud (*Megillah* 7b) records, "Rava said: A person is obligated to drink on Purim until he does not know the difference between 'Cursed be Haman' and 'Blessed be Mordecai' " — encouragement to feed the spirit with spirits. Whether this ruling was accepted by all authorities is beside the point. Even as sober a character as Maimonides codifies as Halakhah the statement of Rava — but his personality comes through when he adds: "What is the obligation of the [Purim] feast? It is that one should drink wine until he is drunk *and falls asleep from drunkenness*" (*Mishneh Torah, Hilkhot Megillah* 2:15). The Rama, several centuries later, comments: "There are others who say that one need not become *that* drunk, but rather that one should drink more than is one's custom ... whether one drinks more or drinks less, the main thing, is that his intention is for the sake of Heaven" (*Shulhan Arukh, Orah Hayyim* 695:2). (My own interpretation of Rava's statement is that the difference between "Cursed be Haman" and "Blessed be Mordecai" is really not that great! One is effectively a restatement of the other.) The fact remains that the statement of Rava is quite unusual, and it may be that the popularity of this dictum paved the way for the halakhic toleration of the loosening of the usual strictness, at least at on Purim proper.

* * *

I am once again indebted to Rabbi Menachem Genack, General Editor of the OU Press, whose vision inspired this series. Finally, I owe special and public commendation to the editor of this volume and of my *Royal Table: A Passover Haggadah*, Dr. Joel Wolowelsky, whose keen intellect is enhanced by his pleasantness of demeanor, and whose editorial skill is equaled only by his profound comprehension of the material involved — and exceeded only by his personal dedication to the goal he shares with me as author, namely, the teaching of Torah by all means.

Norman Lamm

מַעֲרִיב

The prayer of *Ma'ariv* is halakhically different from the other two daily prayers, *Shaharit* and *Minhah*, in that the latter two are considered obligatory, whereas the *Ma'ariv* service is considered voluntary — in the sense that one may dispense with the prayer if another occasion of mitzvah presents itself at the same time. Normally, it is taken that *Ma'ariv* is therefore less important than the other two prayers. But the contrary may be true: *Ma'ariv* is more precious, more difficult, and more demanding, for it is a far greater challenge to hold your own, to keep the faith, when the sun has set, when it is dark all about, when night signals danger. It is for this reason that this prayer is considered voluntary rather than obligatory. Except for very rare cases, the Torah does not legislate heroism as obligatory. It is, rather, a privilege to be able to know of the coming dawn when the sun has begun to set. So let us prayerfully know and understand that the darkness will yet end, and we shall be safe and secure and strong, despite the sudden night that has descended upon the world.

מַעֲרִיב לְפוּרִים

וְהוּא רַחוּם יְכַפֵּר עָוֹן וְלֹא יַשְׁחִית, וְהִרְבָּה לְהָשִׁיב אַפּוֹ וְלֹא יָעִיר כָּל חֲמָתוֹ. יְיָ הוֹשִׁיעָה הַמֶּלֶךְ יַעֲנֵנוּ בְיוֹם קָרְאֵנוּ:

ש"ץ: בָּרְכוּ אֶת יְיָ הַמְבוֹרָךְ:

קהל וש"ץ: בָּרוּךְ יְיָ הַמְבוֹרָךְ לְעוֹלָם וָעֶד:

בָּרוּךְ אַתָּה יְיָ, אֱלֹהֵינוּ מֶלֶךְ הָעוֹלָם, אֲשֶׁר בִּדְבָרוֹ מַעֲרִיב עֲרָבִים, בְּחָכְמָה פּוֹתֵחַ שְׁעָרִים, וּבִתְבוּנָה מְשַׁנֶּה עִתִּים, וּמַחֲלִיף אֶת הַזְּמַנִּים, וּמְסַדֵּר אֶת הַכּוֹכָבִים, בְּמִשְׁמְרוֹתֵיהֶם בָּרָקִיעַ כִּרְצוֹנוֹ. בּוֹרֵא יוֹם וָלָיְלָה, גּוֹלֵל אוֹר

וּמְסַדֵּר אֶת הַכּוֹכָבִים *and arranges the stars.* When the artist Van Gogh was asked about his famous expressionistic painting *The Starry Night,* he said, "I felt a need of — shall I say the word? — religion, and so I went out and painted the stars." It is the very permanence of the stars and the solace they offer to an unstable society that makes them the symbol of religion. It is this fixity amidst flux that Torah offers and that the Messiah will teach. The religion of Torah does not change with the times. It is not subject to the whims of the public opinion poll. Its strength derives from its perennial reliability.

Nevertheless, we must also stress that while Torah is changeless, it must always be relevant to a changing society. It must not be so changeless that it has nothing to do with man who is always in a state of change. Judaism must address man in his changing conditions, it must speak to man of value and faith, of loyalty and honor and meaning, as they apply to his times and his society. But Judaism cannot do this if the teachers of Torah turn their backs on the rest of mankind. This is what we mean when we appeal for the relevance of Judaism, and this is our argument with those who would cut themselves off from modern society completely.

The stars can guide man only when they are visible. If clouds of distrust and diffidence cover the stars, they are of precious little use to man. So the advocates of Torah must speak to modern man in his

MA'ARIV FOR PURIM

And He, being merciful, forgives iniquity, and does not destroy. Many a time He turns His anger away, and does not stir up all His wrath. Save, Lord! May the King answer us on the day when we call.

Leader: **Bless the Lord, the blessed One.**

Cong. and Leader: **Blessed is the Lord, the blessed One, forever and ever.**

Blessed are You, O Lord our God, King of the Universe, Who at His word brings on the evening twilight, with wisdom opens the gates of the heavens, and with understanding changes times and varies the seasons, and arranges the stars in their watches in the sky, according to His will. He creates day and night, rolling away

---

own idiom, they must respect his intelligence, and feel with him in his misery. When the Rabbis of old complained that "Torah lies neglected In a hidden corner" (*Kiddushin* 66a), they did not mean for us to crawl into that corner with it and turn our backs on the world. Rather, they meant for us to take Torah out of that *keren zavit*, that hidden corner, and bring it into the center of the world scene, into the maelstrom of daily events, into the midst of the raging torrents of the times, and with it to offer man abiding faith and enduring stability.

Torah must not be a sealed book written in an ancient and undecipherable language, nor must it be a running commentary of religious journalese. It must be the *sefer ha-hayyim*, the Book of Life. That is a difficult task — to be permanent and yet relevant, changeless and yet germane. It means that while affirming the unchanging nature of Halakhah, we must be able to explain it in terms of a changing society; that while teaching the timeless truths of Torah, we must relate them to issues that are timely. Above all, we must not be afraid to say that we do not have all the answers, and yet we must never cease searching for them.

מִפְּנֵי חֹשֶׁךְ, וְחֹשֶׁךְ מִפְּנֵי אוֹר. וּמַעֲבִיר יוֹם וּמֵבִיא לַיְלָה, וּמַבְדִּיל בֵּין יוֹם
וּבֵין לַיְלָה, יְיָ צְבָאוֹת שְׁמוֹ. אֵל חַי וְקַיָּם, תָּמִיד יִמְלוֹךְ עָלֵינוּ לְעוֹלָם וָעֶד.
בָּרוּךְ אַתָּה יְיָ, הַמַּעֲרִיב עֲרָבִים:

אַהֲבַת עוֹלָם בֵּית יִשְׂרָאֵל עַמְּךָ אָהָבְתָּ, תּוֹרָה וּמִצְוֹת, חֻקִּים וּמִשְׁפָּטִים,
אוֹתָנוּ לִמַּדְתָּ. עַל כֵּן יְיָ אֱלֹהֵינוּ, בְּשָׁכְבֵנוּ וּבְקוּמֵנוּ נָשִׂיחַ בְּחֻקֶּיךָ, וְנִשְׂמַח
בְּדִבְרֵי תוֹרָתֶךָ וּבְמִצְוֹתֶיךָ לְעוֹלָם וָעֶד. כִּי הֵם חַיֵּינוּ וְאֹרֶךְ יָמֵינוּ, וּבָהֶם
נֶהְגֶּה יוֹמָם וָלַיְלָה, וְאַהֲבָתְךָ אַל תָּסִיר מִמֶּנּוּ לְעוֹלָמִים. בָּרוּךְ אַתָּה יְיָ,
אוֹהֵב עַמּוֹ יִשְׂרָאֵל:

___

אַהֲבַת עוֹלָם *With everlasting love.* Religious feelings are a response to God's concern for man. The love that we feel for God is a reaction to the love God has for us — even as, in our *Shaharit* and *Ma'ariv* services, we read first the *Ahavah Rabbah* or *Ahavat Olam*, the declaration of divine love for us, and then we read the *Shema*, which is immediately followed by "*v'ahavta et Hashem Elohekha*, you shall love the Lord your God" (Deuteronomy 6:5), the love of man for God. God's love for man evokes man's love for God; there is a holy reciprocity between the Creator and His creatures.

אוֹהֵב עַמּוֹ יִשְׂרָאֵל *Who loves His people Israel.* Divine solitude evokes in us our own sense of loneliness in the universe, and not only when we face death. As we meet God, loneliness encounters loneliness; and as each of us offers his loneliness as a gift to the other, we experience relief, as it were, from cosmic loneliness. It is not, of course, that God literally experiences loneliness as we do; we are, certainly, beyond such crude anthropomorphisms. Rather, in our religious imagination we project our own loneliness upon God, conceiving of Him too as suffering from this vast and incredible loneliness, and thus allowing man and God to sympathize with each other. Both God and human beings deserve *rachmones*, pity — we, for our failure and pain and suffering, and God, for being abandoned by this creature created in His very own image

the light from before the darkness, and the darkness from before the light. He makes the day to pass and the night to approach, and divides the day from the night; the Lord of Hosts is His Name. A God living and enduring continually, may He reign over us forever and ever. Blessed are You, O Lord, Who brings on the evening twilight.

With everlasting love You have loved the house of Israel, Your people. Torah and commandments, statutes and judgments You taught us. Therefore, O Lord our God, when we lie down and when we rise up we will speak of Your statutes, and we will rejoice in the words of Your Torah and in Your commandments forever. For they are our life and the length of our days, and we will meditate on them day and night. And never take away Your love from us. Blessed are You, O Lord, Who loves His people Israel.

---

and endowed with the gift of free will that we misuse and abuse. And so each waits and longs for the other. The way to bridge the brooding cosmic loneliness, to find our way to each other, is through love. It is this sense of mutual sympathy that gives rise to love of God who reaches out for us with love, as affirmed in the blessing immediately preceding the *Shema*: "Blessed are You, O Lord, who chooses His people Israel *in love*." And we, recognizing that "the Lord is One," that the Creator is alone, yearning for our companionship, respond with love immediately after proclaiming God's utter oneness: "You shall *love* the Lord your God with all your heart …"

Both love and justice exist in God's world. Both are necessary. But we, in our lives, must emphasize the aspect of love. We do not *worship* God's love. We love to worship, and therefore imitate Him in His love. We do not wax poetic about love. We try to practice it prosaically. It is not, for us, some distant *ideal*. It is a *principle* that governs our daily behavior. We are not satisfied with dwelling upon it in our prayers. Rather, we emphasize it in Torah, make it part of our Halakhah, and therefore it becomes for us more real and relevant.

(יחיד אומר: אֵל מֶלֶךְ נֶאֱמָן)

שְׁמַע יִשְׂרָאֵל, יְיָ אֱלֹהֵינוּ, יְיָ אֶחָד:

בלחש: בָּרוּךְ שֵׁם כְּבוֹד מַלְכוּתוֹ לְעוֹלָם וָעֶד

וְאָהַבְתָּ אֵת יְיָ אֱלֹהֶיךָ, בְּכָל־לְבָבְךָ, וּבְכָל־נַפְשְׁךָ, וּבְכָל־מְאֹדֶךָ. וְהָיוּ הַדְּבָרִים הָאֵלֶּה, אֲשֶׁר אָנֹכִי מְצַוְּךָ הַיּוֹם, עַל־לְבָבֶךָ: וְשִׁנַּנְתָּם לְבָנֶיךָ, וְדִבַּרְתָּ בָּם בְּשִׁבְתְּךָ בְּבֵיתֶךָ, וּבְלֶכְתְּךָ בַדֶּרֶךְ וּבְשָׁכְבְּךָ,

---

בָּרוּךְ שֵׁם כְּבוֹד מַלְכוּתוֹ לְעוֹלָם וָעֶד *Blessed be the Name of His glorious kingdom is for ever and ever.* The three major themes found in *Barukh shem kevod* aptly reflect the first verse of the *Shema*, which explains why this traditional verse is paired with the Biblical verse, the *Shema* itself. The *Shema* obviously expresses praise of the Creator. It also implies God's eternity: the three mentions of the divine Name in the *Shema* refer to God's sovereignty before creation, during the existence of the universe, and after the destruction of all creation. And the *Shema* and *Barukh shem kevod* are paired as responsive affirmations of the holiness of God, both sanctifying the divine Name.

עַל לְבָבֶךָ *upon your heart.* The Rabbi of Kotzk asked: Why, in the *Shema*, do we read:

"These words shall be al *levavekha*, on your heart" and not "*bi-levave-kha*, in your heart"? And he answers: It is not too often that the heart is open and that the words of God can enter directly into it. Usually the heart is closed, indifferent, and even callous. The Torah demands that if the words of the Lord cannot come right into an open heart, then at least they shall be placed on the closed heart, so that during those moments of greatness and inspiration when the human heart suddenly opens up, the words of Torah which had been piled on it will tumble in and fill the heart with the seeds of true greatness and sublimity. The reward for the strenuous efforts made during the long, dreary, dismal, and uninspired times comes during these rare but precious moments of spiritual greatness.

וְשִׁנַּנְתָּם *You shall teach them diligently. Ve-shinantam,* generally translated

(*When prayers are not said with a minyan, add:* God, faithful King!)

Hear, O Israel: the Lord is our God, the Lord is One.

In an undertone: Blessed be the Name of His glorious kingdom is forever and ever.

And you shall love the Lord your God with all your heart, and with all your soul, and with all your might. These words, which I command you this day, shall be upon your heart. You shall teach them diligently to your children, and you shall talk of them when you sit in your house, and when you walk by the way, and when

---

as "you shall teach them [i.e., the words of the Torah] diligently to your children," derives from a Hebrew word meaning "sharp" or "acute." This diligence characterizes a teacher who seeks not merely to stuff quantities of information into a student's head, but who trains him in the intricacies of reasoning, who teaches him an approach to dialectical thinking, and who introduces him to the joys of intellectual and spiritual activity. "Your children" does not necessarily refer to one's own children, maintains the *Sifrei*, but to one's students as well: "Even as one's students are called his children, so is he called their father" (*Sifrei, Va'ethanan* 37). Thus, while it is certainly meritorious to teach Torah to one's own children, the mitzvah extends to all Jewish children.

וּבְלֶכְתְּךָ בַדֶּרֶךְ *and when you walk by the way.* In its halakhic analysis, the Talmud sees in this verse an exclusion: When you sit and walk, that is, when you are engaged in mundane, permissible activities, then you are required to read the *Shema*; but if you are occupied with obligatory activities, i.e., the performance of a mitzvah, then you are exempt from reciting the *Shema* (*Berakhot* 11a). This expresses the halakhic principle that one who is already engaged in performing a mitzvah is excused from other positive mitzvot that may come his way at the same time. In regard to reciting the *Shema*, the Talmud offers the special case of a groom on his wedding night: Because his mind is preoccupied with thoughts of his bride and the consummation of their relationship — a mitzvah — he need not recite the *Shema* that night, for it may be assumed that he will not have proper *kavvanah* in his recitation.

וּבְקוּמֶךָ. וּקְשַׁרְתָּם לְאוֹת עַל־יָדֶךָ, וְהָיוּ לְטֹטָפֹת בֵּין עֵינֶיךָ, וּכְתַבְתָּם עַל
מְזֻזֹת בֵּיתֶךָ וּבִשְׁעָרֶיךָ:

Nevertheless, an early authority advocates the reverse point of view: Pseudo-Targum Jonathan, an early translator of Scripture into Aramaic, sees in the words "when you sit in your house" a veiled reference to one building a new home or family, i.e., a groom on his wedding night. Thus, the verse is inclusive rather than exclusionary: it includes the groom in the ranks of those required to read the *Shema* ("You talk of it") *at all times.*

וּבְשָׁכְבְּךָ וּבְקוּמֶךָ *and when you lie down, and when you rise up.* According to the scholars of the House of Hillel, the terms "when you lie down" and "when you rise up" refer to evening and morning, respectively (*Berakhot* 10b). Why then did the Torah not say so explicitly, "you shall talk of them … in the evening and in the morning"?

An insightful answer is provided by Rabbi Zadok Hakohen of Lublin: "evening" and "morning" refer to the natural world; they are astronomical terms, with no special relevance to human beings. Thus, were the Torah to specify "evening" and "morning," we might have interpreted the conjunction *vav* as meaning "or" rather than "and," and we would have deduced that it is sufficient to recite the *Shema*, the acceptance of the yoke of the Kingdom of Heaven, only once a day. But since the Torah speaks explicitly of going to sleep *and* (the letter *vav)* getting up, speaking in human terms, we know that we are commanded to recite the *Shema* twice during the course of our day.

For human beings, day and night are qualitatively and functionally different. Upon rising in the morning, we face a workday; when we go to sleep, we are ready for rest, for physical rejuvenation and mental refreshment. Hence, in the morning we need to recite the *Shema* and accept upon ourselves the yoke of the Kingdom of Heaven so that we succeed in dedicating our varied activities of the day for the sake of Heaven. That is, we pray that our mundane work, whatever its nature, be impregnated with higher meaning, that it fit into a transcendental context. We set our intention on hoping that our major mundane occupations be consonant with our ultimate values. However, when we retire, facing the quotidian period of sleep and rest, we need a different

you lie down, and when you rise up. And you shall bind them for a sign upon your hand, and they shall be for frontlets between your eyes. And you shall write them upon the door posts of your house, and upon your gates.

---

affirmation, namely, that we are submitting ourselves to the yoke of Heaven. Here our need to recite the *Shema* is more subtle, for even when lying in bed and preparing for sleep, a person must know "before Whom he lies." This is a far more difficult task, for it is easier to focus on an action than to dedicate a period of rest and physical inactivity to a higher end.

וּכְתַבְתָּם עַל מְזֻזוֹת בֵּיתֶךָ וּבִשְׁעָרֶיךָ *And you shall write them upon the door posts of your house, and upon your gates.* The concluding passage of the first paragraph of the *Shema* deals with the second of the two "practical," or ceremonial, mitzvot singled out for mention in the *Shema*. The principle behind the mitzvah of *mezuzah* is essentially the same as that for *tefillin*: it is a sign of our love for God. But whereas *tefillin* applies to the personal self, the individual *qua* individual, the mitzvah of *mezuzah* applies to our home — our family and, by extension, our community, city, and country. The belief in the absolute unity of God and the consequent command to love Him are incumbent upon the Jew in all the concentric circles that define his daily existence and endeavors. Not only must the *mezuzah* be affixed to "the posts of your house" but, equally, "upon your gates." The latter term comprises all forms of domicile: "whether it be the gates of courtyards or the gates of alley-ways or the gates of towns and cities — all are required to have a *mezuzah* affixed to them," writes Maimonides in his halakhic code (*Hilkhot Sefer Torah* 6:8). Regarding the purpose of the mitzvah, Maimonides continues: "whenever he comes in or goes out, he will encounter the unity of the Name of the Holy One, and he will recall his love for Him and bestir himself from his slumber and his idle thoughts about his temporal vanities; and he will know that nothing endures forever and ever, save the knowledge of the Rock of Ages. Thus, he will regain his senses and walk in the way of the righteous." Here again, as in the case of *tefillin*, Maimonides emphasizes the love for God as a leitmotif of *mezuzah*. It is interesting to note that in Maimonides' halakhic *magnum opus*, divided into

וְהָיָה אִם־שָׁמֹעַ תִּשְׁמְעוּ אֶל־מִצְוֹתַי, אֲשֶׁר אָנֹכִי מְצַוֶּה אֶתְכֶם הַיּוֹם,
לְאַהֲבָה אֶת יְיָ אֱלֹהֵיכֶם, וּלְעָבְדוֹ בְּכָל־לְבַבְכֶם וּבְכָל נַפְשְׁכֶם. וְנָתַתִּי מְטַר־
אַרְצְכֶם בְּעִתּוֹ, יוֹרֶה וּמַלְקוֹשׁ, וְאָסַפְתָּ דְגָנֶךָ וְתִירשְׁךָ וְיִצְהָרֶךָ. וְנָתַתִּי
עֵשֶׂב בְּשָׂדְךָ לִבְהֶמְתֶּךָ, וְאָכַלְתָּ וְשָׂבָעְתָּ. הִשָּׁמְרוּ לָכֶם פֶּן־יִפְתֶּה לְבַבְכֶם,
וְסַרְתֶּם וַעֲבַדְתֶּם אֱלֹהִים אֲחֵרִים וְהִשְׁתַּחֲוִיתֶם לָהֶם. וְחָרָה אַף־יְיָ בָּכֶם,
וְעָצַר אֶת־הַשָּׁמַיִם וְלֹא־יִהְיֶה מָטָר, וְהָאֲדָמָה לֹא תִתֵּן אֶת־יְבוּלָהּ וַאֲבַדְתֶּם
מְהֵרָה מֵעַל הָאָרֶץ הַטֹּבָה אֲשֶׁר יְיָ נֹתֵן לָכֶם: וְשַׂמְתֶּם אֶת דְּבָרַי אֵלֶּה עַל־
לְבַבְכֶם וְעַל־נַפְשְׁכֶם וּקְשַׁרְתֶּם אֹתָם לְאוֹת עַל־יֶדְכֶם, וְהָיוּ לְטוֹטָפֹת בֵּין
עֵינֵיכֶם: וְלִמַּדְתֶּם אֹתָם אֶת־בְּנֵיכֶם, לְדַבֵּר בָּם, בְּשִׁבְתְּךָ בְּבֵיתֶךָ, וּבְלֶכְתְּךָ
בַדֶּרֶךְ, וּבְשָׁכְבְּךָ וּבְקוּמֶךָ: וּכְתַבְתָּם עַל־מְזוּזוֹת בֵּיתֶךָ וּבִשְׁעָרֶיךָ: לְמַעַן
יִרְבּוּ יְמֵיכֶם וִימֵי בְנֵיכֶם עַל הָאֲדָמָה אֲשֶׁר נִשְׁבַּע יְיָ לַאֲבֹתֵיכֶם לָתֵת לָהֶם,
כִּימֵי הַשָּׁמַיִם עַל־הָאָרֶץ:

---

fourteen separate "books," the second book, *Sefer Ahavah*, "The Book of Love," begins with the Laws of the *Shema*. It then continues with the Laws of Prayer, *Tefillin*, *Mezuzah*, the Scroll of the Torah, the *Tzitzit*, the Blessings, and Circumcision; all of these, in one way or another, are intimately connected to the *Grundprinzip* of the love for God. Thus we find that the whole of the first paragraph of the *Shema* — from the proclamation of God's unity through the commandment to love Him and, finally, to the mitzvot of *tefillin* and *mezuzah* — form one cohesive whole.

וְאָסַפְתָּ דְגָנֶךָ וְתִירשְׁךָ וְיִצְהָרֶךָ *that you may gather in your grain, and your wine, and your oil.* The Talmud presents to us a remarkable idea (*Berakhot* 35b). Rabbi Ishmael makes the following comment: We know that Torah must be studied constantly, "and you shall meditate in it by day and by night." But if that is the case, and if we are to take the Bible with all seriousness, then man must study all the time, whether by day or by night, and have no time to pursue any other interests or activities, even to working to support himself and his family. How, then, do we know that man is indeed permitted to work for a living? He answers: We read in the second passage of the *Shema* the verse "and you shall gather in

And it shall come to pass, if you shall hearken diligently to My commandments which I command you this day, to love the Lord your God and to serve Him with all your heart and with all your soul, that I will give rain in your land in its season, the early rain and the late rain, that you may gather in your grain, and your wine, and your oil. And I will give grass in your field for your cattle, and you shall eat and be satisfied. Take heed to yourselves, lest your heart be seduced, and you turn aside, and serve other gods, and worship them. Then the anger of the Lord will be kindled against you, and He will shut up the heaven, so that there will be no rain, and that the land will not yield her fruit; and you will perish quickly from off the good land which the Lord gives you. Therefore, you shall lay these my words on your heart and on your soul; and you shall bind them for a sign upon your hand, and they shall be for frontlets between your eyes. And you shall teach them to your children, talking of them when you sit in your house, and when you walk by the way, and when you lie down, and when you rise up. And you shall write them upon the doorposts of your house, and upon your gates, so that your days and the days of your children may be multiplied upon the land which the Lord swore to your ancestors to give them, as the days of the heavens above the earth.

---

your corn and your wine and your oil." Thus, the Bible explicitly tells us that we are permitted to work at profane activities, to gather in our harvest, to make a living. From this we know, concludes Rabbi Ishmael, that a man is permitted to spend time away from Torah in order to advance his livelihood. What this means, therefore, is that Torah is the main activity of life, and we may do other things only because they enhance this major activity of our existence. It is not that we must study a little Torah during a lifetime which is devoted primarily to business or profession, but that the time we spend in our secular activities is only a *hetter*, a special dispensation, for time taken away from our only legitimate activity, namely, Talmud Torah.

וַיֹּאמֶר יְיָ אֶל־מֹשֶׁה לֵּאמֹר: דַּבֵּר אֶל־בְּנֵי יִשְׂרָאֵל וְאָמַרְתָּ אֲלֵהֶם: וְעָשׂוּ
לָהֶם צִיצִת עַל־כַּנְפֵי בִגְדֵיהֶם לְדֹרֹתָם, וְנָתְנוּ עַל־צִיצִת הַכָּנָף פְּתִיל
תְּכֵלֶת. וְהָיָה לָכֶם לְצִיצִת, וּרְאִיתֶם אֹתוֹ וּזְכַרְתֶּם אֶת־כָּל־מִצְוֹת יְיָ,
וַעֲשִׂיתֶם אֹתָם, וְלֹא תָתוּרוּ אַחֲרֵי לְבַבְכֶם וְאַחֲרֵי עֵינֵיכֶם, אֲשֶׁר־אַתֶּם
זֹנִים אַחֲרֵיהֶם: לְמַעַן תִּזְכְּרוּ וַעֲשִׂיתֶם אֶת־כָּל־מִצְוֹתָי, וִהְיִיתֶם קְדֹשִׁים
לֵאלֹהֵיכֶם: אֲנִי יְיָ אֱלֹהֵיכֶם, אֲשֶׁר הוֹצֵאתִי אֶתְכֶם מֵאֶרֶץ מִצְרַיִם, לִהְיוֹת
לָכֶם לֵאלֹהִים, אֲנִי יְיָ אֱלֹהֵיכֶם: אֱמֶת

תְּכֵלֶת *blue*. The Sages quote God as saying, "I will punish one who affixes a thread dyed blue and announces that it really is *tekhelet*" (*Bava Metzia* 61b). *Tekhelet*, coming from the rare mollusk *halazon*, is expensive and scarce; *kala ilan* is a common and cheap vegetable dye called indigo. One who dyes his fringes with *kala ilan* and proclaims it to be *tekhelet* is therefore palming off the artificial as genuine. The statement in the Talmud is, therefore, a protest against hypocrisy and deception.

But it is worth pondering what was said on this Talmudic passage by the late and sainted thinker and scholar Rabbi Abraham Chen ("*Be-Malkhut ha-Yahadut*"): The reverse is true as well! God is also displeased with one who possesses the genuine *tekhelet* and yet proclaims that it is merely the artificial *kala ilan*. God will punish not only the hypocrite who passes off the artificial as genuine, but He also dislikes the coward who disguises the authentic as the inauthentic. In other words, there is a strong, neurotic tendency for some people to have the courage only of other people's opinions — but not their own! They are afflicted with a moral weakness: they are ashamed of their elementary decency, they are apprehensive lest they have too good a reputation; they are fearful lest their virtue prove antisocial. There are, apparently, those who wear *tekhelet* but proclaim that it is only *kala ilan*. It is much like a man who enters a restaurant in the company of colleagues or business associates and is handed the menu, and, with nervous eyes darting in all directions, clears his throat and apologetically whispers that he is a vegetarian. We must not submit to the moral cowardice of disguising our *tekhelet* as *kala ilan*. Let us show our true Jewish colors — and be proud of them.

And the Lord spoke to Moses, saying, Speak to the children of Israel, and bid them to make a fringe upon the corners of their garments, throughout their generations; and that they put upon the fringe of each corner a cord of blue. And it shall be to you for a fringe, that you may look upon it and remember all the commandments of the Lord, and do them; and that you not go about after your own heart and your own eyes, after which you use to go astray: that you may remember and do all My commandments, and be holy to your God. I am the Lord your God, Who brought you out of the land of Egypt, to be your God: I am the Lord your God. True —

אֲשֶׁר הוֹצֵאתִי אֶתְכֶם מֵאֶרֶץ מִצְרַיִם *Who brought you out of the land of Egypt.* There are times when God's relations with the world are more intense than normal, when they are extraordinary, far above the usual. These are the times when, but for God's direct intervention and concern with man, the "normal" course of events would inexorably drive him to certain perdition. There are certain critical moments in history, such as the Exodus from Egypt, when all natural laws and historical processes seem to be suspended, as the Eternal pierces the present, and the timeless parts the curtains of time and steps onto the stage of history.

It is in these unique moments when we suddenly become aware of the fact that God's love for us is more than the constant and consistent love of God for man, that which gives man his very existence and breath and being, but is a special, fiery, passionate, ineffable kind of love that is sacred, unquenchable, and inextinguishable, and in which God reveals Himself to human beings, and especially to the people of Israel. And then the Jew comes to a new understanding, an appreciation of the love that God has for him; then his only response is, in turn, a fiery and passionate reaching out for God. Then all of existence seems to be transformed to a new level of transcendence, when suddenly, climactically, and dramatically a new vision ennobles man's soul, a new understanding grips his mind, and a powerful love elevates his heart to unprecedented heights. Then man, too, offers up a love of fire for his beloved Redeemer.

At this moment the soul of the Jew strives to wrench loose from its

הש״ץ חוזר ואומר: יְיָ אֱלֹהֵיכֶם אֱמֶת

וֶאֱמוּנָה כָּל זֹאת, וְקַיָּם עָלֵינוּ, כִּי הוּא יְיָ אֱלֹהֵינוּ וְאֵין זוּלָתוֹ, וַאֲנַחְנוּ יִשְׂרָאֵל
עַמּוֹ. הַפּוֹדֵנוּ מִיַּד מְלָכִים, מַלְכֵּנוּ הַגּוֹאֲלֵנוּ מִכַּף כָּל הֶעָרִיצִים. הָאֵל הַנִּפְרָע
לָנוּ מִצָּרֵינוּ, וְהַמְשַׁלֵּם גְּמוּל לְכָל אֹיְבֵי נַפְשֵׁנוּ, הָעוֹשֶׂה גְדוֹלוֹת עַד אֵין
חֵקֶר, וְנִפְלָאוֹת עַד אֵין מִסְפָּר. הַשָּׂם נַפְשֵׁנוּ בַּחַיִּים, וְלֹא נָתַן לַמּוֹט רַגְלֵנוּ,
הַמַּדְרִיכֵנוּ עַל בָּמוֹת אוֹיְבֵינוּ, וַיָּרֶם קַרְנֵנוּ, עַל כָּל שׂוֹנְאֵנוּ, הָעוֹשֶׂה לָּנוּ נִסִּים
וּנְקָמָה בְּפַרְעֹה, אוֹתוֹת וּמוֹפְתִים בְּאַדְמַת בְּנֵי חָם. הַמַּכֶּה בְעֶבְרָתוֹ כָּל
בְּכוֹרֵי מִצְרָיִם, וַיּוֹצֵא אֶת עַמּוֹ יִשְׂרָאֵל מִתּוֹכָם, לְחֵרוּת עוֹלָם. הַמַּעֲבִיר
בָּנָיו בֵּין גִּזְרֵי יַם סוּף, אֶת רוֹדְפֵיהֶם וְאֶת שׂוֹנְאֵיהֶם, בִּתְהוֹמוֹת טִבַּע, וְרָאוּ

---

bodily bearings and, like a leaping flame of fire which strains to tear itself away from the wick, as if reaching for some mysterious, invisible lover, man's soul ecstatically grasps upward, yearning for the world of the Infinite, for the delights of pure spirit. It is a kind of love which is alternating in intensity and depression: one moment the Jew's spirit lying exhausted, when he fears that all his love for God and Torah is based upon a phantom, when he suspects that his religious loyalties are the result of some kind of psychological aberration, that they are mere fantasies; and the next moment the fire of the spirit breaks into life again, when he conquers his fears, and a new sense of certainty surges up and strengthens him, and he soars upward once again in a holy love of God. Then the Jew is no longer satisfied with his regular, normal, ordinary observance of the mitzvot. For this higher kind of love, the love that beckons man on to unscaled heights, can be expressed not through the usual modes of Jewish religious behavior, but only through a profound study of Torah. It is here, in the seemingly dry fields of the intellect, that Jewish religious experience reaches its most fervent climax. For Torah is the word of God. The study of Torah is, therefore, the most direct attachment to God Himself available to us. Torah is the locus for contact between natural man and supernatural God.

אֱמֶת *True. Emet,* truth, is a virtue if tempered with graciousness. *Emet* is important enough to be the connecting link between the *Shema* and the *Amidah,* yet we must remember that this *emet* is not mentioned

The leader repeats: The Lord your God is true.

and trustworthy is all this, and it is established with us that He is the Lord our God, and there is none beside Him, and that we, Israel, are His people. It is He Who redeems us from the hand of kings, our King Who delivers us from the grasp of all the terrible tyrants. He is the God Who on our behalf deals out punishment to our adversaries, and requites all the enemies of our soul; Who does great things past finding out, and wonders without number; Who held our soul in life, and did not suffer our feet to slip; Who made us tread upon the high places of our enemies, and exalted our horn over all them that hate us; Who wrought for us miracles and vengeance upon Pharaoh; signs and wonders in the land of the children of Ham; Who smote in His wrath all the first-born of Egypt, and brought forth His people Israel from among them to everlasting freedom; Who made His children pass between the divisions of the Reed Sea, sinking their pursuers and their enemies in the depths. Then His children beheld His might; they

---

alone. Along with it we enumerate in *Shaharit* a whole list of qualities which tend to make truth more palatable, which moderate the often frightening quality of *emet* and make it human. *Emet* must also be *yatziv ve-nakhon ve-kayam ve-yashar*, proper and straight; it must be *ne'eman va'ahuv vehaviv ve'nehmad, ve'yafeh*, loyally and pleasantly and attractively presented! even if it is *nora v'adir*, an awesome and powerful truth, still it must be *metukan u-mekubal*, prepared for and acceptable to human sensitivity, and above all, *ve'tov ve'yafeh*, expressed in a manner that is good and beautiful. Only then may we be sure that *ha-davar ha-zeh alenu le-olam va-ed*, that this truth will remain with us forever. That is why the Halakhah maintained that the law of *hokheiah tokhiah*, of reproaching the sinner, must be executed with a great deal of delicacy and sensitive attention to the individual's feelings. There is, in Judaism, an ethic of criticism. A frank reproof may be in itself unavoidably painful, but one should minimize the anguish and the guilt and the feelings of inferiority and worthlessness that may needlessly result from it.

בָּנָיו גְּבוּרָתוֹ. שִׁבְּחוּ וְהוֹדוּ לִשְׁמוֹ. וּמַלְכוּתוֹ בְּרָצוֹן קִבְּלוּ עֲלֵיהֶם, מֹשֶׁה
וּבְנֵי יִשְׂרָאֵל לְךָ עָנוּ שִׁירָה בְּשִׂמְחָה רַבָּה, וְאָמְרוּ כֻלָּם:

מִי כָמֹכָה בָּאֵלִים יְיָ, מִי כָּמֹכָה נֶאְדָּר בַּקֹּדֶשׁ, נוֹרָא תְהִלֹּת, עֹשֵׂה פֶלֶא:
מַלְכוּתְךָ רָאוּ בָנֶיךָ, בּוֹקֵעַ יָם לִפְנֵי מֹשֶׁה, זֶה אֵלִי עָנוּ וְאָמְרוּ: יְיָ יִמְלוֹךְ

שִׁירָה *a song.* Why is *shirah* accorded such a place of honor in the Jewish
tradition? How can one win eternity for a song? The answer cannot be
merely the aesthetic quality of *shirah*, for other peoples, speaking in
other tongues, have produced poetry and music equal to and perhaps
superior to that of Israel. The significance of *shirah* lies not in the senses
but in the spirit, not in the art but in the heart, not in the sound but
in the vision. *Shirah* is the expression of insight. It reveals an added
dimension of experience: an awareness of hidden truths, a sensitivity to
mysteries usually veiled and obscure in the normal course of mundane,
prosaic life. It is the ability to perceive what is beyond the apparent,
the capacity to see the world right-side up even if it is, as it usually is,
upside down.

Shirah is necessary especially because the world in which we live
is an *olam ha-shekker*, a world of lies. It is a world which too often
rewards vice and punishes virtue. Not always, but much too frequently,
the weighty and worthy are neglected by the world, allowed to sink into
oblivion, while the light and flighty, the unworthy and the frivolous, are
those who are raised to positions of eminence and influence, and cher-
ished as successful and wise. The function of *shirah* in such a world is to
enable us to perceive what is truly worthy and weighty and what is only
superficial and meaningless, to see through the sham, past the artificial,
beyond illusion, behind the facade, and to discover the authentic and
the real and the genuine.

The *shirah* said at the Red Sea abounds in such insights. Here is
Pharaoh, who, like a successor-tyrant some 3,000 years later, believed
his reign would last a thousand years. His bragging was legend. All
arrogance, his egotism and his power remain stilled and silenced, covered forever by the dark waters of the Red Sea. When the facade is
ripped off, when man's cruel acting is revealed as nothing more than a
play, a deceitful sham, then we attain the insight: "*Mi kamokha ba-elim*

praised and gave thanks to His Name and willingly accepted His Sovereignty. Moses and the children of Israel sang a song to You with great joy, saying, all of them,

"Who is like You, O Lord, among the mighty ones? Who is like You, glorious in holiness, awesome in praises, doing wonders?" Your children beheld Your sovereign power, as You split the sea before Moses: they exclaimed, "This is my God!" and said, "The

---

Hashem, who is like You, Lord, among the mighty?" It is God, the Lord of history, who will declare and determine the destiny of men and nations; Pharaoh and his fellow potentates are but a passing phantom.

In our everyday world, it is the Pharaohs who are loud. They exact the tribute of the masses and dominate the scene, while God and the Godly are silent, seeming to sit on the sidelines of life's great spectacles. Ultimately, however, we become aware of the silent but unyielding truth that God prevails. And it is *shirah* which lets us peer behind the curtain, hear above the din, and learn God's honest truth. *Shirah* makes us take life more seriously — and ourselves less seriously. It inspires us to see beyond the fleeting to the final, beyond the passing to the permanent, beyond the tentative to the ultimate. It encourages us to peer behind the curtain of illusion that so often is lowered onto the stage of human activity and enterprise and that separates man from the genuine truth needed to sustain him. It is a poetic insight without which human beings cannot be truly human, without which Jews cannot be truly Jewish.

זֶה אֵלִי *"This is my God!"* On the words "This is my God," the *Mekhilta* says: "A mere maid-servant on the shores of the Red Sea was able to see more than Ezekiel and the other prophets" (*Mekhilta de-Rabbi Yishmael, Be-Shallah, Masehta Deshira* 3). The lowliest of the Israelites who experienced the Exodus had, as it were, a direct vision of God, whereas the prophets perceived Him in symbols and "riddles." Why is this so? And what do the Rabbis mean to say by this? I suggest that they offered a commentary on human nature in general, and also a subtle, implied criticism of the prophets.

During the normal course of humdrum life, only the highly perceptive and intelligent exercise foresight and vision and can see the truly

לְעוֹלָם וָעֶד. וְנֶאֱמַר: כִּי פָּדָה יְיָ אֶת יַעֲקֹב, וּגְאָלוֹ מִיַּד חָזָק מִמֶּנּוּ. בָּרוּךְ אַתָּה יְיָ גָּאַל יִשְׂרָאֵל:

הַשְׁכִּיבֵנוּ יְיָ אֱלֹהֵינוּ לְשָׁלוֹם, וְהַעֲמִידֵנוּ מַלְכֵּנוּ לְחַיִּים וּפְרוֹשׂ עָלֵינוּ סֻכַּת שְׁלוֹמֶךָ וְתַקְּנֵנוּ בְּעֵצָה טוֹבָה מִלְּפָנֶיךָ, וְהוֹשִׁיעֵנוּ לְמַעַן שְׁמֶךָ, וְהָגֵן בַּעֲדֵנוּ, וְהָסֵר מֵעָלֵינוּ אוֹיֵב, דֶּבֶר, וְחֶרֶב, וְרָעָב וְיָגוֹן, וְהָסֵר שָׂטָן מִלְּפָנֵינוּ וּמֵאַחֲרֵנוּ, וּבְצֵל כְּנָפֶיךָ תַּסְתִּירֵנוּ. כִּי אֵל שׁוֹמְרֵנוּ וּמַצִּילֵנוּ אָתָּה, כִּי אֵל מֶלֶךְ חַנּוּן וְרַחוּם אָתָּה, וּשְׁמוֹר צֵאתֵנוּ וּבוֹאֵנוּ, לְחַיִּים וּלְשָׁלוֹם, מֵעַתָּה וְעַד עוֹלָם. בָּרוּךְ אַתָּה יְיָ, שׁוֹמֵר עַמּוֹ יִשְׂרָאֵל לָעַד:

---

great issues, those that are real but not yet apparent. However, *hoi polloi*, the ordinary masses, go on unaware of that which is happening quietly and imperceptibly. The people sleep while the prophet dreams. The people yawn, while the prophet cries out and demands and protests. But in the extreme moments of history — whether moments of miraculous redemption or moments of critical danger — the prophet, so accustomed to visions and the extraordinary, to hyperbole and the supernatural, is sometimes insensitive. He is too high in heaven to see what lies before him on earth. And here the maid-servant may sometimes see the issues with startling clarity. The maid-servants, in an intuitive flash of cognition, saw what the prophets failed to see.

Yet, this having been said, it is important to remember that it is Ezekiel and the other prophets who remain the textbooks of our faith. We read Ezekiel, we chant Haftorahs from Isaiah, we draw inspiration from Amos. Nothing, except for the words *zeh Eli*, survives of the visions of the maid-servants on the shores of the Red Sea. The crisis, gut-reaction of the maid-servant has its place — but it is a very limited place, and is only of momentary duration. Woe to the people who make a cult of a maid-servant's wisdom! The perpetuation of hysteria is neither prophetic nor profitable. It is irresponsible.

Now is not the time for the House of Israel to be led by maid-servants. Ephemeral ecstasies are not the stuff of true leadership. The flash-in-the-pan may illuminate momentarily — but it cannot become the "light unto the nations" for all eternity. No, not the simple excitement

Lord shall reign forever and ever!" And it is said, For the Lord has redeemed Jacob, and delivered him from the hand of him that was stronger than he. Blessed are You, O Lord, Who redeemed Israel.

Cause us to lie down, O Lord our God, in peace, and raise us up, O our King, to life. Spread over us the tabernacle of Your peace. Direct us aright through Your own good counsel, and save us for Your Name's sake. Shield us, remove from us every enemy, pestilence, sword, famine, and sorrow; and remove the adversary from before us and from behind us; and shelter us beneath the shadow of your wings — for You, O God, are our Guardian and our Deliverer; You, O God, are a gracious and merciful King. Guard our going out and our coming in, for life and for peace, from this time forth and forever. Blessed are You, O Lord, Who guards His people Israel for ever.

---

and sloganeering of the maid-servants, not the words "Never Again" whispered threateningly into a telephone, or shouted angrily through a car window as a missile is hurled out — those are not the stuff of mature policy. The Jewish "Never Again" as proclaimed by the true prophets is what ought to concern us.

Listen to how the prophet Ezekiel rises above his initial failure, meets his critics, and in chapter 36 proclaims his "Never Again": "Your cities will be repopulated and your ruins will be rebuilt, and I will resettle you upon your land as in the days of your ancient glory.... Never again will I permit the vilification of the nations to be heard against you.... Never again will you have to bear the shame wished upon you by the peoples of the world. Never again will your people Israel be driven from the mountains of Israel.... These are the words of the Lord God" (Ezekiel 36:10–15).

Such are the words of the Lord God — as spoken not by a maid-servant but by *a* true prophet of the Lord. This is authentic Jewish leadership.

שׁוֹמֵר עַמּוֹ יִשְׂרָאֵל *Who guards His people Israel for ever.* Tradition teaches us that there is a custom to study all night on Shavuot and not to sleep

בָּרוּךְ יְיָ לְעוֹלָם, אָמֵן וְאָמֵן. בָּרוּךְ יְיָ מִצִּיּוֹן שֹׁכֵן יְרוּשָׁלָיִם הַלְלוּיָהּ. בָּרוּךְ יְיָ אֱלֹהִים אֱלֹהֵי יִשְׂרָאֵל, עֹשֵׂה נִפְלָאוֹת לְבַדּוֹ. וּבָרוּךְ שֵׁם כְּבוֹדוֹ לְעוֹלָם, וְיִמָּלֵא כְבוֹדוֹ אֶת כָּל הָאָרֶץ, אָמֵן וְאָמֵן. יְהִי כְבוֹד יְיָ לְעוֹלָם, יִשְׂמַח יְיָ בְּמַעֲשָׂיו. יְהִי שֵׁם יְיָ מְבוֹרָךְ, מֵעַתָּה וְעַד עוֹלָם, כִּי לֹא יִטֹּשׁ יְיָ אֶת עַמּוֹ בַּעֲבוּר שְׁמוֹ הַגָּדוֹל, כִּי הוֹאִיל יְיָ לַעֲשׂוֹת אֶתְכֶם לוֹ לְעָם. וַיַּרְא כָּל הָעָם וַיִּפְּלוּ עַל פְּנֵיהֶם, וַיֹּאמְרוּ: יְיָ הוּא הָאֱלֹהִים, יְיָ הוּא הָאֱלֹהִים. וְהָיָה יְיָ לְמֶלֶךְ עַל כָּל הָאָרֶץ, בַּיּוֹם הַהוּא יִהְיֶה יְיָ אֶחָד וּשְׁמוֹ אֶחָד. יְהִי חַסְדְּךָ יְיָ עָלֵינוּ, כַּאֲשֶׁר יִחַלְנוּ לָךְ. הוֹשִׁיעֵנוּ יְיָ אֱלֹהֵינוּ, וְקַבְּצֵנוּ מִן הַגּוֹיִם, לְהוֹדוֹת לְשֵׁם קָדְשֶׁךָ, לְהִשְׁתַּבֵּחַ בִּתְהִלָּתֶךָ. כָּל גּוֹיִם אֲשֶׁר עָשִׂיתָ יָבֹאוּ וְיִשְׁתַּחֲווּ לְפָנֶיךָ אֲדֹנָי, וִיכַבְּדוּ לִשְׁמֶךָ. כִּי גָדוֹל אַתָּה וְעֹשֵׂה נִפְלָאוֹת אַתָּה אֱלֹהִים לְבַדֶּךָ. וַאֲנַחְנוּ עַמְּךָ וְצֹאן מַרְעִיתֶךָ, נוֹדֶה לְּךָ לְעוֹלָם, לְדוֹר וָדוֹר נְסַפֵּר תְּהִלָּתֶךָ. בָּרוּךְ יְיָ בַּיּוֹם, בָּרוּךְ יְיָ בַּלַּיְלָה, בָּרוּךְ יְיָ בְּשָׁכְבֵנוּ, בָּרוּךְ יְיָ בְּקוּמֵנוּ. כִּי בְיָדְךָ נַפְשׁוֹת הַחַיִּים וְהַמֵּתִים, אֲשֶׁר בְּיָדוֹ נֶפֶשׁ כָּל חָי וְרוּחַ כָּל בְּשַׂר אִישׁ. בְּיָדְךָ

---

in order to make up for a rather startling occurrence. That is, the people of Israel, who used to get up at the crack of dawn in the desert of Sinai, slept late on the morning that they were to receive the Torah at Sinai. God had to wake them with thunder and lightning, a kind of celestial alarm clock. Tradition informs us of the relationship of sleep and Torah — they are in contrast with each other!

How, then, shall we keep ourselves awake, alive, and engaged? To become alive and alert one must reach out to others and assume responsibility for his fellow humans. Of God Himself we are told: "Behold, the Guardian of Israel neither sleeps nor slumbers, the Lord shall watch over you and be your shadow over your right hand" (Psalms 121:4–5). God's sleeplessness, His quality of alertness, is expressed by His *shemirah,* His care and concern for others: He is the Guardian of Israel. So is it for us. If we wish to live fully, deeply, we must live for others as well as for ourselves.

The study of Torah is the best way to be awake. Without it, life for the

Blessed be the Lord forever, Amen and Amen. Blessed be the Lord out of Zion, Who dwells in Jerusalem, Praise the Lord. Blessed be the Lord God, the God of Israel, Who alone does wondrous things: and blessed be His glorious Name for ever; and let the whole earth be filled with His glory, Amen and Amen. Let the glory of the Lord endure for ever; let the Lord rejoice in His works. Let the Name of the Lord be blessed from this time forth and forever. For the Lord will not forsake His people for His great Name's sake; because the Lord has vowed to make you His people. And when all the people saw it, they fell on their faces: and they said, "The Lord, He is God; the Lord, He is God." And the Lord shall be King over all the earth: in that day shall the Lord be One, and His Name One. Let Your loving-kindness, O Lord, be upon us, according as we have hoped for You. Save us, O Lord Our God, and gather us and deliver us from the nations, to give thanks to Your holy Name, and to glory in Your praise. All nations whom You have made shall come and bow before You, O Lord; and they shall glorify Your Name: for You are great and do marvelous things; You are God alone. But we are Your people and the sheep of Your pasture; we will give thanks to You forever: we will recount Your praise for all generations. Blessed be the Lord by day; blessed be the Lord by night. Blessed be the Lord when we lie down; blessed be the Lord when we rise up. For in Your hand are the souls of the living and the dead, [as it is written,] "In His hand is the soul of every living thing, and the spirit of all human flesh." Into Your hand I commend my spirit; You have redeemed

---

Jew is full of voids and vacuums, and life can be one long yawn occasionally interrupted by brief periods of semi-consciousness. But with the study of Torah, with the awareness of its summons and demands, its promises and consolations, its intellectual stimulation and moral challenge — we are fully and deliciously alive.

אַפְקִיד רוּחִי, פָּדִיתָה אוֹתִי יְיָ אֵל אֱמֶת. אֱלֹהֵינוּ שֶׁבַּשָּׁמַיִם, יַחֵד שִׁמְךָ, וְקַיֵּם מַלְכוּתְךָ תָּמִיד, וּמְלוֹךְ עָלֵינוּ לְעוֹלָם וָעֶד:

יִרְאוּ עֵינֵינוּ, וְיִשְׂמַח לִבֵּנוּ, וְתָגֵל נַפְשֵׁנוּ, בִּישׁוּעָתְךָ בֶּאֱמֶת, בֶּאֱמוֹר לְצִיּוֹן מָלַךְ אֱלֹהָיִךְ. יְיָ מֶלֶךְ, יְיָ מָלָךְ, יְיָ יִמְלוֹךְ לְעוֹלָם וָעֶד, כִּי הַמַּלְכוּת שֶׁלְּךָ הִיא, וּלְעוֹלְמֵי עַד תִּמְלוֹךְ בְּכָבוֹד, כִּי אֵין לָנוּ מֶלֶךְ אֶלָּא אָתָּה. בָּרוּךְ אַתָּה יְיָ, הַמֶּלֶךְ בִּכְבוֹדוֹ, תָּמִיד יִמְלוֹךְ עָלֵינוּ לְעוֹלָם וָעֶד, וְעַל כָּל מַעֲשָׂיו:

חצי קדיש

שׁ"ץ: יִתְגַּדַּל וְיִתְקַדַּשׁ שְׁמֵהּ רַבָּא. בְּעָלְמָא דִי בְרָא כִרְעוּתֵהּ, וְיַמְלִיךְ מַלְכוּתֵהּ בְּחַיֵּיכוֹן וּבְיוֹמֵיכוֹן וּבְחַיֵּי דְכָל בֵּית יִשְׂרָאֵל. בַּעֲגָלָא וּבִזְמַן קָרִיב וְאִמְרוּ אָמֵן:

קהל ושׁ"ץ: יְהֵא שְׁמֵהּ רַבָּא מְבָרַךְ לְעָלַם וּלְעָלְמֵי עָלְמַיָּא:

שׁ"ץ: יִתְבָּרַךְ וְיִשְׁתַּבַּח, וְיִתְפָּאַר וְיִתְרוֹמַם וְיִתְנַשֵּׂא וְיִתְהַדָּר וְיִתְעַלֶּה וְיִתְהַלָּל שְׁמֵהּ דְּקֻדְשָׁא בְּרִיךְ הוּא. לְעֵלָּא מִן כָּל בִּרְכָתָא וְשִׁירָתָא, תֻּשְׁבְּחָתָא וְנֶחֱמָתָא, דַּאֲמִירָן בְּעָלְמָא, וְאִמְרוּ אָמֵן:

עמידה

אֲדֹנָי שְׂפָתַי תִּפְתָּח וּפִי יַגִּיד תְּהִלָּתֶךָ:

בָּרוּךְ אַתָּה יְיָ אֱלֹהֵינוּ וֵאלֹהֵי אֲבוֹתֵינוּ, אֱלֹהֵי אַבְרָהָם, אֱלֹהֵי יִצְחָק, וֵאלֹהֵי יַעֲקֹב. הָאֵל הַגָּדוֹל הַגִּבּוֹר וְהַנּוֹרָא, אֵל עֶלְיוֹן, גּוֹמֵל חֲסָדִים טוֹבִים, וְקוֹנֵה

me, O Lord God of truth. Our God Who is in heaven, assert the unity of Your Name, and establish Your kingdom continually, and reign over us forever and ever.

May our eyes behold, our hearts rejoice, and our souls be glad in Your true salvation, when it shall be said to Zion, "your God reigns." The Lord reigns; the Lord has reigned; the Lord shall reign forever and ever: for the kingdom is Yours, and to eternity will You reign in glory; for we have no King but You. Blessed are You, O Lord, the King, Who constantly in His glory will reign over us and over all His works forever and ever.

HALF KADDISH

Leader: Magnified and sanctified may His great Name be, in the world which He has created according to His will. May He establish His kingdom during your life and during your days, and during the life of all the house of Israel, even speedily and at a near time, and say, Amen.

Cong. and Leader: May His great Name be blessed forever and to all eternity.

Leader: Blessed, praised, glorified, exalted, extolled, honored, magnified, and lauded be the Name of the Holy One, Blessed be He, beyond all the blessings and hymns, praises and consolations, which are uttered in the world; and say, Amen.

AMIDAH

O Lord, open my lips, and my mouth shall declare Your praise.

Blessed are You, O Lord our God and God of our forefathers, God of Abraham, God of Isaac, and God of Jacob, the great, mighty and revered God, the most high God, Who bestows loving-kindnesses, and possesses all things; Who remembers the pious deeds

הַכֹּל, וְזוֹכֵר חַסְדֵּי אָבוֹת, וּמֵבִיא גוֹאֵל לִבְנֵי בְנֵיהֶם לְמַעַן שְׁמוֹ בְּאַהֲבָה: מֶלֶךְ עוֹזֵר וּמוֹשִׁיעַ וּמָגֵן: בָּרוּךְ אַתָּה יְיָ, מָגֵן אַבְרָהָם:

אַתָּה גִּבּוֹר לְעוֹלָם אֲדֹנָי, מְחַיֵּה מֵתִים אַתָּה, רַב לְהוֹשִׁיעַ: מַשִּׁיב הָרוּחַ וּמוֹרִיד הַגֶּשֶׁם: מְכַלְכֵּל חַיִּים בְּחֶסֶד, מְחַיֵּה מֵתִים בְּרַחֲמִים רַבִּים, סוֹמֵךְ נוֹפְלִים, וְרוֹפֵא חוֹלִים, וּמַתִּיר אֲסוּרִים, וּמְקַיֵּם אֱמוּנָתוֹ לִישֵׁנֵי עָפָר, מִי כָמוֹךָ בַּעַל גְּבוּרוֹת וּמִי דוֹמֶה לָּךְ, מֶלֶךְ מֵמִית וּמְחַיֶּה וּמַצְמִיחַ יְשׁוּעָה: וְנֶאֱמָן אַתָּה לְהַחֲיוֹת מֵתִים. בָּרוּךְ אַתָּה יְיָ, מְחַיֵּה הַמֵּתִים:

אַתָּה קָדוֹשׁ וְשִׁמְךָ קָדוֹשׁ וּקְדוֹשִׁים בְּכָל יוֹם יְהַלְלוּךָ, סֶלָה. בָּרוּךְ אַתָּה יְיָ, הָאֵל הַקָּדוֹשׁ.

אַתָּה חוֹנֵן לְאָדָם דַּעַת, וּמְלַמֵּד לֶאֱנוֹשׁ בִּינָה.

———•———

למוצאי שבת:

אַתָּה חוֹנַנְתָּנוּ לְמַדַּע תּוֹרָתֶךָ, וַתְּלַמְּדֵנוּ לַעֲשׂוֹת חֻקֵּי רְצוֹנֶךָ, וַתַּבְדֵּל יְיָ

וַתַּבְדֵּל *You have made a distinction.* We need to exercise one particular faculty of the human psyche: the power to discern and discriminate and distinguish between the real and the fictional, the genuine and the artificial, right and wrong, licit and illicit. In a word, we need *Havdalah.* When we recite this prayer, we bless God who distinguishes between sacred and profane, light and dark, Israel and the nations, Sabbath and weekday. Jewish practice calls for us to recite the *Havdalah* on Saturday nights and at the end of holidays, not only over a cup of wine, but also during the *Amidah* of the evening prayer which marks the transition from holy day to weekday. And the Talmud requires that the *Havdalah* be recited specifically in the blessing which begins "Atah honen le-adam da'at," the blessing in which we pray to the Almighty for the gift of wisdom and knowledge and understanding (*Berakhot* 33a).

What is the relevance of *Havdalah* to this specific blessing? The Rabbis answer: "*Im ein deiah, havdalah minayin,* if there is no knowledge,

of the patriarchs, and in love brings a Redeemer to their children's children for His Name's sake. O King, Helper, Savior, and Shield. Blessed are You, O Lord, the Shield of Abraham.

You, O Lord, are mighty forever. You revive the dead; You are mighty to save; Who causes the wind to blow and the rain to fall; Who sustains the living with loving-kindness, revives the dead with great mercy, supports the fallen, heals the sick, releases the captives, and keeps faith with those who sleep in the dust. Who is like You, Lord of mighty acts, and who resembles You, O King, Who brings death and bestows life and makes salvation sprout! You are faithful to revive the dead. Blessed are You, O Lord, Who revives the dead.

You are holy, and Your Name is holy, and holy beings praise You daily, Selah! Blessed are You, O Lord, the holy God.

You favor humanity with knowledge, and teach mortals understanding.

—◦•◦—

At the conclusion of the Sabbath say:

You have favored us with knowledge of your Torah, and have taught us to perform the statutes of Your will. You have made a distinction, O Lord our God, between holy and secular, between

---

whence the ability to distinguish?" (*Yerushalmi, Berakhot* 39b). In other words, the ability to discern different values, to discriminate and to distinguish between competing claims, and therefore the ability to emerge whole from the confusions that reign in life, requires *deiah* — special insights and intellectual gifts. And yet, if we examine the passage of the *Havdalah* carefully, we remain with the question: why so? Apparently, it should be rather easy to make these distinctions. Any child can tell the difference between light and dark; reference to identity of the parents will tell us if one is Jewish or non-Jewish; the difference between the Sabbath and weekdays is nothing more complicated than consulting a

אֱלֹהֵינוּ בֵּין קֹדֶשׁ לְחוֹל, בֵּין אוֹר לְחוֹשֶׁךְ, בֵּין יִשְׂרָאֵל לָעַמִּים בֵּין יוֹם הַשְּׁבִיעִי לְשֵׁשֶׁת יְמֵי הַמַּעֲשֶׂה. אָבִינוּ מַלְכֵּנוּ, הָחֵל עָלֵינוּ הַיָּמִים הַבָּאִים לִקְרָאתֵנוּ לְשָׁלוֹם, חֲשׂוּכִים מִכָּל חֵטְא, וּמְנֻקִּים מִכָּל עָוֹן, וּמְדֻבָּקִים בְּיִרְאָתֶךָ. וְ-

━━◆━━

חָנֵּנוּ מֵאִתְּךָ דֵּעָה, בִּינָה וְהַשְׂכֵּל. בָּרוּךְ אַתָּה יְיָ, חוֹנֵן הַדָּעַת.

הֲשִׁיבֵנוּ אָבִינוּ לְתוֹרָתֶךָ, וְקָרְבֵנוּ מַלְכֵּנוּ לַעֲבוֹדָתֶךָ, וְהַחֲזִירֵנוּ בִּתְשׁוּבָה שְׁלֵמָה לְפָנֶיךָ. בָּרוּךְ אַתָּה יְיָ, הָרוֹצֶה בִּתְשׁוּבָה.

calendar; and even the distinction between sacred and profane is not overly taxing — who cannot tell apart, for instance, a *Sefer Torah* from a novel? Why, then, the special requirement for *deiah*, or knowledge, for intellectual grace, in order to perform *Havdalah*?

The answer is that for those who are superficial or who dwell in only one realm, *da'at* is indeed unnecessary. If we associate only with *kodesh* (holiness), Israel, *ore* (light), and Sabbath, or only with *hol* (the profane), the nations, *hoshekh* (darkness), and weekday, it is easy to discern distinctions, and life is much less confusing. The full agnostic has few problems. There is little to confuse him. He swallows all of contemporary life, and therefore he has no difficulty in trying to tell apart its various strands. Similarly, at the other end of the spectrum, the Jew who does not step out of his self-imposed boundaries of the sacred, of Israel, of the light of Torah, rejects all that is new and secular and alien in the contemporary culture, and he too has little to confuse him.

However, *deiah* is needed, and *Havdalah* is vital for those of us who choose to live in both realms and reject neither — for those of us who opt both for light and darkness, for Israel and the nations, for Sabbath and weekday, for the sacred and the profane. This category describes most of us, who will not succumb to the blandishments of the materialistic and hedonistic and agnostic society, and yet refuse the easy comforts of intellectual ghettoization; who believe that the function and the mission of the Jew in the world is to illuminate the *hoshekh* (darkness); to sanctify the *hol* (profane); to bring the Jewish message

light and darkness, between Israel and other nations, between the seventh day and the six working days. O our Father, our King, grant that the days which are approaching us may begin for us in peace, and that we may be withheld from all sin and cleansed from all iniquity, and cleave to the fear of You. And

—•—

O favor us with knowledge, understanding, and discernment from You. Blessed are You, O Lord, gracious Giver of knowledge.

Cause us to return, O our Father, to your Torah; draw us near, O our King, to Your service, and bring us back in perfect repentance to You. Blessed are You, O Lord, Who desires repentance.

---

to the nations; and to introduce the warmth and meaningfulness of the Sabbath to all the days of the week.

For those who are involved in this great mission was the dictum of the Rabbis meant: *im ein deiah, havdalah minayin*. It is those who straddle both worlds, who are therefore subject to the danger of confusion, and who therefore need the special divine gift of *deiah* or knowledge, insight, in order to be able to perform *Havdalah*, always to distinguish between the light and the dark, even when we try to illuminate the shadows of life; to know what separates the holy and the profane, even when we try to consecrate the secular.

הָרוֹצֶה בִּתְשׁוּבָה *Who desires repentance.* What is the relationship of *teshuvah* (repentance) and *selihah* (forgiveness, or the request for forgiveness)? Does not *selihah* follow automatically upon *teshuvah*? And if so, why is it that in the *Amidah* prayer the two are assigned to two separate blessings, *ha-rotse be-teshuvah* and *ha-marbe lisloah*?

I find the answer in two different midrashim (both quoted by the author of *Shvilei Leket*) relating each blessing to a different incident of sin and repentance in the life of the patriarchal family of Jacob. The first midrash relates that when Reuben sinned against his father Jacob by sleeping with Bilhah, it was ordained that he be punished by death, but

סְלַח לָנוּ, אָבִינוּ, כִּי חָטָאנוּ, מְחַל לָנוּ, מַלְכֵּנוּ כִּי פָשָׁעְנוּ, כִּי מוֹחֵל וְסוֹלֵחַ אָתָּה. בָּרוּךְ אַתָּה יְיָ, חַנּוּן הַמַּרְבֶּה לִסְלֹחַ.

---

afterwards he repented, whereupon the ministering angels proclaimed the blessing of "God Who desires repentance."

Judah sinned against Tamar and pronounced the verdict, "Take her out and let her be burnt" (Genesis 38:24). But when Tamar showed him proof that she had not sinned, he immediately confessed and said "She is right and I am wrong," and he was forgiven for that sin. Whereupon, the ministering angels proclaimed the blessing of "God Who graciously forgives greatly." So the ministering angels teach us that the concepts of *teshuvah* and *selihah* are not identical, and they relate them to the two archetypical dramas of sin and repentance.

What is the difference between these two stories? Let us analyze each and compare them. The sin of Reuben was not as simple as it sounds. After Rachel died, Jacob moved into the tent of Bilhah, the servant of Rachel. Reuben was insulted. He had to keep his peace when his mother, Leah, was slighted in favor of Rachel, her sister who was a full wife. But he could not suffer his mother's hurt when a mere maid-servant was given priority over her, a full wife of Jacob. He therefore demanded that Leah become first in the affection and respect of Jacob. The Netziv maintains that Reuben slept in the tent of Bilhah, that is, stayed over in her tent the whole night, to make sure that Jacob could not enter. The whole night he stayed there, waiting, and for a long, long night, he had constant opportunity to reconsider his forceful intrusion into the life of his father. But he did nothing. His sin was deliberate, a conscious and fully aware act of disrespect toward and disobedience against his father.

Now let us consider his *teshuvah*. When Reuben heard that his brothers wanted to kill Joseph, he saved him from their hands, saying, "Let us not kill him." The sin was in Reuben's defending his mother against Rachel and what belonged to Rachel. The repentance was his taking up the cudgels on behalf of Joseph, the son of Rachel. Reuben's *teshuvah* was slow, deliberate, long-developing. It was not superficial, it was not an outburst in one heroic act. Thus, we read that after Joseph was sold by the brothers, Reuben returned to the pit into which the brothers had

Forgive us, O our Father, for we have sinned; pardon us, O our King, for we have transgressed; for You pardon and forgive. Blessed are You, O Lord, the gracious One Who abundantly forgives.

---

cast Joseph. Rashi asks: Where was Reuben during the time that Joseph was sold? Rashi answers that he was not present, because, according to one version, he was deeply engrossed in his sackcloth and fasting, in remorse for having intruded and rearranged the bed of his father. His *teshuvah* was the result of prolonged introspection, from pangs of conscience. Moreover, it bedeviled him: Reuben's attempt at *teshuvah* by saving Joseph was frustrated by his very feelings of *teshuvah*, by his very act of contrition in "his sackcloth and his fasting" for his sin against his father. His *teshuvah* defeats itself, it is painful and tragic. No wonder, that after the result of this kind of process of *teshuvah*, the ministering angels should offer the blessing to God Who desires such repentance!

חַנּוּן הַמַּרְבֶּה לִסְלֹחַ *the gracious One Who abundantly forgives*. Now we turn to Judah's *teshuvah*. Picture that scene as Tamar walked up to Judah at the gates of the city where he presided. Up she walks, slowly and deliberately. Judah notices her every step, and his righteous indignation builds up. This woman was a blot on his family, a stain on his record. And then — the surprise: Tamar spreads it all out on his table before him, the robe and the seal and the staff. His judicial composure is shattered. All becomes clear to him, as clear as day, as clear as the searing sun. What a clash of plans and thoughts clutch Judah at that moment. No doubt he must have thought: "She is embarrassing me. She wants to destroy me! I can get rid of her now, and send her to her death before anyone realizes what is happening. I could rise and call out again, 'Take her out and let her be burnt!' If anyone notices these items, I can accuse her of being a thief as well as an adulteress. No one will object, no one will say a word, no one will know what has happened." But no! Judah decides against expediency, against self-interest. The Divine Image stirs within Judah and — he confesses! He is, after all, the son of Jacob, the grandson of Abraham and Isaac. There shall be no miscarriage of justice. "And Judah recognized them and he said, 'She is right and I am wrong'" (Genesis 38:26). At that moment he was forgiven for that

רְאֵה בְעָנְיֵנוּ, וְרִיבָה רִיבֵנוּ, וּגְאָלֵנוּ מְהֵרָה לְמַעַן שְׁמֶךָ, כִּי גּוֹאֵל חָזָק אָתָּה. בָּרוּךְ אַתָּה יְיָ, גּוֹאֵל יִשְׂרָאֵל.

רְפָאֵנוּ. יְיָ, וְנֵרָפֵא, הוֹשִׁיעֵנוּ וְנִוָּשֵׁעָה, כִּי תְהִלָּתֵנוּ אָתָּה, וְהַעֲלֵה רְפוּאָה שְׁלֵמָה לְכָל מַכּוֹתֵינוּ. כִּי אֵל מֶלֶךְ רוֹפֵא נֶאֱמָן וְרַחֲמָן אָתָּה. בָּרוּךְ אַתָּה יְיָ, רוֹפֵא חוֹלֵי עַמּוֹ יִשְׂרָאֵל.

---

dreadful sin. Whereupon the ministering angels proclaimed, "Blessed are You, O Lord, Who is gracious and forgives greatly."

How different is the contrition of Judah from the repentance of Reuben! Indeed there are two kinds of *teshuvah*, and they are different psychologically and spiritually. That of Judah is a result of the sudden outburst of innate decency which swells up like a mighty river after a cloudburst and overflows all dams. Or, it is like lightning, which in its suddenness and brilliance gives him the vision of truth and beauty. The *teshuvah* of Reuben is slow and halting, deliberate and painful. It is not like a cloudburst or a mighty river, but like little streams of conscience and tiny rivulets of renewal which come together slowly and patiently. It is not lightning, but a gradual enlightenment, like the rise of dawn after a long night, when sometimes he does not know if it is dark or light.

Hence, for Judah, there is only *selihah*, forgiveness. For Reuben, there is full repentance. Judah's sin was slow and deliberate; his *teshuvah* was quick and heroic. Therefore he is forgiven only as a result of God's grace: But his act is not something for which God, as it were, yearns. Reuben's *teshuvah*, like his sin, was prolonged, deep, and thorough. Therefore Reuben is accepted on his own merits, even without special "grace." For a return of this kind, God yearns and pines.

Consider how brilliantly the Sages formulated the prayers: The blessing of *selihah* speaks only of sin and pardon. It is a one-issue blessing. The blessing of *teshuvah* reveals a whole process: "O Father, return us to Your Torah; draw us near, O King, to Your service; return us in full repentance to You." It is a multifaceted procedure, going from the study of Torah to prayer and service, to the religious experience of divine closeness itself. Notice too that the blessing of *teshuvah* follows the blessing of understanding. Intelligence or understanding leads to repentance. It is only when a full and thorough and comprehensive

Look upon our affliction, and plead our cause, and redeem us speedily for Your Name's sake; for You are a mighty Redeemer. Blessed are You, O Lord, the Redeemer of Israel.

Heal us, O Lord, and we shall be healed; save us and we shall be saved; for You are our praise. Grant perfect healing to all our wounds; for You, God, King, are a faithful and merciful Healer. Blessed are You, O Lord, Who heals the sick of His people Israel.

---

teshuvah is not operative that we have to fall back on *hanun ha-marbe lisloah,* which is only a second best.

Unlike Judah, who confessed only when the evidence was piled up, we must, like Reuben, hear even the intangible, faint, gossamer whispers of contrition and strive for genuine *teshuvah,* beginning with *hashivenu avinu le-Toratekha,* and on to *le-avodatekha,* and ultimately to *hahazirenu be-teshuvah sheleimah lefanekha.*

רוֹפֵא חוֹלֵי עַמּוֹ יִשְׂרָאֵל *Who heals the sick of His people Israel.* We know that there are fundamentalist sects which do not approve of the use of medicine and surgery. Often we laugh at them, but if we are fair we will recognize that there is a logical consistency in their religious premise. Perhaps what is wrong with them is that they are *too* consistent! If we believe that God is Master of the world, then indeed how dare we change His decree or rule, and if He decreed that one be sick, by what right do we interfere in the process and heal him? The Rabbis recognized the apparent justice of this argument and therefore pointed to two Biblical words which are the warrant for our right to interfere: "*ve'rapo yerape,* man shall heal" (Exodus 21:19). The Rabbis added: "From this we know that the physician has the right to exercise the healing arts" (*Bava Kamma* 85a). So the physician may interfere in the natural design. But Nahmanides deduces from this that once we have established that it is *permissible* to interfere, it automatically and immediately becomes *obligatory* to do so! The principle of the commandment to preserve and enhance life makes it not only permissible but obligatory to heal and cure. God is the ultimate Healer, but man must always take his step first. We must initiate the concern and activity for health, and only then does God help.

45 ↩

בָּרֵךְ עָלֵינוּ, יְיָ אֱלֹהֵינוּ, אֶת הַשָּׁנָה הַזֹּאת וְאֶת כָּל מִינֵי תְבוּאָתָהּ לְטוֹבָה וְתֵן טַל וּמָטָר לִבְרָכָה

עַל פְּנֵי הָאֲדָמָה, וְשַׂבְּעֵנוּ מִטּוּבֶךָ, וּבָרֵךְ שְׁנָתֵנוּ כַּשָּׁנִים הַטּוֹבוֹת. בָּרוּךְ אַתָּה יְיָ, מְבָרֵךְ הַשָּׁנִים.

תְּקַע בְּשׁוֹפָר גָּדוֹל לְחֵרוּתֵנוּ, וְשָׂא נֵס לְקַבֵּץ גָּלֻיּוֹתֵינוּ, וְקַבְּצֵנוּ יַחַד מֵאַרְבַּע כַּנְפוֹת הָאָרֶץ. בָּרוּךְ אַתָּה יְיָ, מְקַבֵּץ נִדְחֵי עַמּוֹ יִשְׂרָאֵל.

הָשִׁיבָה שׁוֹפְטֵינוּ כְּבָרִאשׁוֹנָה וְיוֹעֲצֵינוּ כְּבַתְּחִלָּה, וְהָסֵר מִמֶּנּוּ יָגוֹן וַאֲנָחָה, וּמְלוֹךְ עָלֵינוּ אַתָּה, יְיָ, לְבַדְּךָ בְּחֶסֶד וּבְרַחֲמִים, וְצַדְּקֵנוּ בַּמִּשְׁפָּט. בָּרוּךְ אַתָּה יְיָ, מֶלֶךְ אוֹהֵב צְדָקָה וּמִשְׁפָּט.

וְלַמַּלְשִׁינִים אַל תְּהִי תִקְוָה, וְכָל הָרִשְׁעָה כְּרֶגַע תֹּאבֵד, וְכָל אוֹיְבֶיךָ מְהֵרָה יִכָּרֵתוּ, וְהַזֵּדִים מְהֵרָה תְעַקֵּר וּתְשַׁבֵּר וּתְמַגֵּר וְתַכְנִיעַ בִּמְהֵרָה בְיָמֵינוּ. בָּרוּךְ אַתָּה יְיָ, שֹׁבֵר אֹיְבִים וּמַכְנִיעַ זֵדִים.

עַל הַצַּדִּיקִים וְעַל הַחֲסִידִים וְעַל זִקְנֵי עַמְּךָ בֵּית יִשְׂרָאֵל, וְעַל פְּלֵיטַת סוֹפְרֵיהֶם, וְעַל גֵּרֵי הַצֶּדֶק וְעָלֵינוּ, יֶהֱמוּ נָא רַחֲמֶיךָ, יְיָ אֱלֹהֵינוּ, וְתֵן שָׂכָר טוֹב לְכָל הַבּוֹטְחִים בְּשִׁמְךָ בֶּאֱמֶת, וְשִׂים חֶלְקֵנוּ עִמָּהֶם לְעוֹלָם, וְלֹא נֵבוֹשׁ כִּי בְךָ בָּטָחְנוּ. בָּרוּךְ אַתָּה יְיָ, מִשְׁעָן וּמִבְטָח לַצַּדִּיקִים.

וְלִירוּשָׁלַיִם עִירְךָ בְּרַחֲמִים תָּשׁוּב, וְתִשְׁכּוֹן בְּתוֹכָהּ כַּאֲשֶׁר דִּבַּרְתָּ, וּבְנֵה אוֹתָהּ בְּקָרוֹב בְּיָמֵינוּ בִּנְיַן עוֹלָם, וְכִסֵּא דָוִד מְהֵרָה לְתוֹכָהּ תָּכִין. בָּרוּךְ אַתָּה יְיָ, בּוֹנֵה יְרוּשָׁלָיִם.

תְּקַע בְּשׁוֹפָר גָּדוֹל לְחֵרוּתֵנוּ *Sound the great horn for our freedom.* We read in Isaiah (27:13), "On that day [of the redemption] a great shofar will be sounded, and those who are lost in the land of Ashur [Assyria] and those who are dispersed in the land of Egypt will return to the Holy Land." The greatest exile — as one eminent rabbi taught — occurs when we do not know that we are in exile. The more we forget our exile, the deeper we are caught in its web.

Bless this year for us, O Lord our God, together with every kind of its produce, for our welfare. Give dew and rain for a blessing upon the face of the earth, and satisfy us with Your goodness, and bless our year like the best years. Blessed are You, O Lord, Who blesses the years.

Sound the great horn for our freedom, lift up the banner to gather our exiles, and gather us together from the four corners of the earth. Blessed are You, O Lord, Who gathers the dispersed ones of His people Israel.

Restore our judges as at first, and our counselors as at the beginning; and remove from us grief and sighing; and reign over us, O Lord, You alone, in loving-kindness and tender mercy, and justify us in judgment. Blessed are You O Lord, the King Who loves righteousness and judgment.

And for slanderers let there be no hope, and let all wickedness perish in an instant; and let all Your enemies be speedily cut off. Speedily uproot, crush, cast down, and humble the dominion of arrogance speedily in our days. Blessed are You, O Lord, Who breaks the enemies and humbles the arrogant.

Towards the righteous, the pious, the elders of Your people the house of Israel, the remnant of their scholars, the righteous converts, and us may Your tender mercies be stirred, O Lord our God; grant a good reward to all who faithfully trust in Your Name; set our portion with them forever, so that we may not be put to shame; for we have trusted in You. Blessed are You, O Lord, the Support and Trust of the righteous.

And to Jerusalem, Your city, return in mercy, and dwell within it as You have spoken; rebuild it soon in our days as an everlasting structure, and speedily set up within it the throne of David. Blessed are You, O Lord, Who rebuilds Jerusalem.

אֶת צֶמַח דָּוִד עַבְדְּךָ מְהֵרָה תַצְמִיחַ, וְקַרְנוֹ תָּרוּם בִּישׁוּעָתֶךָ, כִּי לִישׁוּעָתְךָ קִוִּינוּ כָּל הַיּוֹם. בָּרוּךְ אַתָּה יְיָ, מַצְמִיחַ קֶרֶן יְשׁוּעָה.

שְׁמַע קוֹלֵנוּ, יְיָ אֱלֹהֵינוּ, חוּס וְרַחֵם עָלֵינוּ, וְקַבֵּל בְּרַחֲמִים וּבְרָצוֹן אֶת תְּפִלָּתֵנוּ, כִּי אֵל שׁוֹמֵעַ תְּפִלּוֹת וְתַחֲנוּנִים אָתָּה, וּמִלְּפָנֶיךָ, מַלְכֵּנוּ, רֵיקָם אַל תְּשִׁיבֵנוּ. כִּי אַתָּה שׁוֹמֵעַ תְּפִלַּת עַמְּךָ יִשְׂרָאֵל בְּרַחֲמִים . בָּרוּךְ אַתָּה יְיָ, שׁוֹמֵעַ תְּפִלָּה.

רְצֵה, יְיָ אֱלֹהֵינוּ, בְּעַמְּךָ יִשְׂרָאֵל וּבִתְפִלָּתָם, וְהָשֵׁב אֶת הָעֲבוֹדָה לִדְבִיר בֵּיתֶךָ, וְאִשֵּׁי יִשְׂרָאֵל, וּתְפִלָּתָם בְּאַהֲבָה תְקַבֵּל בְּרָצוֹן, וּתְהִי לְרָצוֹן תָּמִיד עֲבוֹדַת יִשְׂרָאֵל עַמֶּךָ. וְתֶחֱזֶינָה עֵינֵינוּ בְּשׁוּבְךָ לְצִיּוֹן בְּרַחֲמִים. בָּרוּךְ אַתָּה יְיָ, הַמַּחֲזִיר שְׁכִינָתוֹ לְצִיּוֹן.

מוֹדִים אֲנַחְנוּ לָךְ, שָׁאַתָּה הוּא, יְיָ אֱלֹהֵינוּ וֵאלֹהֵי אֲבוֹתֵינוּ, לְעוֹלָם וָעֶד, צוּר חַיֵּינוּ, מָגֵן יִשְׁעֵנוּ, אַתָּה הוּא לְדוֹר וָדוֹר נוֹדֶה לְךָ וּנְסַפֵּר תְּהִלָּתֶךָ. עַל חַיֵּינוּ הַמְּסוּרִים בְּיָדֶךָ, וְעַל נִשְׁמוֹתֵינוּ הַפְּקוּדוֹת לָךְ, וְעַל נִסֶּיךָ שֶׁבְּכָל יוֹם עִמָּנוּ, וְעַל נִפְלְאוֹתֶיךָ וְטוֹבוֹתֶיךָ שֶׁבְּכָל עֵת, עֶרֶב וָבֹקֶר וְצָהֳרָיִם, הַטּוֹב כִּי לֹא כָלוּ רַחֲמֶיךָ, וְהַמְרַחֵם כִּי לֹא תַמּוּ חֲסָדֶיךָ מֵעוֹלָם קִוִּינוּ לָךְ.

עַל הַנִּסִּים, וְעַל הַפֻּרְקָן, וְעַל הַגְּבוּרוֹת, וְעַל הַתְּשׁוּעוֹת, וְעַל הַמִּלְחָמוֹת, שֶׁעָשִׂיתָ לַאֲבוֹתֵינוּ בַּיָּמִים הָהֵם בַּזְּמַן הַזֶּה.

בִּימֵי מָרְדְּכַי וְאֶסְתֵּר בְּשׁוּשַׁן הַבִּירָה, כְּשֶׁעָמַד עֲלֵיהֶם הָמָן הָרָשָׁע, בִּקֵּשׁ

כְּשֶׁעָמַד עֲלֵיהֶם הָמָן הָרָשָׁע *when the wicked Haman rose up against them.* There is a remarkable passage in the Talmud (*Hullin* 139b): "How do we know Haman is mentioned in the Torah?" And the Talmud cites a verse in Genesis: After Adam and Eve have eaten of the forbidden fruit of the Tree of Knowledge, God said to Adam: "Did you eat from the tree…?" (Genesis 3:11). The first word in this accusation is *ha-min,* which, in a play on words, sounds like *Haman.* Thus we know of Haman from this verse.

Now, this is a remarkably peculiar passage — unless it is but an

Speedily cause the offspring of Your servant David to flourish, and let his pride be exalted by Your salvation, because we wait for Your salvation all the day. Blessed are You, O Lord, Who causes the pride of salvation to flourish.

Hear our voice, O Lord our God; spare us and have mercy upon us, and accept our prayer in mercy and favor; for You are God Who listens to prayers and supplications: From Your presence, O our King, do not turn us away empty-handed; for You listen to the prayer of Your people Israel in mercy. Blessed are You, O Lord, Who listens to prayer.

Be favorable, O Lord our God, toward Your people Israel and their prayer; restore the service to Your most holy Temple; receive in love and favor both the fire-offerings of Israel and their prayer; and may the service of Your people Israel always be favorable to You. And let our eyes behold Your return to Zion in mercy. Blessed are You, O Lord, Who restores His divine Presence to Zion.

We give thanks to You, for You are the Lord our God and the God of our ancestors forever and ever; You are the Rock of our lives, the Shield of our salvation through every generation. We will give thanks to You and declare Your praise — for our lives which are committed into Your hand, and for our souls which are in Your charge, and for Your miracles which are with us every day, and for Your wonders and Your benefits which are with us at all times — evening, morning and afternoon. O You Who are all-good, Whose mercies never fail; You, merciful Being, Whose loving-kindnesses never cease, we have always put our hope in You.

[We thank You] for the miracles, for the redemption, for the mighty deeds, for the salvations, and for the military victories which You performed for our ancestors in those days, at this season.

In the days of Mordecai and Esther, in Shushan the capital, when

לְהַשְׁמִיד, לַהֲרֹג וּלְאַבֵּד אֶת כָּל הַיְּהוּדִים, מִנַּעַר וְעַד זָקֵן, טַף וְנָשִׁים, בְּיוֹם אֶחָד בִּשְׁלֹשָׁה עָשָׂר לְחֹדֶשׁ שְׁנֵים עָשָׂר, הוּא חֹדֶשׁ אֲדָר, וּשְׁלָלָם לָבוֹז. וְאַתָּה בְּרַחֲמֶיךָ הָרַבִּים הֵפַרְתָּ אֶת עֲצָתוֹ, וְקִלְקַלְתָּ אֶת מַחֲשַׁבְתּוֹ, וַהֲשֵׁבוֹתָ לּוֹ גְּמוּלוֹ בְּרֹאשׁוֹ, וְתָלוּ אוֹתוֹ וְאֶת בָּנָיו עַל הָעֵץ.

וְעַל כֻּלָּם יִתְבָּרַךְ וְיִתְרוֹמַם שִׁמְךָ, מַלְכֵּנוּ, תָּמִיד לְעוֹלָם וָעֶד. וְכֹל הַחַיִּים יוֹדוּךָ סֶלָה, וִיהַלְלוּ אֶת שִׁמְךָ בֶּאֱמֶת, הָאֵל יְשׁוּעָתֵנוּ וְעֶזְרָתֵנוּ סֶלָה. בָּרוּךְ אַתָּה יְיָ, הַטּוֹב שִׁמְךָ וּלְךָ נָאֶה לְהוֹדוֹת.

שָׁלוֹם רָב עַל יִשְׂרָאֵל עַמְּךָ תָּשִׂים לְעוֹלָם, כִּי אַתָּה הוּא מֶלֶךְ אָדוֹן לְכָל הַשָּׁלוֹם. וְטוֹב בְּעֵינֶיךָ לְבָרֵךְ אֶת עַמְּךָ יִשְׂרָאֵל בְּכָל עֵת וּבְכָל שָׁעָה בִּשְׁלוֹמֶךָ. בָּרוּךְ אַתָּה יְיָ, הַמְבָרֵךְ אֶת עַמּוֹ יִשְׂרָאֵל בַּשָּׁלוֹם.

יִהְיוּ לְרָצוֹן אִמְרֵי פִי וְהֶגְיוֹן לִבִּי לְפָנֶיךָ, יְיָ צוּרִי וְגֹאֲלִי.

---

example of Talmudlc humor, which it may be occasionally but certainly not always. Why does the Talmud have to seek a source for Haman in the Torah? The answer — and it is a remarkably perspicacious insight — was offered by the late sage of Kletsk and then Lakewood, Rabbi Aaron Kotler. The Talmud, he tells us, is pointing to a remarkable similarity between Haman and Adam in their approaches to life. Both Adam and Haman are guilty of partially unfulfilled rising expectations, causing them to insist that they must get everything, without exception. Thus, Adam in the Garden of Eden would seem to have had everything a man could want: an inexhaustible food supply, the loveliness of Paradise, a wife, rivers and trees and mountains of gold and silver, everything — except for one little tree the fruit of which is forbidden to him. Everything he has means nothing; it is only that one tree which he must have. Hence, his expulsion from Paradise.

Haman goes through a similar process. He has everything that a politician can want: power, glory, the envy of his colleagues and subordinates, riches, and a large household. He is a man who effectively runs the entire Persian Empire, because the king is, after all, a fool. Only one little thing is denied Haman: a solitary Jew outside the court refuses to bow to him. This proves to be such a maddening factor to Haman that

the wicked Haman rose up against them, and sought to destroy, to slay, and exterminate all the Jews, both young and old, little children and women, on one day, on the thirteenth day of the twelfth month, which is the month of Adar, and to plunder their possessions. Then You, in Your abundant mercy, nullified his counsel, frustrated his design, and caused his scheme to return upon his own head; and they hanged him and his sons upon the gallows.

For all these things Your Name, O our King, shall be continually blessed and exalted forever and ever. And everything that lives shall give thanks to You, Selah! and shall praise Your Name in truth, O God, our salvation and our help, Selah! Blessed are You, O Lord, Whose Name is "All-good," and to Whom it is fitting to give thanks.

Grant abundant peace to Israel Your people for ever; for You are the sovereign Lord of all peace; and may it be good in Your eyes to bless Your people Israel at all times and in every hour with Your peace. Blessed are You, O Lord, Who blesses His people Israel with peace.

Let the words of my mouth and the meditation of my heart be acceptable before You, O Lord, my Rock and my Redeemer.

---

he proposes a plan for genocide and ultimately is ruined and executed because of it. Each of them is, therefore, undone by rising expectations.

Rising expectations, while certainly justifiable and necessary for constituting a moral and fair and equitable society, entail dangers in the realms of psychology, politics, and morality. Perhaps the most moral and Jewish approach to rising expectations, both of the Purim epoch and our own, should lead us to a modification of this theme. Rising expectations, yes — but not expectations of others; rather, of ourselves.

יְהִיוּ לְרָצוֹן אִמְרֵי פִי *Let the words of my mouth ... be acceptable.* Hasidim tell the following story: There was a small hamlet to which travelers from the outside world came only very rarely. One day the townspeople noticed that their watches were not synchronized, Each one showed a

אֱלֹהַי, נְצוֹר לְשׁוֹנִי מֵרָע. וּשְׂפָתַי מִדַּבֵּר מִרְמָה: וְלִמְקַלְלַי נַפְשִׁי תִדֹּם,
וְנַפְשִׁי כֶּעָפָר לַכֹּל תִּהְיֶה. פְּתַח לִבִּי בְּתוֹרָתֶךָ, וּבְמִצְוֹתֶיךָ תִּרְדּוֹף נַפְשִׁי.
וְכָל הַחוֹשְׁבִים עָלַי רָעָה, מְהֵרָה הָפֵר עֲצָתָם וְקַלְקֵל מַחֲשַׁבְתָּם. עֲשֵׂה
לְמַעַן שְׁמֶךָ, עֲשֵׂה לְמַעַן יְמִינֶךָ, עֲשֵׂה לְמַעַן קְדֻשָּׁתֶךָ. עֲשֵׂה לְמַעַן תּוֹרָתֶךָ.
לְמַעַן יֵחָלְצוּן יְדִידֶיךָ, הוֹשִׁיעָה יְמִינְךָ וַעֲנֵנִי. יִהְיוּ לְרָצוֹן אִמְרֵי פִי וְהֶגְיוֹן
לִבִּי לְפָנֶיךָ, יְיָ צוּרִי וְגוֹאֲלִי. עֹשֶׂה שָׁלוֹם בִּמְרוֹמָיו, הוּא יַעֲשֶׂה שָׁלוֹם עָלֵינוּ,
וְעַל כָּל יִשְׂרָאֵל וְאִמְרוּ: אָמֵן.

יְהִי רָצוֹן מִלְּפָנֶיךָ, יְיָ אֱלֹהֵינוּ וֵאלֹהֵי אֲבוֹתֵינוּ, שֶׁיִּבָּנֶה בֵּית הַמִּקְדָּשׁ בִּמְהֵרָה
בְיָמֵינוּ, וְתֵן חֶלְקֵנוּ בְּתוֹרָתֶךָ, וְשָׁם נַעֲבָדְךָ בְּיִרְאָה כִּימֵי עוֹלָם וּכְשָׁנִים
קַדְמוֹנִיּוֹת. וְעָרְבָה לַיְיָ מִנְחַת יְהוּדָה וִירוּשָׁלָיִם כִּימֵי עוֹלָם וּכְשָׁנִים
קַדְמוֹנִיּוֹת.

different time, so that most likely none had the right time. As a result,
all the people except one put their watches on their shelves and failed
to wind them. This one man said: "Although I am sure I do not have the
right time, nevertheless, I will keep my watch wound." Several months
later, a traveler chanced upon the hamlet. The people surrounded him
and asked him for news from the outside world, and then — for the
right time. He took out his watch and told them. The people ran back

O my God! guard my tongue from evil and my lips from speaking guile; and to those who curse me let my soul be silent, let my soul be to all as the dust. Open my heart to Your Torah, and let my soul pursue Your commandments. If any design evil against me, speedily nullify their counsel, and frustrate their designs. Do it for the sake of Your Name, do it for the sake of Your right hand, do it for the sake of Your holiness, do it for the sake of Your Torah. In order that Your beloved ones may be delivered, O save with Your right hand, and answer me. Let the words of my mouth and the meditation of my heart be acceptable before You, O Lord, my Rock and my Redeemer. He Who makes peace in His high places, may He make peace for us and for all Israel, and say, Amen.

May it be Your will, O Lord our God and God of our ancestors, that the Temple be speedily rebuilt in our days, and grant our portion in Your Torah. And there we will serve You with awe, as in the days of old, and as in former years. Then shall the offering of Judah and Jerusalem be pleasant to the Lord, as in the days of old, and as in former years.

---

to recover their watches and set them properly But none of the watches would work, for they had grown rusty — except the watch which this one man had kept winding all along despite the ridicule of his friends.

So it is with prayer, or Torah, or any other religious duty. Unless we keep it "running" constantly, it will be of no avail to us in the moments of crisis when we really need it.

קדיש שלם

ש"ץ: יִתְגַּדַּל וְיִתְקַדַּשׁ שְׁמֵהּ רַבָּא. בְּעָלְמָא דִּי בְרָא כִרְעוּתֵהּ, וְיַמְלִיךְ מַלְכוּתֵהּ בְּחַיֵּיכוֹן וּבְיוֹמֵיכוֹן וּבְחַיֵּי דְכָל בֵּית יִשְׂרָאֵל. בַּעֲגָלָא וּבִזְמַן קָרִיב וְאִמְרוּ אָמֵן:

יִתְגַּדַּל וְיִתְקַדַּשׁ *Magnified and sanctified.* The *Kaddish* has its origin in the Bible when the spirit of prophecy moves Ezekiel, and the prophet speaks the words "*Hitgadalti ve'hitkadashti,* Thus will I be magnified and sanctified and known in the eyes of the nations" (Ezekiel 38:23). From these words we derive "*Yitgadal ve'yitkadash,* may His great Name be magnified and sanctified." The leading theme of both the prayer and the prophecy is one which is fascinating in its theological and practical aspects, and is known to us as *Kiddush Hashem,* the sanctification of God's Name. *Kiddush Hashem* is one of the leading motifs in all Jewish life. Millions of our people throughout history have readily given their lives for *Kiddush Hashem.* Halakhah places it on par, with respect to its negation or transgression, with the three cardinal sins of idolatry, bloodshed, and incest.

Let us delineate one important aspect of *Kiddush Hashem* in the hope that this magnificent religious ideal will become more and more intelligible and, hence, more meaningful to us. Our verse says that God will be magnified and sanctified and known in the eyes of the nations, and later we read that "the nations shall know that I am the Lord, the Holy One of Israel" (Ezekiel 39:7). Not only in Ezekiel, but in many books of the Bible, do we meet up with this desire to prove to the nations that our religion is right. When Israel was threatened with extinction in the desert, Moses turned to God and said, "Why should the Egyptians have the opportunity of pointing a finger at us?" And centuries later David wondered aloud, "What will the gentile nations say about this?" Indeed, how strange all this is! Why should a prophet suddenly be so concerned with impressing the gentiles? Did he thrive on the compliments of the non-Jews and suffer when they sneered? What is this connection between sanctification and the gentiles, between *Kiddush Hashem* and God's prestige, between *Kiddush Hashem* and Israel's welfare?

And yet, that is the clue to the very essence of *Kiddush Hashem!* For

FULL KADDISH

Leader: Magnified and sanctified may His great Name be, in the world which He has created according to His will. May He establish His kingdom during your life and during your days, and during the life of all the house of Israel, even speedily and at a near time, and say, Amen.

---

the glory of God is His acceptance by all the world and the practice of His ordained rules of ethical conduct by all His creatures. God's sanctification comes about when His people, whom He has promised to help and redeem, prosper and fare well. For in the eyes of the world, when Israel prospers, it is a sign that the divine promises to Abraham, Isaac, and Jacob are being kept and hence that the God of Israel is the God of Truth. The sanctification of God, and His glorification by the peoples of the earth, flows from the well-being of Israel.

However, when Israel suffers and is pillaged and pilloried, the nations of the world ask, Where is your God and all His promises? Then they disbelieve the chosenness of Israel, the Torah — and then the Jewish concept of God in its entirety. And that is *hillul Hashem*, the desecration of God's Name, the opposite of *Kiddush Hashem*.

The saying of the *Kaddish* includes both. We say "*Yitgadal ve-yitkadash she- meih rabba be'alma di'vera khirutei,* may His Name be glorified in the world which He created" — and then, in the Sephardic tradition, "*ve-yitzmakh purkanei vi-yekarev meshihei,* by bringing the redemption of Israel and bringing close the coming of the Messiah." We thus ask for *Kiddush Hashem* in the first manner. Then we respond, "*Yehei shemei rabba* ... may God's Name be blessed in this world." When I act like a Jew, God's Name is blessed. When I attend a synagogue regularly, God's Name is blessed. When I *daven* because I want to and not because I have to, God's Name is doubly sanctified. When I am decent and generous, God is blessed. Here are two of the ways of establishing God's Kingdom, of sanctifying His Name.

And there is yet a third way. Moses was leading his disgruntled people through the terrible desert on their way to an unknown Promised Land. At one point, the thirst was terrible. But Israel's complaining was even

קהל וש״ץ: יְהֵא שְׁמֵהּ רַבָּא מְבָרַךְ לְעָלַם וּלְעָלְמֵי עָלְמַיָּא:

ש״ץ: יִתְבָּרַךְ וְיִשְׁתַּבַּח, וְיִתְפָּאַר וְיִתְרוֹמַם וְיִתְנַשֵּׂא וְיִתְהַדָּר וְיִתְעַלֶּה
וְיִתְהַלָּל שְׁמֵהּ דְּקֻדְשָׁא בְּרִיךְ הוּא. לְעֵלָּא מִן כָּל בִּרְכָתָא וְשִׁירָתָא,
תֻּשְׁבְּחָתָא וְנֶחֱמָתָא, דַּאֲמִירָן בְּעָלְמָא, וְאִמְרוּ אָמֵן:

תִּתְקַבֵּל צְלוֹתְהוֹן וּבָעוּתְהוֹן דְּכָל (בֵּית) יִשְׂרָאֵל קֳדָם אֲבוּהוֹן דִּי בִשְׁמַיָּא
וְאִמְרוּ אָמֵן: יְהֵא שְׁלָמָא רַבָּא מִן שְׁמַיָּא וְחַיִּים עָלֵינוּ וְעַל כָּל יִשְׂרָאֵל,
וְאִמְרוּ אָמֵן: עֹשֶׂה שָׁלוֹם בִּמְרוֹמָיו הוּא יַעֲשֶׂה שָׁלוֹם עָלֵינוּ וְעַל כָּל
יִשְׂרָאֵל, וְאִמְרוּ אָמֵן:

---

more terrible. God told Moses to address a rock and that a miracle
would occur — water would gush forth from it. Instead, Moses, in
the company of his brother Aaron, approached the rock and struck it,
saying, "From this rock shall we bring forth water" (Numbers 20:10).
God was angry with Moses. He had committed the sin of *hillul Hashem*,
a sin so severe that he would die before crossing the Jordan, and be
deprived of leading his people into the Promised Land.

What was the sin of Moses which incurred God's wrath? Most of us
have been taught that the sin consisted of his striking rather than talking to the rock. Perhaps such is Rashi's explanation. But that does not

Cong. and Leader: May His great Name be blessed forever and to all eternity.

Leader: Blessed, praised, glorified, exalted, extolled, honored, magnified, and lauded be the Name of the Holy One, Blessed be He, beyond all the blessings and hymns, praises and consolations, which are uttered in the world; and say, Amen.

May the prayers and supplications of all of Israel be accepted before their Father Who is in Heaven; and say, Amen.

May there be abundant peace from Heaven, and life for us and for all Israel; and say, Amen.

He Who makes peace in His high places, may He make peace for us and for all Israel; and say, Amen.

---

account for God's speaking of Moses' not performing *Kiddush Hashem.* Rambam has a much deeper commentary: The sin lay in the "we shall bring forth the water." What they should have said is "God will bring forth the water." In other words, the sin consisted of their failure to attribute the miracle to God. So the third method of achieving *Kiddush Hashem* is to ascribe all life, all action, all creativity to its true source: God.

Thus we say at the end of the *Kaddish,* "*Yehei shlama rabba min shemaya, May peace come from heaven*" — not from our own mind or might. Only when it is realized that national prosperity and universal peace stem from God is His Name sanctified and glorified.

MEGILLAT ESTHER

The Inside Story of the *Megillah*

Who is the real hero of the *Megillah*? Of course, if we refer the question to the folk-consciousness of our people, there is no doubt that the answer is either Esther or Mordecai. Remarkably, however, if we refer to the *Megillah* itself, we discover that the name mentioned most frequently throughout the entire book is that of King Ahashverosh. One nineteenth-century Jewish scholar went to the trouble of counting the number of times that the term *melekh*, king, appears in this little book. His study showed that the name appears no less than one hundred eight-seven times. King Ahashverosh is a central figure, the axis of the whole plot. All revolves about him, nothing occurs without him. At almost every point we are apprised of the feelings and emotions of Ahashverosh: the king is happy, the king is angry; the king is restless, the king is upset; the king is fuming, the king is drunk; the king commands, the king consents. Even the greatness of Mordecai is tied to the king. At the very end of the book, we read that "Mordecai the Jew was next unto King Ahashverosh."

Yet, despite the fact that nothing seems to happen in this book without the ubiquitous king, he appears as a man who is feeble, spineless, unimaginative, and powerless. In the ten chapters of *Megillat Esther*, not one single act of importance is initiated by Ahashverosh — except, of course, his merry-making at parties and his romantic adventures. Even in these he shows no original-ity. He is angry at Vashti — but it is Memukhan who suggests that she be punished. He looks for a new queen — but only after the young men of his court have recommended it. He makes the deci-sion to commit genocide against the Jewish people only because Haman has proposed it. Soon he gives his royal ring to Haman, thus making him, for all practical purposes, the ruler of the realm. Later he will give the same ring to Mordecai, thus gearing the whole apparatus of government to a new policy. And when he is fuming against Haman, he hangs him only because the idea is planted in his mind by one of his ministers. The Book of Esther shows a remarkable paradox: On the one hand, the king is an essential figure; on the other hand, he is a mere follower, a weakling, a king who reigns but does not rule. He is, in the words of our rabbinic tradition, *a melekh tipesh* — a foolish and ineffectual sovereign. He is a royal puppet; others hold the strings.

How does one account for this paradox? If Ahashverosh is really a nonentity, why does everything seem to revolve about him? The answer is that the *Megillah,* as a document promulgated by Mordecai and Esther, was, of necessity, addressed to two separate audiences. Primarily, it was written to and for their fellow Jews both of that age and all ages. But secondarily, it was a document which had to satisfy, or at least not offend, Ahashverosh, his royal court, and especially the official religion of the empire. The Jews of Persia triumphed, they were victorious, but they could not afford to assert their independence as openly as were the Maccabees able to do in a later era. They were still in *galut*. Hence, the tale must be subdued. It must be written on two levels: revealed and concealed, open and hidden, an outer and an inner story. And hence, in the words of Mordecai himself, the *Megillah* was sent to the Jewish communities of one hundred and twenty-seven provinces as *divrei shalom ve-emet* — "words of peace and truth." To the Jews the story of the *Megillah* was *emet* — truth, the real story which they had to discover by a patient and careful perusal of the text. But the apparent story of the *Megillah* was not the same as the inner, true story for purposes of *shalom*, peacefulness and a desire not to offend the ruling circles and established religion. In other words, the *Megillah* is an unusually splendid example of a diplomatic document which tries to accommodate the competing demands of *shalom* and *emet*.

Let us try to analyze both levels, both stories. Look at the *Megillah* superficially, and you will notice that the royal court of Ahashverosh and the king himself are glorified, while the distinctively Jewish religious elements — which must have been offensive to Persian paganism — are subdued and only hinted at vaguely. Ahashverosh was probably proud of the praise of the *melekh* in the *Megillah*. He probably regarded it as a public relations coup, as a propaganda victory, as a worthy chronicle for the sovereign of one hundred and twenty-seven lands from India to Ethiopia.

Of the thirty-four times that the word *mishteh* (party or banquet) appears in all of Scripture, seventeen of them are in the Book of Esther. There is good reason for the elaborate description in the *Megillah* of the king's court and his lavish banquets. The royal party was evidently a status symbol for Persian kings. The bigger the king, the bigger and the better his parties. The one described at the beginning of Megillat Esther lasted for no less than one hundred and eighty days. Vashti's downfall occurred at a *mishteh*. Esther plans the destruction of Haman and the frustration of the pogrom at a *mishteh*. And when Mordecai and Esther declare for all generations the holiday of Purim, it consists, primarily, of a *mishteh*. These constant references to lavish parties, to the riches of Ahashverosh, to the extent of his realm, and attributing all actions to him, these are part of the attempt to appease the absolute monarch of this ancient empire. These are the words of *shalom*.

For the same reason, whatever there is of Judaism and Jewish religion in the *Megillah* is only in disguise. Thus, we are told that Mordecai refused to bow down to Haman. Our tradition tells us the reason — it was because Haman wore, around his neck, the statue of an idol. The *Megillah* itself, however, makes no mention of these religious scruples of Mordecai. A three-day fast assembly is declared by Esther and Mordecai. The *Megillah* mentions nothing about prayer, and certainly nothing about Him to Whom the prayers are directed. At the end we are told of the declaration of Purim as a holiday — but, aside from more parties, gifts, and charity, is there no thanksgiving? The *Megillah* tells nothing of this, or of Him to Whom thanks are given. There is only the vaguest hint: *le-hiyot osim et shnei ha-yamin ha-elah* — to "do" the two days of Purim. Those who know Jewish tradition will recognize that this refers to certain religious practices. But it is only a hint. It is certainly not explicit.

In the same manner, Haman's accusations against the Jews were no doubt far more elaborate than they appear in the *Megillah*. The *Megillah* has toned them down, and recorded that Haman accused us only of being dispersed and "different." In all probability, Haman told Ahashverosh that the Jews were dispersed and disunited — and that they were united only in their stubborn opposition to Persian paganism. Yet the *Megillah* does not mention this.

Finally, the clearest indication that we have here a "diplomatic" document with an inner story that is only hinted at, comes in the verses which describe Mordecai's message to Esther when he discovers the nefarious plans of Haman's program. Mordecai tells Esther that she must appear before the king to request his royal intervention lest succor come from another place (*makom aher*) and "who knows, *u-mi yode'a*," whether you have not come to royal estate for such a time as this. These expressions — "another place" and "who knows" — are euphemisms for God. The Name of God does not appear at all in this book — strange for a Biblical book, is it not? So that God and Judaism are hinted at, but nowhere are they spelled out clearly.

Thus, insofar as the apparent story of the *Megillah* is concerned, Ahashverosh is at the center, whereas Judaism is deemphasized and peripheral. It is an apologetic document calculated to satisfy any third-rate Persian super-patriot. Still, the Jews knew the real meaning of the *Megillah*. They saw the *emet* despite the attempt at *shalom*. They did not need an interpreter. For the real story of the *Megillah* is the one that is concealed, not the superficial tale. And here there is no need to mention the Name of God, for the whole story is Godly, providential, and holy. The real story, the *emet* of the story of the *Megillat Esther*, is, as in all of the Torah — especially the story of Joseph — that every individual lives and acts on two levels On the lower, conscious, human level, he makes free-will decisions for which he is fully responsible. But they appear out of context, seemingly as if man is the true sovereign of the universe and there is no God Who has larger designs. Yet on a higher level, all these free, single, individual decisions and acts fall into an overall pattern determined and predestined by God Himself. Here man acts out the role already written by God. The true story, therefore, is that man is both puppet and puppeteer, master and servant of his fate, molder of and molded by his destiny.

This is the inner, real story of the *Megillah*. It tells us to look at the grandiose figure cut by Ahashverosh, the Persian potentate. In reality he is a weakling, a despicably ineffectual piece of putty in the hands of his underlings and especially the hands of his Creator. He thinks he directs the current of events when in fact he is swept along the mighty tides and swift streams of history like driftwood on a raging river.

Take each individual event of the *Megillah*'s story and it may appear insignificant. But put them together, and you have the marvelous unfolding of the will of the *Hashgahah* — Divine Providence. No individual detail seems to make too much sense in and of itself. But when you finish the reading of the story, they all fit into their places and assume a meaning that surpasses what the individual actors could possibly have known at the time they were performing their normal deeds. And throughout the story, the king who might otherwise — insofar as *shalom* is concerned — appear as the Great Man, appears to us, in *emet*, as a pawn and a puppet. He plays only a minor role in which there are greater actors, and in which the director and producer is the Almighty.

No wonder that the Book of Esther is part of *Kitvei Kodesh*, Holy Scripture. And no wonder that the Rabbis, asking, "*Remez le-Esther min ha-Torah minayin*, where do we find a hint or reference to Esther in the Bible?" answer: With the verse "*ve-anokhi haster astir panai*, and I shall hide my face on that day" (*Hullin* 139b). The name of Esther is etymologically related to the word *hastir*, to hide or conceal. The story of Esther is a story that is concealed within the book. Behind the veil of mundane events, in which man arrogantly assumes that he is the sole master of his own destiny and that all that counts is power and might, God smilingly, but in His mysterious way, guides His universe and directs the flow of history. The Book of Esther is, indeed, the story of *hastir*.

Megillat Esther, the document of *divrei shalom ve-emet*, words of peace and truth, is most appropriate to our own day. For we, not only one day a year, but throughout the twelve months, live a life of Purim. We will recall that the derivation of the word "Purim" is from the *pur*, the lots that Haman threw. Purim therefore means "fateful days," and in these fateful days, with the imminent threat of cosmic catastrophe, all human beings, but especially Jews, must learn the two lessons of the Book of Esther. They are, first, that we must seek to accommodate the principles of *shalom* and *emet*; that it is possible for them to co-exist, to maintain the integrity of *emet*, or truth, and at the same time live a life of *shalom*, or peacefulness, as we have explained.

But even more important is the story of *emet* as such, the real, inner, concealed story of the *Megillah*. It is that, despite all appearances, nothing we do is insignificant or inconsequential in the eyes of God. Despite occasional feelings of inferiority and flashes of meaninglessness, we are all actors in a great, divine drama. Not all is as it appears to be. What sometimes appears as great might and overwhelming power is often only a mirage in the desert of life. And in that desert, the real oasis is the will of God, and the human aspiration to reach out for the Almighty and follow His ways. This is what Mordecai and Esther have taught us. And that is why, in the words of the *Megillah*, "their memories shall not vanish from their children" — nor from our children and our children's children unto the end of time.

קריאת המגילה

בָּרוּךְ אַתָּה יְיָ אֱלֹהֵינוּ מֶלֶךְ הָעוֹלָם, אֲשֶׁר קִדְּשָׁנוּ בְּמִצְוֹתָיו וְצִוָּנוּ עַל מִקְרָא מְגִלָּה.

בָּרוּךְ אַתָּה יְיָ אֱלֹהֵינוּ מֶלֶךְ הָעוֹלָם, שֶׁעָשָׂה נִסִּים לַאֲבוֹתֵינוּ בַּיָּמִים הָהֵם בַּזְּמַן הַזֶּה.

בָּרוּךְ אַתָּה יְיָ אֱלֹהֵינוּ מֶלֶךְ הָעוֹלָם, שֶׁהֶחֱיָנוּ וְקִיְּמָנוּ וְהִגִּיעָנוּ לַזְּמַן הַזֶּה:

THE READING OF THE MEGILLAH

Before reading the Megillah, the reader recites the following blessings:

Blessed are You, O Lord our God, King of the Universe, Who has sanctified us through His commandments, and has commanded us regarding the reading of the Megillah.

Blessed are You, O Lord our God, King of the Universe, Who performed miracles for our ancestors in those days, at this season.

Blessed are You, O Lord our God, King of the Universe, Who has kept us alive, and has preserved us, and enabled us to reach this season.

מגילת אסתר

פרק א

א וַיְהִי בִּימֵי אֲחַשְׁוֵרוֹשׁ הוּא אֲחַשְׁוֵרוֹשׁ הַמֹּלֵךְ מֵהֹדּוּ וְעַד־כּוּשׁ שֶׁבַע
וְעֶשְׂרִים וּמֵאָה מְדִינָה: ב בַּיָּמִים הָהֵם כְּשֶׁבֶת| הַמֶּלֶךְ אֲחַשְׁוֵרוֹשׁ עַל
כִּסֵּא מַלְכוּתוֹ אֲשֶׁר בְּשׁוּשַׁן הַבִּירָה: ג בִּשְׁנַת שָׁלוֹשׁ לְמָלְכוֹ עָשָׂה מִשְׁתֶּה
לְכָל־שָׂרָיו וַעֲבָדָיו חֵיל| פָּרַס וּמָדַי הַפַּרְתְּמִים וְשָׂרֵי הַמְּדִינוֹת לְפָנָיו: ד
בְּהַרְאֹתוֹ אֶת־עֹשֶׁר כְּבוֹד מַלְכוּתוֹ וְאֶת־יְקָר תִּפְאֶרֶת גְּדוּלָּתוֹ יָמִים רַבִּים

עָשָׂה מִשְׁתֶּה *he made a feast.* When, according to the Talmud (*Megillah*
12a), Rabbi Simeon bar Yohai's students asked him "Why were the Jews
of the generation [of the Purim incident] found worthy of destruction,"
he challenged them to offer a reason. They responded: "Because they
consented to join in the great feast tendered by the evil Ahashverosh,"
about which we read at the beginning of the *Megillah*. Indeed, Mordecai,
according to the Midrash, warned them not to participate, so as not to
give any excuse for Satan to accuse Israel of wrongdoing.

The general idea of this passage is that man sometimes invites retribution and hatred. He too often "gives an opening to the mouth of
Satan." Of course, there is no real excuse for Haman. Morally, we can
never forgive a criminal of this sort. But if the victim incites him, dares
him, seduces him, and then leaves himself defenseless before him, we
can understand the criminal — psychologically if not morally. In a
word, Haman is always inexcusable, but we must never give an excuse
to the Hamans of the world! This means that we Jews must follow a
two-pronged attack against anti-Semitism: First, we must battle it on
moral and all other relevant grounds — political, economic, and social.
And second, we must seek to prevent its occurrence by avoiding any
unnecessary provocations.

Why should sociability, the willingness of the Jews to join in the
banquet of Ahashverosh, especially when commanded by the king, be
identified as a cause of genocide? Did not Haman himself later charge
Jews with the exact reverse, blaming them for being divided and spread
amongst all the peoples and their laws differ from those of all other

Megillat Esther

Chapter 1

1 Now it came to pass in the days of Ahashverosh — this is Ahashverosh who reigned, from India to Ethiopia, over one hundred and twenty-seven provinces — **2** that in those days, when the king Ahashverosh sat on the throne of his kingdom, which was in Shushan the capital, **3** in the third year of his reign, he made a feast for all his princes and his servants; the army of Persia and Media, the nobles and princes of the provinces, being before him; **4** when he showed the riches of his

---

peoples? Why do the Rabbis blame their gregariousness and friendship, whereas Haman does the opposite? I suggest, first, that the Rabbis may have been engaging in irony: The more Jews tried to "pass" as pure Persians and Medes, the more the Hamans and Ahasheroshes considered them different! The more they tried to blur their identities in wine and drunkenness, the more their Jewishness stood out.

But perhaps there is also a second explanation of this Talmudic passage. Maybe their presence at the banquet tendered by the evil king was in itself a contributing factor in Haman's genocidal plot. I wonder how these 18,500 Jews of Shushan disported themselves at that banquet. I wonder, if we may project from the present backwards into history, whether most of them were not the nouveaux riches of a prosperous Shushanite Jewish community, who were only too willing to display all the signs of their newfound affluence and social acceptability. And when Jews are demonstrative and ostentatious, they become more visible, more provocative, and thus more vulnerable. Neither assimilation nor ostentation helps. On the contrary, they harm!

There never is a moral excuse for anti-Semitism. The Haman who seized on our Jewish ostentation or assimilation or immorality or corruption to plan to kill and destroy and undo all Jews in a genocidal catastrophe remains a monster — and all anti-Semitism is monstrous. But we Jews must be careful not to provide excuses for such anti-Semitism. Every Jew must remember that we are all co-responsible one for the other, whether we like it or not.

שְׁמוֹנִים וּמְאַת יוֹם: ה וּבִמְלֹאות| [וּבִמְלוֹאת כ'] הַיָּמִים הָאֵלֶּה עָשָׂה
הַמֶּלֶךְ לְכָל־הָעָם הַנִּמְצְאִים בְּשׁוּשַׁן הַבִּירָה לְמִגָּדוֹל וְעַד־קָטָן מִשְׁתֶּה
שִׁבְעַת יָמִים בַּחֲצַר גִּנַּת בִּיתַן הַמֶּלֶךְ: ו חוּר| כַּרְפַּס וּתְכֵלֶת אָחוּז בְּחַבְלֵי־
בוּץ וְאַרְגָּמָן עַל־גְּלִילֵי כֶסֶף וְעַמּוּדֵי שֵׁשׁ מִטּוֹת| זָהָב וָכֶסֶף עַל רִצְפַת
בַּהַט־וָשֵׁשׁ וְדַר וְסֹחָרֶת: ז וְהַשְׁקוֹת בִּכְלֵי זָהָב וְכֵלִים מִכֵּלִים שׁוֹנִים וְיֵין
מַלְכוּת רָב כְּיַד הַמֶּלֶךְ: ח וְהַשְּׁתִיָּה כַדָּת אֵין אֹנֵס כִּי־כֵן| יִסַּד הַמֶּלֶךְ עַל
כָּל־רַב בֵּיתוֹ לַעֲשׂוֹת כִּרְצוֹן אִישׁ־וָאִישׁ: ס ט גַּם וַשְׁתִּי הַמַּלְכָּה עָשְׂתָה

וּבִמְלֹאת הַיָּמִים הָאֵלֶּה עָשָׂה הַמֶּלֶךְ מִשְׁתֶּה שִׁבְעַת יָמִים *And when these days were
fulfilled, the king made a feast for all the people that were present in
Shushan the capital, both great and small, seven days.* Megillat Esther
manifests a remarkable phenomenon of duplication. The repetition of
certain things twice seems to crop up all through the work in a manner
that begs explanation. Thus there are two drinking parties, one for the
nobility and one for the masses. There are two feasts, one for Vashti and
one for Esther. Even more astounding, because it is inherently irrational
(for which reason the Sages and commentaries offer a variety of explanations), there is a repetition of the gathering of the maidens at a beauty
contest to choose a queen — even though Esther had already been
chosen after her predecessor, Vashti, was disposed of. Esther invites the
king and Haman twice — even though she could have accused Haman
at the first party. The legislation of two days of Purim, one for closed
cities and one for open cities, is a distinction which has no parallel
elsewhere in the Torah and which defies easy explanation. Mordecai
and Esther twice legislate the reading of the *Megillah* and the attendant
mitzvot of Purim — even though once would have sufficed. How shall
we explain all this?

I am indebted to the late Rabbi Zev Goethold for the following
insight. Perhaps it is a subtle reaction — but one which most Persian
Jews of that time would have been sensitive to and have understood
immediately — against the dominant Persian pagan religion. It has
been commented often that *Megillat Esther* goes out of its way not to
emphasize the Jewish religion; thus, there is no explicit mention of God.

glorious kingdom and the honor of his excellent majesty, many days, even a hundred and eighty days. **5** And when these days were fulfilled, the king made a feast for all the people that were present in Shushan the capital, both great and small, seven days, in the court of the garden of the king's palace; **6** there were hangings of white, fine cotton, and blue, bordered with cords of fine linen and purple, upon silver rods and pillars of marble; the couches were of gold and silver, upon a pavement of green, and white, and shell, and onyx marble. **7** And they gave them drink in vessels of gold — the vessels being diverse one from another — and royal wine in abundance, according to the bounty of the king. **8** And the drinking was according to the law; none did compel; for so the king had appointed to all the officers of his house, that they should do according to every man's pleasure. **9** Also Vashti the queen made a feast for the women in the royal house which

---

The references to Him are vague and indirect. This is so, apparently, because the Jews of that era were still in exile, and did not want to upset the local authorities and masses who would not want the Jewish God to be credited with the redemption of Israel and the humiliation of a prominent fellow citizen.

For the same reason, the *Megillah* included a subtle polemic, sardonic and satiric and even humorous in nature, against the dualism of ancient Persian religion. By emphasizing the number two in the story of Jewish redemption, it meant to emphasize that the very number that characterized the Persian religion — the *shetei reshuyot,* or dualism — was the one utilized by the One God of Israel to secure His people's triumph against the Persian tyrant. (Had the *Megillah* been composed in a Christian country, perhaps all the above events would have happened and been described three times.) Just as the pagan deities of ancient Egypt — the Nile, the frogs, and so on — became the instrument of the redemption of Israel, so was the dualism of Persia the medium for the salvation of the Jews by the One God. The tendency to assert the principle of Judaism even under the most unfavorable political and social conditions is thus beautifully expressed in *Megillat Esther* in this disguised numerical polemic.

מִשְׁתֵּה נָשִׁים בֵּית הַמַּלְכוּת אֲשֶׁר לַמֶּלֶךְ אֲחַשְׁוֵרוֹשׁ: ' בַּיּוֹם הַשְּׁבִיעִי כְּטוֹב לֵב־הַמֶּלֶךְ בַּיָּיִן אָמַר לִמְהוּמָן בִּזְּתָא חַרְבוֹנָא בִּגְתָא וַאֲבַגְתָא זֵתַר וְכַרְכַּס שִׁבְעַת הַסָּרִיסִים הַמְשָׁרְתִים אֶת־פְּנֵי הַמֶּלֶךְ אֲחַשְׁוֵרוֹשׁ: יא לְהָבִיא אֶת־וַשְׁתִּי הַמַּלְכָּה לִפְנֵי הַמֶּלֶךְ בְּכֶתֶר מַלְכוּת לְהַרְאוֹת הָעַמִּים וְהַשָּׂרִים אֶת־יָפְיָהּ כִּי־טוֹבַת מַרְאֶה הִיא: יב וַתְּמָאֵן הַמַּלְכָּה וַשְׁתִּי לָבוֹא בִּדְבַר הַמֶּלֶךְ אֲשֶׁר בְּיַד הַסָּרִיסִים וַיִּקְצֹף הַמֶּלֶךְ מְאֹד וַחֲמָתוֹ בָּעֲרָה בוֹ: ס יג וַיֹּאמֶר הַמֶּלֶךְ לַחֲכָמִים יֹדְעֵי הָעִתִּים כִּי־כֵן דְּבַר הַמֶּלֶךְ לִפְנֵי כָּל־יֹדְעֵי דָּת וָדִין: יד וְהַקָּרֹב אֵלָיו כַּרְשְׁנָא שֵׁתָר אַדְמָתָא תַרְשִׁישׁ מֶרֶס מַרְסְנָא מְמוּכָן שִׁבְעַת שָׂרֵי | פָּרַס וּמָדַי רֹאֵי פְּנֵי הַמֶּלֶךְ הַיֹּשְׁבִים רִאשֹׁנָה בַּמַּלְכוּת: טו כְּדָת מַה־לַעֲשׂוֹת בַּמַּלְכָּה וַשְׁתִּי עַל | אֲשֶׁר לֹא־עָשְׂתָה אֶת־מַאֲמַר הַמֶּלֶךְ אֲחַשְׁוֵרוֹשׁ בְּיַד הַסָּרִיסִים: ס טז וַיֹּאמֶר מְמוּכָן [מוֹמְכָן כ'] לִפְנֵי

לְהָבִיא אֶת־וַשְׁתִּי הַמַּלְכָּה לִפְנֵי הַמֶּלֶךְ בְּכֶתֶר מַלְכוּת *To bring Vashti the queen before the king with the crown royal.* The psychological and political consequences of rising expectations are exemplified in the Purim story. Vashti was dethroned because of her negative response to Ahashverosh's royal command, and she certainly was right. In his drunken fit, and in his empty boasting, he demanded that the queen appear before him and his royal court in nothing but her royal crown. She refused.

There is not much more we know from the text of the Book of Esther. But here the midrashim, Jewish legend and tradition, fill in the gaps in the *Megillah* story. Apparently, the conflict turned largely on the matter we would call in Hebrew and Yiddish *yihus*, nobility of ancestry. Vashti was the daughter of Belshazzar and the granddaughter of Nebuchadnezzar, the great emperors of Babylonia, whereas Ahashverosh was a commoner who had usurped the throne. And so, the conflict: Vashti was anxious to demonstrate her superiority over the commoner who was her husband, and Ahashverosh was equally eager to manifest his superiority even over the scion of the emperor's family. Hence, when Ahashverosh made his demand upon Vashti — which now seems to have been psychologically and politically motivated as well as the result of his inebriation and boasting — her response was not merely negative, but arrogant. She sent a messenger to the king calling

belonged to king Ahashverosh. 10 On the seventh day, when the heart of the king was merry with wine, he commanded Mehuman, Bizzetha, Harbona, Bigtha, and Abagtha, Zethar, and Carcas, the seven chamberlains that ministered in the presence of Ahashverosh the king, 11 to bring Vashti the queen before the king with the crown royal, to show the peoples and the princes her beauty; for she was fair to look on. 12 But the queen Vashti refused to come at the king's commandment by the chamberlains; therefore was the king very wrathful, and his anger burned in him. 13 Then the king said to the wise men, who knew the times — for so was the king's manner toward all that knew law and judgment; 14 and the next to him was Carshena, Shethar, Admatha, Tarshish, Meres, Marsena, and Memucan, the seven princes of Persia and Media, who saw the king's face, and sat the first in the kingdom: 15 "What shall we do to the queen Vashti according to law, as she has not done the bidding of the king Ahashverosh by the chamberlains?" 16 And Memucan answered before the king and the princes: "Vashti

---

him a lush and a fool, reminding him that if her father and grandfather had been alive, they would never have consented to her marriage to a man who could not hold his liquor and was a consummate idiot.

Further, there was a subtle political element. Vashti had her own power-play and expectations. She was anti-Jewish and had thwarted the attempt to rebuild the Temple. In order to demonstrate the subjugation of the Jews in her realm, she forced her Jewish female subjects to work on Shabbat in a state of humiliation. So she herself was punished in kind: On the seventh day of the royal party she was commanded to submit to the same humiliation by Ahashverosh. From later remarks, it is obvious that she was thinking not only of defending women's rights, but of the domination of the kingdom by herself and all other women. Truly, this was a case of sexual politics in antiquity. Vashti's rising expectations about her own power were countered by Ahashverosh's escalation in his move to exercise his power. The rising expectations of each thus resulted in a comical and absurd, yet fateful, conflict between the primitive forces of what now would be known as women's liberation against male chauvinism.

הַמֶּלֶךְ וְהַשָּׂרִים לֹא עַל־הַמֶּלֶךְ לְבַדּוֹ עָוְתָה וַשְׁתִּי הַמַּלְכָּה כִּי עַל־כָּל־
הַשָּׂרִים וְעַל־כָּל־הָעַמִּים אֲשֶׁר בְּכָל־מְדִינוֹת הַמֶּלֶךְ אֲחַשְׁוֵרוֹשׁ: יז כִּי־יֵצֵא
דְבַר־הַמַּלְכָּה עַל־כָּל־הַנָּשִׁים לְהַבְזוֹת בַּעְלֵיהֶן בְּעֵינֵיהֶן בְּאָמְרָם הַמֶּלֶךְ
אֲחַשְׁוֵרוֹשׁ אָמַר לְהָבִיא אֶת־וַשְׁתִּי הַמַּלְכָּה לְפָנָיו וְלֹא־בָאָה: יח וְהַיּוֹם
הַזֶּה תֹּאמַרְנָה| שָׂרוֹת פָּרַס־וּמָדַי אֲשֶׁר שָׁמְעוּ אֶת־דְּבַר הַמַּלְכָּה לְכֹל
שָׂרֵי הַמֶּלֶךְ וּכְדַי בִּזָּיוֹן וָקָצֶף: יט אִם־עַל־הַמֶּלֶךְ טוֹב יֵצֵא דְבַר־מַלְכוּת
מִלְּפָנָיו וְיִכָּתֵב בְּדָתֵי פָרַס־וּמָדַי וְלֹא יַעֲבוֹר אֲשֶׁר לֹא־תָבוֹא וַשְׁתִּי לִפְנֵי
הַמֶּלֶךְ אֲחַשְׁוֵרוֹשׁ וּמַלְכוּתָהּ יִתֵּן הַמֶּלֶךְ לִרְעוּתָהּ הַטּוֹבָה מִמֶּנָּה: כ וְנִשְׁמַע
פִּתְגָם הַמֶּלֶךְ אֲשֶׁר־יַעֲשֶׂה בְּכָל־מַלְכוּתוֹ כִּי רַבָּה הִיא וְכָל־הַנָּשִׁים יִתְּנוּ
יְקָר לְבַעְלֵיהֶן לְמִגָּדוֹל וְעַד־קָטָן: כא וַיִּיטַב הַדָּבָר בְּעֵינֵי הַמֶּלֶךְ וְהַשָּׂרִים
וַיַּעַשׂ הַמֶּלֶךְ כִּדְבַר מְמוּכָן: כב וַיִּשְׁלַח סְפָרִים אֶל־כָּל־מְדִינוֹת הַמֶּלֶךְ אֶל־
מְדִינָה וּמְדִינָה כִּכְתָבָהּ וְאֶל־עַם וָעָם כִּלְשׁוֹנוֹ לִהְיוֹת כָּל־אִישׁ שֹׂרֵר בְּבֵיתוֹ
וּמְדַבֵּר כִּלְשׁוֹן עַמּוֹ: פ

פרק ב

א אַחַר הַדְּבָרִים הָאֵלֶּה כְּשֹׁךְ חֲמַת הַמֶּלֶךְ אֲחַשְׁוֵרוֹשׁ זָכַר אֶת־וַשְׁתִּי וְאֵת
אֲשֶׁר־עָשָׂתָה וְאֵת אֲשֶׁר־נִגְזַר עָלֶיהָ: ב וַיֹּאמְרוּ נַעֲרֵי־הַמֶּלֶךְ מְשָׁרְתָיו
יְבַקְשׁוּ לַמֶּלֶךְ נְעָרוֹת בְּתוּלוֹת טוֹבוֹת מַרְאֶה: ג וְיַפְקֵד הַמֶּלֶךְ פְּקִידִים בְּכָל־
מְדִינוֹת מַלְכוּתוֹ וְיִקְבְּצוּ אֶת־כָּל־נַעֲרָה־בְתוּלָה טוֹבַת מַרְאֶה אֶל־שׁוּשַׁן
הַבִּירָה אֶל־בֵּית הַנָּשִׁים אֶל־יַד הֵגֶא סְרִיס הַמֶּלֶךְ שֹׁמֵר הַנָּשִׁים וְנָתוֹן
תַּמְרוּקֵיהֶן: ד וְהַנַּעֲרָה אֲשֶׁר תִּיטַב בְּעֵינֵי הַמֶּלֶךְ תִּמְלֹךְ תַּחַת וַשְׁתִּי וַיִּיטַב
הַדָּבָר בְּעֵינֵי הַמֶּלֶךְ וַיַּעַשׂ כֵּן: ה ס אִישׁ יְהוּדִי הָיָה בְּשׁוּשַׁן הַבִּירָה וּשְׁמוֹ
מָרְדֳּכַי בֶּן יָאִיר בֶּן־שִׁמְעִי בֶּן־קִישׁ אִישׁ יְמִינִי: ו אֲשֶׁר הָגְלָה מִירוּשָׁלַיִם

בֶּן קִישׁ *the son of Kish*. The person on whose shoulders falls the grave
responsibility of leadership must be willing to accept that responsibility.
Leadership is frustrating, disappointing, and heartbreaking. The temp-
tation is all too great for anyone jetted into this position to throw up his
hands and cry "Let them do whatever they please. I'm going to retire" or

the queen has not done wrong to the king only, but also to all the princes, and to all the peoples, that are in all the provinces of the king Ahashverosh. **17** For this deed of the queen will come abroad to all women, to make their husbands contemptible in their eyes, when it will be said: 'The king Ahashverosh commanded Vashti the queen to be brought in before him, but she came not.' **18** And this day will the princesses of Persia and Media who have heard of the deed of the queen say the same to all the king's princes. So will there arise enough contempt and wrath. **19** If it please the king, let there go forth a royal commandment from him, and let it be written among the laws of the Persians and the Medes, that it be not altered, that Vashti come no more before king Ahashverosh, and that the king give her royal estate to another that is better than she. **20** And when the king's decree which he shall make shall be published throughout all his kingdom, great though it be, all the wives will give to their husbands honor, both to great and small." **21** And the word pleased the king and the princes; and the king did according to the word of Memucan; **22** for he sent letters into all the king's provinces, into every province according to the writing thereof, and to every people after their language, that every man should bear rule in his own house, and speak according to the language of his people.

Chapter 2

1 After these things, when the wrath of king Ahashverosh was assuaged, he remembered Vashti, and what she had done, and what was decreed against her. **2** Then said the king's servants that ministered to him: "Let there be sought for the king young virgins fair to look on; **3** and let the king appoint officers in all the provinces of his kingdom, that they may gather together all the fair young virgins to Shushan the capital, to the house of the women, to the custody of Hegai the king's chamberlain, keeper of the women; and let their ointments be given them; **4** and let the maiden that pleases the king be queen instead of Vashti." And the thing pleased the king; and he did so. **5** There was a certain Jew in Shushan the capital, whose name was Mordecai the son of Jair the son of Shimei the son of Kish, a Benjamite, **6** who had been

עִם־הַגֹּלָה אֲשֶׁר הָגְלְתָה עִם יְכָנְיָה מֶלֶךְ־יְהוּדָה אֲשֶׁר הֶגְלָה נְבוּכַדְנֶאצַּר מֶלֶךְ בָּבֶל: ז וַיְהִי אֹמֵן אֶת־הֲדַסָּה הִיא אֶסְתֵּר בַּת־דֹּדוֹ כִּי אֵין לָהּ אָב וָאֵם וְהַנַּעֲרָה יְפַת־תֹּאַר וְטוֹבַת מַרְאֶה וּבְמוֹת אָבִיהָ וְאִמָּהּ לְקָחָהּ מָרְדֳּכַי לוֹ לְבַת: ח וַיְהִי בְּהִשָּׁמַע דְּבַר־הַמֶּלֶךְ וְדָתוֹ וּבְהִקָּבֵץ נְעָרוֹת רַבּוֹת אֶל־ שׁוּשַׁן הַבִּירָה אֶל־יַד הֵגַי וַתִּלָּקַח אֶסְתֵּר אֶל־בֵּית הַמֶּלֶךְ אֶל־יַד הֵגַי שֹׁמֵר הַנָּשִׁים: ט וַתִּיטַב הַנַּעֲרָה בְעֵינָיו וַתִּשָּׂא חֶסֶד לְפָנָיו וַיְבַהֵל אֶת־תַּמְרוּקֶיהָ וְאֶת־מָנוֹתֶהָ לָתֵת לָהּ וְאֵת שֶׁבַע הַנְּעָרוֹת הָרְאֻיוֹת לָתֶת־לָהּ מִבֵּית הַמֶּלֶךְ וַיְשַׁנֶּהָ וְאֶת־נַעֲרוֹתֶיהָ לְטוֹב בֵּית הַנָּשִׁים: י לֹא־הִגִּידָה אֶסְתֵּר אֶת־עַמָּהּ וְאֶת־מוֹלַדְתָּהּ כִּי מָרְדֳּכַי צִוָּה עָלֶיהָ אֲשֶׁר לֹא־תַגִּיד: יא וּבְכָל־יוֹם וָיוֹם מָרְדֳּכַי מִתְהַלֵּךְ לִפְנֵי חֲצַר בֵּית־הַנָּשִׁים לָדַעַת אֶת־שְׁלוֹם אֶסְתֵּר וּמַה־ יֵּעָשֶׂה בָּהּ: יב וּבְהַגִּיעַ תֹּר נַעֲרָה וְנַעֲרָה לָבוֹא| אֶל־הַמֶּלֶךְ אֲחַשְׁוֵרוֹשׁ מִקֵּץ הֱיוֹת לָהּ כְּדָת הַנָּשִׁים שְׁנֵים עָשָׂר חֹדֶשׁ כִּי כֵּן יִמְלְאוּ יְמֵי מְרוּקֵיהֶן שִׁשָּׁה חֳדָשִׁים בְּשֶׁמֶן הַמֹּר וְשִׁשָּׁה חֳדָשִׁים בַּבְּשָׂמִים וּבְתַמְרוּקֵי הַנָּשִׁים: יג וּבָזֶה הַנַּעֲרָה בָּאָה אֶל־הַמֶּלֶךְ אֵת כָּל־אֲשֶׁר תֹּאמַר יִנָּתֵן לָהּ לָבוֹא עִמָּהּ מִבֵּית הַנָּשִׁים עַד־בֵּית הַמֶּלֶךְ: יד בָּעֶרֶב| הִיא בָאָה וּבַבֹּקֶר הִיא שָׁבָה אֶל־בֵּית הַנָּשִׁים שֵׁנִי אֶל־יַד שַׁעַשְׁגַז סְרִיס הַמֶּלֶךְ שֹׁמֵר הַפִּילַגְשִׁים לֹא־תָבוֹא עוֹד

"I'm going into business" or "I'm going to enjoy a life of freedom for a change." But there is a moral duty which binds those chosen to do what they must in guiding their charges.

That Mordecai was such a person is immediately evident. His secret instructions to Esther when she is taken into the king's household, and his careful planning even before Haman hatches his actual plot, all point to a feeling of responsibility on Mordecai's part. Our Rabbis saw this even more clearly in the listing of his genealogy. We are told that Mordecai was the great-grandson of Kish, who was the father of King Saul. And our Rabbis seem puzzled. That is impossible, they say, for there were many more generations between these two. Actually there were nine generations between Mordecai and Kish, not four. And, they answer, the name "Kish" is important not as an ancestor of Mordecai, but as indication of his character, *She-hekish*, he would forcefully knock

carried away from Jerusalem with the captives that had been carried away with Jeconiah king of Judah, whom Nebuchadnezzar the king of Babylon had carried away. **7** And he brought up Hadassah, that is, Esther, his uncle's daughter; for she had neither father nor mother, and the maiden was of beautiful form and fair to look on; and when her father and mother were dead, Mordecai took her for his own daughter. **8** So it came to pass, when the king's commandment and his decree was published, and when many maidens were gathered together to Shushan the capital, to the custody of Hegai, that Esther was taken into the king's house, to the custody of Hegai, keeper of the women. **9** And the maiden pleased him, and she obtained kindness of him; and he speedily gave her her ointments, with her portions, and the seven maidens, who were chosen to be given her out of the king's house; and he advanced her and her maidens to the best place in the house of the women. **10** Esther had not made known her people nor her kindred; for Mordecai had charged her that she should not tell it. **11** And Mordecai walked every day before the court of the women's house, to know how Esther did, and what would become of her. **12** Now when the turn of every maiden was come to go in to king Ahashverosh, after that it had been done to her according to the law for the women, twelve months — for so were the days of their anointing accomplished, to wit, six months with oil of myrrh, and six month with sweet odours, and with other ointments of the women — **13** when then the maiden came to the king, whatsoever she desired was given her to go with her out of the house of the women to the king's house. **14** In the evening she went, and on the morrow she returned into the second house of the women, to the custody

on the doors of prayer which were then opened to him. Mordecai likewise pushed himself to the fore; he, so to speak, demanded of God that something be done for his people; he was not satisfied with remaining in the background. He forced his way through the Gates of Prayer, accepting the burden of national leadership, and he was therefore successful — his prayers were accepted.

אֶל־הַמֶּלֶךְ כִּי אִם־חָפֵץ בָּהּ הַמֶּלֶךְ וְנִקְרְאָה בְשֵׁם: טו וּבְהַגִּיעַ תֹּר־אֶסְתֵּר
בַּת־אֲבִיחַיִל דֹּד מָרְדֳּכַי אֲשֶׁר לָקַח־לוֹ לְבַת לָבוֹא אֶל־הַמֶּלֶךְ לֹא בִקְשָׁה
דָּבָר כִּי אִם אֶת־אֲשֶׁר יֹאמַר הֵגַי סְרִיס־הַמֶּלֶךְ שֹׁמֵר הַנָּשִׁים וַתְּהִי אֶסְתֵּר
נֹשֵׂאת חֵן בְּעֵינֵי כָּל־רֹאֶיהָ: טז וַתִּלָּקַח אֶסְתֵּר אֶל־הַמֶּלֶךְ אֲחַשְׁוֵרוֹשׁ אֶל־
בֵּית מַלְכוּתוֹ בַּחֹדֶשׁ הָעֲשִׂירִי הוּא־חֹדֶשׁ טֵבֵת בִּשְׁנַת־שֶׁבַע לְמַלְכוּתוֹ:
יז וַיֶּאֱהַב הַמֶּלֶךְ אֶת־אֶסְתֵּר מִכָּל־הַנָּשִׁים וַתִּשָּׂא־חֵן וָחֶסֶד לְפָנָיו מִכָּל־
הַבְּתוּלֹת וַיָּשֶׂם כֶּתֶר־מַלְכוּת בְּרֹאשָׁהּ וַיַּמְלִיכֶהָ תַּחַת וַשְׁתִּי: יח וַיַּעַשׂ
הַמֶּלֶךְ מִשְׁתֶּה גָדוֹל לְכָל־שָׂרָיו וַעֲבָדָיו אֵת מִשְׁתֵּה אֶסְתֵּר וַהֲנָחָה לַמְּדִינוֹת
עָשָׂה וַיִּתֵּן מַשְׂאֵת כְּיַד הַמֶּלֶךְ: יט וּבְהִקָּבֵץ בְּתוּלוֹת שֵׁנִית וּמָרְדֳּכַי יֹשֵׁב
בְּשַׁעַר־הַמֶּלֶךְ: כ אֵין אֶסְתֵּר מַגֶּדֶת מוֹלַדְתָּהּ וְאֶת־עַמָּהּ כַּאֲשֶׁר צִוָּה עָלֶיהָ
מָרְדֳּכַי וְאֶת־מַאֲמַר מָרְדֳּכַי אֶסְתֵּר עֹשָׂה כַּאֲשֶׁר הָיְתָה בְאָמְנָה אִתּוֹ: ס
כא בַּיָּמִים הָהֵם וּמָרְדֳּכַי יֹשֵׁב בְּשַׁעַר־הַמֶּלֶךְ קָצַף בִּגְתָן וָתֶרֶשׁ שְׁנֵי־סָרִיסֵי
הַמֶּלֶךְ מִשֹּׁמְרֵי הַסַּף וַיְבַקְשׁוּ לִשְׁלֹחַ יָד בַּמֶּלֶךְ אֲחַשְׁוֵרֹשׁ: כב וַיִּוָּדַע הַדָּבָר
לְמָרְדֳּכַי וַיַּגֵּד לְאֶסְתֵּר הַמַּלְכָּה וַתֹּאמֶר אֶסְתֵּר לַמֶּלֶךְ בְּשֵׁם מָרְדֳּכָי: כג
וַיְבֻקַּשׁ הַדָּבָר וַיִּמָּצֵא וַיִּתָּלוּ שְׁנֵיהֶם עַל־עֵץ וַיִּכָּתֵב בְּסֵפֶר דִּבְרֵי הַיָּמִים
לִפְנֵי הַמֶּלֶךְ: פ

פרק ג׳

א אַחַר | הַדְּבָרִים הָאֵלֶּה גִּדַּל הַמֶּלֶךְ אֲחַשְׁוֵרוֹשׁ אֶת־הָמָן בֶּן־הַמְּדָתָא
הָאֲגָגִי וַיְנַשְּׂאֵהוּ וַיָּשֶׂם אֶת־כִּסְאוֹ מֵעַל כָּל־הַשָּׂרִים אֲשֶׁר אִתּוֹ: ב וְכָל־עַבְדֵי
הַמֶּלֶךְ אֲשֶׁר־בְּשַׁעַר הַמֶּלֶךְ כֹּרְעִים וּמִשְׁתַּחֲוִים לְהָמָן כִּי־כֵן צִוָּה־לוֹ הַמֶּלֶךְ

הָמָן בֶּן הַמְּדָתָא הָאֲגָגִי *Haman the son of Hammedatha the Agagite.* Underneath
all the obvious fun of wielding the *groggers* and the stamping are expressions of vindictiveness. Doesn't this open the floodgates to hatred
against real people here and now? And is not hatred unreservedly evil
and morally corrupting?

But just as there is a mitzvah to love God, our neighbor, or the
stranger, so there is a mitzvah to hate. For instance, we must hate
Amalek. And yet, the Halakhah provides immediate correctives and

of Shaashgaz, the king's chamberlain, who kept the concubines; she would come to the king no more, except the king delighted in her, and she were called by name. **15** Now when the turn of Esther, the daughter of Abihail the uncle of Mordecai, who had taken her for his daughter, came to go in to the king, she required nothing but what Hegai the king's chamberlain, the keeper of the women, appointed. And Esther obtained favor in the sight of all that looked upon her. **16** So Esther was taken to king Ahashverosh into his house royal in the tenth month, which is the month Tebeth, in the seventh year of his reign. **17** And the king loved Esther above all the women, and she obtained grace and favor in his sight more than all the virgins; so that he set the royal crown upon her head, and made her queen instead of Vashti. **18** Then the king made a great feast for all his princes and his servants, Esther's feast; and he granted a release to the provinces, and gave gifts, according to the bounty of the king. **19** And when the virgins were gathered together the second time, and Mordecai sat in the king's gate — **20** Esther had not yet made known her kindred nor her people; as Mordecai had charged her; for Esther obeyed the commandment of Mordecai, as when she was brought up with him — **21** in those days, while Mordecai sat in the king's gate, two of the king's chamberlains, Bigthan and Teresh, of those that kept the door, were angered, and sought to lay hands on the king Ahashverosh. **22** And the thing became known to Mordecai, who told it to Esther the queen; and Esther told the king thereof in Mordecai's name. **23** And when inquiry was made of the matter, and it was found to be so, they were both hanged on a tree; and it was written in the book of the chronicles before the king.

Chapter 3

1 After these things king Ahashverosh promoted Haman the son of Hammedatha the Agagite, and advanced him, and set his seat above all the princes that were with him. **2** And all the king's servants, that were in the king's gate, bowed down, and prostrated themselves before Haman; for the king had so commanded concerning him.

וּמָרְדֳּכַי לֹא יִכְרַע וְלֹא יִשְׁתַּחֲוֶה: ג וַיֹּאמְרוּ עַבְדֵי הַמֶּלֶךְ אֲשֶׁר־בְּשַׁעַר הַמֶּלֶךְ לְמָרְדֳּכָי מַדּוּעַ אַתָּה עוֹבֵר אֵת מִצְוַת הַמֶּלֶךְ: ד וַיְהִי כְּאָמְרָם [בְּאָמְרָם כ'] אֵלָיו יוֹם וָיוֹם וְלֹא שָׁמַע אֲלֵיהֶם וַיַּגִּידוּ לְהָמָן לִרְאוֹת הֲיַעַמְדוּ דִּבְרֵי מָרְדֳּכַי כִּי־הִגִּיד לָהֶם אֲשֶׁר־הוּא יְהוּדִי: ה וַיַּרְא הָמָן כִּי־אֵין מָרְדֳּכַי כֹּרֵעַ וּמִשְׁתַּחֲוֶה לוֹ וַיִּמָּלֵא הָמָן חֵמָה: ו וַיִּבֶז בְּעֵינָיו לִשְׁלֹחַ יָד בְּמָרְדֳּכַי לְבַדּוֹ כִּי־הִגִּידוּ לוֹ אֶת־עַם מָרְדֳּכָי וַיְבַקֵּשׁ הָמָן לְהַשְׁמִיד אֶת־כָּל־הַיְּהוּדִים אֲשֶׁר בְּכָל־מַלְכוּת אֲחַשְׁוֵרוֹשׁ עַם מָרְדֳּכָי: ז בַּחֹדֶשׁ הָרִאשׁוֹן הוּא־חֹדֶשׁ נִיסָן בִּשְׁנַת שְׁתֵּים עֶשְׂרֵה לַמֶּלֶךְ אֲחַשְׁוֵרוֹשׁ הִפִּיל פּוּר הוּא הַגּוֹרָל לִפְנֵי הָמָן מִיּוֹם | לְיוֹם וּמֵחֹדֶשׁ לְחֹדֶשׁ שְׁנֵים־עָשָׂר הוּא־חֹדֶשׁ אֲדָר: ס ח וַיֹּאמֶר הָמָן לַמֶּלֶךְ אֲחַשְׁוֵרוֹשׁ יֶשְׁנוֹ עַם־אֶחָד מְפֻזָּר וּמְפֹרָד בֵּין הָעַמִּים בְּכֹל מְדִינוֹת מַלְכוּתֶךָ וְדָתֵיהֶם שֹׁנוֹת מִכָּל־עָם וְאֶת־דָּתֵי הַמֶּלֶךְ אֵינָם עֹשִׂים

---

restraints so that the practice is far different from the theory. Thus, some authorities maintain that the commandment to destroy Amalek is operative only when the Amalekites refuse first to accept the seven commandments of the sons of Noah, the basic foundations of civilized life. Hence, it is not a genocidal commandment, but it means that we must do battle with those who are so uncivilized as to corrupt and destroy others.

We reserve our actual, living hatred for the unusually hateful individuals who commit historic crimes and whose malice is monstrous and premeditated. Anti-Semites who wish to destroy all the Jewish people; monsters who seek sadistically to wipe out whole populations — such people remain deserving, on purely moral grounds, of actual contempt and hatred. And, of course, we are always bidden to release our hatred against the symbols of evil.

This is the basic motif of the commandment to read the Biblical portion of Amalek, and to observe the festival of Purim. I want to teach my children to hate as well as to love. I want them to know that there is a moral law which requires that those who have placed themselves outside morality deserve not our love but our contempt. I want my children to have available for themselves the psychological relief in hating those who deserve it, so that they can relate to all others constructively

But Mordecai did not bow down, nor did he prostrate himself before him. 3 Then the king's servants, that were in the king's gate, said to Mordecai: "Why do you transgress the king's commandment?" 4 Now it came to pass, when they spoke daily to him, and he did not listen to them, that they told Haman, to see whether Mordecai's words would stand; for he had told them that he was a Jew. 5 And when Haman saw that Mordecai did not bow down, and did not prostrate himself before him, then Haman was full of wrath. 6 But it seemed contemptible in his eyes to lay hands on Mordecai alone; for they had made known to him the people of Mordecai; wherefore Haman sought to destroy all the Jews that were throughout the whole kingdom of Ahashverosh, the people of Mordecai. 7 In the first month, which is the month Nisan, in the twelfth year of king Ahashverosh, they cast pur, that is, the lot, before Haman from day to day, and from month to month, to the twelfth month, which is the month Adar. 8 And Haman said to king Ahashverosh: "There is a certain people scattered abroad and dispersed among the peoples in all the provinces of your kingdom; and their laws are different from those of every people; and they do not

---

and lovingly. I want them to be halakhic Jews, and thus to handle hatred with extreme circumspection and caution and great care; and so, in effect, they will hate without hurt, and express their innate hostility toward evil by stamping and stomping and *groggering* Haman. By restricting our hatred to evil and those who personify it and symbolize by chanting the commandment to obliterate Amalek and by hissing and booing at the mention of Haman's name, we shall learn to act lovingly to all God's other creatures.

וְאֶת דָּתֵי הַמֶּלֶךְ אֵינָם עֹשִׂים *and they do not keep the king's laws.* Haman's accusation is that Jews only appear to be diverse and not able to agree upon anything; actually, they consider themselves one people. Hence, they are subversive in their dogged and haughty loyalty to their own group. We do not eat the foods of other peoples, and we do not intermarry with them. He was furious with us because our many holidays, which do not coincide with the holidays of other people, cause an economic

וְלַמֶּ֫לֶךְ אֵין־שֹׁוֶה לְהַנִּיחָ֑ם: ט אִם־עַל־הַמֶּ֫לֶךְ ט֔וֹב יִכָּתֵ֔ב לְאַבְּדָ֑ם וַעֲשֶׂ֤רֶת
אֲלָפִ֜ים כִּכַּר־כֶּ֗סֶף אֶשְׁקוֹל֙ עַל־יְדֵי֙ עֹשֵׂ֣י הַמְּלָאכָ֔ה לְהָבִ֖יא אֶל־גִּנְזֵ֥י הַמֶּֽלֶךְ:
י וַיָּ֧סַר הַמֶּ֛לֶךְ אֶת־טַבַּעְתּ֖וֹ מֵעַ֣ל יָד֑וֹ וַֽיִּתְּנָ֗הּ לְהָמָ֧ן בֶּֽן־הַמְּדָ֛תָא הָאֲגָגִ֖י צֹרֵ֥ר
הַיְּהוּדִֽים: יא וַיֹּ֤אמֶר הַמֶּ֙לֶךְ֙ לְהָמָ֔ן הַכֶּ֖סֶף נָת֣וּן לָ֑ךְ וְהָעָ֕ם לַעֲשֹׂ֥ות בּ֖וֹ כַּטּ֥וֹב
בְּעֵינֶֽיךָ: יב וַיִּקָּרְאוּ֩ סֹפְרֵ֨י הַמֶּ֜לֶךְ בַּחֹ֣דֶשׁ הָרִאשׁ֗וֹן בִּשְׁלוֹשָׁ֤ה עָשָׂר֙ יוֹם֙ בּ֔וֹ
וַיִּכָּתֵ֣ב כְּֽכָל־אֲשֶׁר־צִוָּ֣ה הָמָ֡ן אֶ֣ל אֲחַשְׁדַּרְפְּנֵֽי־הַ֠מֶּלֶךְ וְֽאֶל־הַפַּחוֹת֩ אֲשֶׁ֨ר|
עַל־מְדִינָ֜ה וּמְדִינָ֗ה וְאֶל־שָׂ֤רֵי עַם֙ וָעָ֔ם מְדִינָ֤ה וּמְדִינָה֙ כִּכְתָבָ֔הּ וְעַ֥ם וָעָ֖ם
כִּלְשׁוֹנ֑וֹ בְּשֵׁ֨ם הַמֶּ֤לֶךְ אֲחַשְׁוֵרֹשׁ֙ נִכְתָּ֔ב וְנֶחְתָּ֖ם בְּטַבַּ֥עַת הַמֶּֽלֶךְ: יג וְנִשְׁל֣וֹחַ
סְפָרִ֡ים בְּיַד֩ הָרָצִ֨ים אֶל־כָּל־מְדִינ֣וֹת הַמֶּ֗לֶךְ לְהַשְׁמִ֤יד לַהֲרֹג֙ וּלְאַבֵּ֣ד אֶת־
כָּל־הַ֠יְּהוּדִים מִנַּ֨עַר וְעַד־זָקֵ֜ן טַ֤ף וְנָשִׁים֙ בְּי֣וֹם אֶחָ֔ד בִּשְׁלוֹשָׁ֥ה עָשָׂ֛ר לְחֹ֥דֶשׁ
שְׁנֵים־עָשָׂ֖ר הוּא־חֹ֣דֶשׁ אֲדָ֑ר וּשְׁלָלָ֖ם לָבֽוֹז: יד פַּתְשֶׁ֣גֶן הַכְּתָ֗ב לְהִנָּ֤תֵֽן דָּת֙
בְּכָל־מְדִינָ֣ה וּמְדִינָ֔ה גָּל֖וּי לְכָל־הָֽעַמִּ֑ים לִהְי֥וֹת עֲתִדִ֖ים לַיּ֥וֹם הַזֶּֽה: טו הָרָצִ֞ים

---

drain upon the larger community. Furthermore, "they do not perform the laws of the king." Jews refuse to celebrate those national holidays which are religious in character and which are pagan in essence. Behind this forensic facade lay what Haman regarded as the fatal flaw of the faithful Jew: "Mordecai would not kneel and would not bow down." Mordecai, symbol of the Jew, will not deify a mere mortal even if he be as powerful as Haman. The Jew will never idolize a mere human being.

How do we plead to this ancient accusation, so much older and so much more serious because it is more rational than the crucifixion libel? Are we guilty, or shall we seek to be "absolved"? Of course, the first human tendency is to plead "not guilty." We feel that we ought to deny the calumny of the anti-Semite and call it false. But not in this case. On the contrary, we are guilty! It is the pride of our people to plead "guilty as charged." The wretched Haman's conclusions may be vile exaggerations and misleading, but in essence what he says is right. And woe to the Jew who seeks to be absolved of Haman's indictment! The *Yalkut* puts the matter this way: "Rabbi Levi said, 'Concerning what Haman

keep the king's laws; therefore it is of no benefit to the king to tolerate them. **9** If it please the king, let it be written that they be destroyed; and I will pay ten thousand talents of silver into the hands of those that have the charge of the king's business, to bring it into the king's treasuries." **10** And the king took his ring from his hand, and gave it to Haman the son of Hammedatha the Agagite, the Jews' enemy. **11** And the king said to Haman: "The silver is given to you, the people also, to do with them as it seems good to you." **12** Then the king's scribes were called in the first month, on the thirteenth day thereof, and there was written, according to all that Haman commanded, to the king's satraps, and to the governors that were over every province, and to the princes of every people; to every province according to the writing thereof, and to every people according to their language; in the name of king Ahashverosh it was written, and it was sealed with the king's ring. **13** And letters were sent by posts into all the king's provinces, to destroy, to slay, and to cause to perish, all Jews, both young and old, little children and women, in one day, on the thirteenth day of the twelfth month, which is the month Adar, and to take the spoil of them for plunder. **14** The copy of the writing, to be given out for a decree in every province, was to be published for all peoples, that they should be ready for that day. **15** The posts went forth in haste by the king's

---

prosecuted Israel for here below, the angel Michael defended us for up above' " (*Yalkut Shimoni, Esther* 654). He implied that up above, before God, the angel presented these very anti-Semitic charges as proof that Israel had retained its spiritual independence and its moral integrity. The very charges of Haman are the demonstrations of Israel's loyalty to its spiritual vocation. What to the king of Persia seems a criminal charge, to the King of the Universe is a lofty compliment — not heinous but holy; not sinister but sublime. It is of the utmost importance that we understand these charges and so order our lives that we become guilty of them if we are not already so.

יָצְאוּ דְחוּפִים בִּדְבַר הַמֶּלֶךְ וְהַדָּת נִתְּנָה בְּשׁוּשַׁן הַבִּירָה וְהַמֶּלֶךְ וְהָמָן יָשְׁבוּ
לִשְׁתּוֹת וְהָעִיר שׁוּשָׁן נָבוֹכָה: פ

פרק ד'

א וּמָרְדֳּכַי יָדַע אֶת־כָּל־אֲשֶׁר נַעֲשָׂה וַיִּקְרַע מָרְדֳּכַי אֶת־בְּגָדָיו וַיִּלְבַּשׁ
שַׂק וָאֵפֶר וַיֵּצֵא בְּתוֹךְ הָעִיר וַיִּזְעַק זְעָקָה גְדֹלָה וּמָרָה: ב וַיָּבוֹא עַד לִפְנֵי
שַׁעַר־הַמֶּלֶךְ כִּי אֵין לָבוֹא אֶל־שַׁעַר הַמֶּלֶךְ בִּלְבוּשׁ שָׂק: ג וּבְכָל־מְדִינָה

נָבוֹכָה *perplexed.* "The city of Shushan," that is, its Jewish population, "was
perplexed." The word "perplexed" is too weak. Perhaps "overwhelmed"
is more accurate. Persian Jewry was completely unprepared for the
possibility of genocide. In Persia, Jews thought, "it can't happen here."
Surely, civilized men and a cultured society cannot suddenly be transformed into beasts. The Jews of Persia were comfortable in their society.
They were being entertained in the "White House" of the Persians and
the Medes. They were accepted as citizens of the empire, subjects of
the king, and they would not stand out as Jews. Probably, when Haman
ascended to the office of prime minister, they thought that despite his
tendency to extremism, his secretiveness, his reputation for aggressive-
ness, he would be good for the empire and especially for business — and
therefore for themselves. And so, their naïveté left them vulnerable,
exposed to the sudden and climactic awareness of human bestiality and
degradation. The bitter truth came as a traumatic revelation, and their
naïveté left them incredulous and defenseless.

My teacher, Rabbi Joseph B. Soleveitchik, of blessed memory, located
the source of this naïveté in the great Jewish faith that man was created in the "image of God." This sublime principle led Jews to delude
themselves into believing that, therefore, man is incapable of senseless
evil, of cruelty, of absurd atrocities, of irrational malice. But creation
in the image of God means only that man has a *capacity* for good, the
potential of moral heroism and saintliness. Every individual, by virtue
of his being a member of the human race, has a certain minimum
core of worthiness and value which derives from the Creator whom
he resembles. But it does not mean that left to his own resorts, man
will do the right thing. For man also has another facet to his complex

commandment, and the decree was given out in Shushan the capital; and the king and Haman sat down to drink; but the city of Shushan was perplexed.

Chapter 4

1 When Mordecai knew all that was done, Mordecai rent his clothes, and put on sackcloth with ashes, and went out into the midst of the city, and cried with a loud and a bitter cry; **2** and he came before the king's gate; for none might enter within the king's gate clothed with sackcloth. **3** And in every province, wherever the king's commandment

---

personality: that of evil. "For the imagination of man's heart is evil from his youth" (Genesis 6:5).

When we forget this, when we ignore the demonic potential of man, we slip into a naive faith which leaves us vulnerable. And that is downright dangerous. This occurred not only in ancient days. In modern times too, we have been shocked when we experienced the horrifying phenomenon of man turning into monster. And, in our naïveté, we Jews forgot that when this occurs, when the demonic in man comes to the forefront, his first victim is usually the Jew! We forgot that all humans are capable of such unreasonable hatred — not only peasants and ignorant red-necks, but also poets and philosophers and statesmen, regardless of social or economic or political or religious or intellectual class or status. We forgot that the evil side of man is often couched in idealistic and utopian visions, and in humanistic rhetoric. Today, after the bloody encounter with the Amalek of the Holocaust, we should have been cured of this naïveté. However, when things are looking bright, when we have reestablished our confidence in man and his benevolent nature, then, and specifically then, when we might be at the mercy of this horrible fallacy, must we recall that man has a propensity for the demonic, that man is potentially an Amalekite. Only by means of such vigilance can we bring on that great day, the day of the Messiah, when the Jewish faith in man, in his image of God, will ultimately be vindicated fully and completely. Only with such realism wedded to idealism, with such faith without naïveté, can we aspire to the day when we shall be happy and joyous, confident and serene as Jews.

וּמְדִינָ֣ה מְק֡וֹם אֲשֶׁר֩ דְּבַר־הַמֶּ֨לֶךְ וְדָת֜וֹ מַגִּ֗יעַ אֵ֤בֶל גָּדוֹל֙ לַיְּהוּדִ֔ים וְצ֥וֹם וּבְכִ֖י וּמִסְפֵּ֑ד שַׂ֣ק וָאֵ֔פֶר יֻצַּ֖ע לָֽרַבִּֽים: ד וַתָּב֩וֹאנָה [וַתָּב֨וֹאֶינָה כ'] נַעֲר֨וֹת אֶסְתֵּ֤ר וְסָרִיסֶ֙יהָ֙ וַיַּגִּ֣ידוּ לָ֔הּ וַתִּתְחַלְחַ֥ל הַמַּלְכָּ֖ה מְאֹ֑ד וַתִּשְׁלַ֨ח בְּגָדִ֜ים לְהַלְבִּ֣ישׁ אֶֽת־מָרְדֳּכַ֗י וּלְהָסִ֥יר שַׂקּ֛וֹ מֵעָלָ֖יו וְלֹ֥א קִבֵּֽל: ה וַתִּקְרָ֣א אֶסְתֵּ֗ר לַהֲתָ֞ךְ מִסָּרִיסֵ֤י הַמֶּ֙לֶךְ֙ אֲשֶׁ֣ר הֶעֱמִ֣יד לְפָנֶ֔יהָ וַתְּצַוֵּ֖הוּ עַֽל־מָרְדֳּכָ֑י לָדַ֥עַת מַה־זֶּ֖ה וְעַל־מַה־זֶּֽה: ו וַיֵּצֵ֥א הֲתָ֖ךְ אֶֽל־מָרְדֳּכָ֑י אֶל־רְח֣וֹב הָעִ֔יר אֲשֶׁ֖ר לִפְנֵ֥י שַֽׁעַר־הַמֶּֽלֶךְ: ז וַיַּגֶּד־ל֣וֹ מָרְדֳּכַ֔י אֵ֖ת כָּל־אֲשֶׁ֣ר קָרָ֑הוּ וְאֵ֣ת| פָּרָשַׁ֣ת הַכֶּ֗סֶף אֲשֶׁ֨ר אָמַ֤ר הָמָן֙ לִ֠שְׁקוֹל עַל־גִּנְזֵ֧י הַמֶּ֛לֶךְ בַּיְּהוּדִ֖ים [בַּיְּהוּדִ֖יים כ'] לְאַבְּדָֽם: ח וְאֶת־פַּתְשֶׁ֣גֶן כְּתָֽב־הַ֠דָּת אֲשֶׁר־נִתַּ֨ן בְּשׁוּשָׁ֤ן לְהַשְׁמִידָם֙ נָ֣תַן ל֔וֹ לְהַרְא֥וֹת אֶת־אֶסְתֵּ֖ר וּלְהַגִּ֣יד לָ֑הּ וּלְצַוּ֣וֹת עָלֶ֗יהָ לָב֨וֹא אֶל־הַמֶּ֧לֶךְ לְהִֽתְחַנֶּן־ל֛וֹ וּלְבַקֵּ֥שׁ מִלְּפָנָ֖יו עַל־עַמָּֽהּ: ט וַיָּב֖וֹא הֲתָ֑ךְ וַיַּגֵּ֣ד לְאֶסְתֵּ֔ר אֵ֖ת דִּבְרֵ֥י מָרְדֳּכָֽי: י וַתֹּ֤אמֶר אֶסְתֵּר֙ לַהֲתָ֔ךְ וַתְּצַוֵּ֖הוּ אֶֽל־מָרְדֳּכָֽי: יא כָּל־עַבְדֵ֣י הַמֶּ֡לֶךְ וְעַם־מְדִינ֨וֹת הַמֶּ֜לֶךְ יֽוֹדְעִ֗ים אֲשֶׁ֣ר כָּל־אִ֣ישׁ וְ֠אִשָּׁה אֲשֶׁ֨ר יָבֽוֹא־אֶל־הַמֶּ֤לֶךְ אֶל־הֶֽחָצֵר֙ הַפְּנִימִ֗ית אֲשֶׁ֣ר לֹֽא־יִקָּרֵ֗א אַחַ֤ת דָּתוֹ֙ לְהָמִ֔ית לְבַ֞ד מֵאֲשֶׁ֨ר יֽוֹשִׁיט־ל֥וֹ הַמֶּ֛לֶךְ אֶת־שַׁרְבִ֥יט הַזָּהָ֖ב וְחָיָ֑ה וַאֲנִ֗י לֹ֤א נִקְרֵ֙אתִי֙ לָב֣וֹא אֶל־הַמֶּ֔לֶךְ זֶ֖ה שְׁלוֹשִׁ֥ים יֽוֹם: יב וַיַּגִּ֣ידוּ לְמָרְדֳּכָ֑י אֵ֖ת דִּבְרֵ֥י אֶסְתֵּֽר: פ יג וַיֹּ֥אמֶר מָרְדֳּכַ֖י לְהָשִׁ֣יב אֶל־אֶסְתֵּ֑ר אַל־תְּדַמִּ֣י בְנַפְשֵׁ֔ךְ לְהִמָּלֵ֥ט בֵּית־הַמֶּ֖לֶךְ מִכָּל־הַיְּהוּדִֽים: יד כִּ֣י אִם־הַחֲרֵ֣שׁ תַּחֲרִישִׁי֮ בָּעֵ֣ת הַזֹּאת֒ רֶ֣וַח וְהַצָּלָ֞ה יַעֲמ֤וֹד לַיְּהוּדִים֙ מִמָּק֣וֹם

Do not think in your heart that אַל־תְּדַמִּ֣י בְנַפְשֵׁ֔ךְ לְהִמָּלֵ֥ט בֵּ֣ית הַמֶּ֖לֶךְ מִכָּל־הַיְּהוּדִֽים **you shall escape in the king's house, more than all the Jews.** Queen Esther, apprised of the nefarious plans of Haman, probably considered them the ranting of a madman. He could not possibly really mean to do what he proclaimed he would! It was only when Mordecai spoke to her in words as strong, cold, cutting as steel that she came to her senses and thus averted a great tragedy. The democracies of the West similarly did not believe that Hitler meant to do what he announced in his *Mein Kampf*. They did not believe it, they were silent, and eighteen million people were killed as testimony to that silence.

We have been plagued by a nagging question: Why did European

and his decree came, there was great mourning among the Jews, and fasting, and weeping, and wailing; and many lay in sackcloth and ashes. 4 And Esther's maidens and her chamberlains came and told it her; and the queen was exceedingly distressed; and she sent raiment to clothe Mordecai; and to take his sackcloth off him; but he did not accept it. 5 Then Esther called for Hathach, one of the king's chamberlains, whom he had appointed to attend upon her, and sent him to Mordecai, to know what this was, and why it was. 6 So Hathach went to Mordecai to the broad place of the city, which was before the king's gate. 7 And Mordecai told him of all that had happened to him, and the exact sum of the money that Haman had promised to pay to the king's treasuries for the Jews, to destroy them. 8 Also he gave him the copy of the writing of the decree that was given out in Shushan to destroy them, to show it to Esther, and to declare it to her; and to charge her that she should go to the king, to make supplication to him, and to make request before him, for her people. 9 And Hathach came and told Esther the words of Mordecai. 10 Then Esther spoke to Hathach, and gave him a message to Mordecai: 11 "All the king's servants, and the people of the king's provinces, know, that whoever, whether man or woman, shall come to the king into the inner court, who is not called, there is one law for him, that he be put to death, except such to whom the king shall hold out the golden scepter, that he may live; but I have not been called to come to the king these thirty days." 12 And they told to Mordecai Esther's words. 13 Then Mordecai commanded them to answer Esther: "Do not think in your heart that you shall escape in the king's house, more than all the Jews. 14 For if you hold your peace at this time, then relief and deliverance will arise to the Jews from another place, but you and your father's house will

---

Jewry not react violently to these plans of destruction? An answer seems to be crystallizing from all the mass of data — that the Jews, because of their own innate character, simply never believed the reports they had been receiving of death camps and crematoria. It could not be true. And so they were silent.

אַחֵר וְאַתְּ וּבֵית־אָבִיךְ תֹּאבֵדוּ וּמִי יוֹדֵעַ אִם־לְעֵת כָּזֹאת הִגַּעַתְּ לַמַּלְכוּת:
טז וַתֹּאמֶר אֶסְתֵּר לְהָשִׁיב אֶל־מָרְדֳּכָי: יז לֵךְ כְּנוֹס אֶת־כָּל־הַיְּהוּדִים
הַנִּמְצְאִים בְּשׁוּשָׁן וְצוּמוּ עָלַי וְאַל־תֹּאכְלוּ וְאַל־תִּשְׁתּוּ שְׁלֹשֶׁת יָמִים
לַיְלָה וָיוֹם גַּם־אֲנִי וְנַעֲרֹתַי אָצוּם כֵּן וּבְכֵן אָבוֹא אֶל־הַמֶּלֶךְ אֲשֶׁר לֹא־כַדָּת
וְכַאֲשֶׁר אָבַדְתִּי אָבָדְתִּי: יח וַיַּעֲבֹר מָרְדֳּכָי וַיַּעַשׂ כְּכֹל אֲשֶׁר־צִוְּתָה עָלָיו
אֶסְתֵּר: ס

פרק ה'

א וַיְהִי | בַּיּוֹם הַשְּׁלִישִׁי וַתִּלְבַּשׁ אֶסְתֵּר מַלְכוּת וַתַּעֲמֹד בַּחֲצַר בֵּית־הַמֶּלֶךְ
הַפְּנִימִית נֹכַח בֵּית הַמֶּלֶךְ וְהַמֶּלֶךְ יוֹשֵׁב עַל־כִּסֵּא מַלְכוּתוֹ בְּבֵית הַמַּלְכוּת
נֹכַח פֶּתַח הַבָּיִת: ב וַיְהִי כִרְאוֹת הַמֶּלֶךְ אֶת־אֶסְתֵּר הַמַּלְכָּה עֹמֶדֶת בֶּחָצֵר
נָשְׂאָה חֵן בְּעֵינָיו וַיּוֹשֶׁט הַמֶּלֶךְ לְאֶסְתֵּר אֶת־שַׁרְבִיט הַזָּהָב אֲשֶׁר בְּיָדוֹ
וַתִּקְרַב אֶסְתֵּר וַתִּגַּע בְּרֹאשׁ הַשַּׁרְבִיט: ס ג וַיֹּאמֶר לָהּ הַמֶּלֶךְ מַה־לָּךְ
אֶסְתֵּר הַמַּלְכָּה וּמַה־בַּקָּשָׁתֵךְ עַד־חֲצִי הַמַּלְכוּת וְיִנָּתֵן לָךְ: ד וַתֹּאמֶר
אֶסְתֵּר אִם־עַל־הַמֶּלֶךְ טוֹב יָבוֹא הַמֶּלֶךְ וְהָמָן הַיּוֹם אֶל־הַמִּשְׁתֶּה אֲשֶׁר־
עָשִׂיתִי לוֹ: ה וַיֹּאמֶר הַמֶּלֶךְ מַהֲרוּ אֶת־הָמָן לַעֲשׂוֹת אֶת־דְּבַר אֶסְתֵּר וַיָּבֹא
הַמֶּלֶךְ וְהָמָן אֶל־הַמִּשְׁתֶּה אֲשֶׁר־עָשְׂתָה אֶסְתֵּר: ו וַיֹּאמֶר הַמֶּלֶךְ לְאֶסְתֵּר
בְּמִשְׁתֵּה הַיַּיִן מַה־שְּׁאֵלָתֵךְ וְיִנָּתֵן לָךְ וּמַה־בַּקָּשָׁתֵךְ עַד־חֲצִי הַמַּלְכוּת
וְתֵעָשׂ: ז וַתַּעַן אֶסְתֵּר וַתֹּאמַר שְׁאֵלָתִי וּבַקָּשָׁתִי: ח אִם־מָצָאתִי חֵן בְּעֵינֵי
הַמֶּלֶךְ וְאִם־עַל־הַמֶּלֶךְ טוֹב לָתֵת אֶת־שְׁאֵלָתִי וְלַעֲשׂוֹת אֶת־בַּקָּשָׁתִי יָבוֹא
הַמֶּלֶךְ וְהָמָן אֶל־הַמִּשְׁתֶּה אֲשֶׁר אֶעֱשֶׂה לָהֶם וּמָחָר אֶעֱשֶׂה כִּדְבַר הַמֶּלֶךְ:
ט וַיֵּצֵא הָמָן בַּיּוֹם הַהוּא שָׂמֵחַ וְטוֹב לֵב וְכִרְאוֹת הָמָן אֶת־מָרְדֳּכַי בְּשַׁעַר
הַמֶּלֶךְ וְלֹא־קָם וְלֹא־זָע מִמֶּנּוּ וַיִּמָּלֵא הָמָן עַל־מָרְדֳּכַי חֵמָה: י וַיִּתְאַפַּק הָמָן
וַיָּבוֹא אֶל־בֵּיתוֹ וַיִּשְׁלַח וַיָּבֵא אֶת־אֹהֲבָיו וְאֶת־זֶרֶשׁ אִשְׁתּוֹ: יא וַיְסַפֵּר לָהֶם
הָמָן אֶת־כְּבוֹד עָשְׁרוֹ וְרֹב בָּנָיו וְאֵת כָּל־אֲשֶׁר גִּדְּלוֹ הַמֶּלֶךְ וְאֵת אֲשֶׁר נִשְּׂאוֹ
עַל־הַשָּׂרִים וְעַבְדֵי הַמֶּלֶךְ: יב וַיֹּאמֶר הָמָן אַף לֹא־הֵבִיאָה אֶסְתֵּר הַמַּלְכָּה
עִם־הַמֶּלֶךְ אֶל־הַמִּשְׁתֶּה אֲשֶׁר־עָשָׂתָה כִּי אִם־אוֹתִי וְגַם־לְמָחָר אֲנִי קָרוּא־
לָהּ עִם־הַמֶּלֶךְ: יג וְכָל־זֶה אֵינֶנּוּ שֹׁוֶה לִי בְּכָל־עֵת אֲשֶׁר אֲנִי רֹאֶה אֶת־

perish; and who knows whether you have not come to royal estate for such a time as this?" **15** Then Esther bade them to answer Mordecai: **16** "Go, gather together all the Jews that are present in Shushan, and fast for me, and neither eat nor drink three days, night or day; I also and my maidens will fast in like manner; and so will I go in to the king, which is not according to the law; and if I perish, I perish." **17** So Mordecai went his way, and did according to all that Esther had commanded him.

Chapter 5

1 Now it came to pass on the third day, that Esther put on her royal apparel, and stood in the inner court of the king's house, against the king's house; and the king sat upon his royal throne in the royal house, opposite the entrance of the house. **2** And, when the king saw Esther the queen standing in the court, she obtained favor in his sight; and the king held out to Esther the golden scepter that was in his hand. And Esther drew near, and touched the top of the scepter. **3** Then the king said to her: "What is your wish, queen Esther? for whatever you request, even to half of the kingdom, it shall be given to you." **4** And Esther said: "If it seem good to the king, let the king and Haman come today to the banquet that I have prepared for him." **5** Then the king said: "Cause Haman to make haste, that it may be done as Esther has said." So the king and Haman came to the banquet that Esther had prepared. **6** And the king said to Esther at the banquet of wine: "Whatever your petition, it shall be granted you; and whatever you request, even to the half of the kingdom, it shall be performed." **7** Then Esther answered, and said: "My petition and my request is — **8** if I have found favor in the eyes of the king, and if it please the king to grant my petition, and to perform my request — let the king and Haman come to the banquet that I shall prepare for them, and I will do tomorrow as the king has said." **9** Then went Haman forth that day joyful and glad of heart; but when Haman saw Mordecai in the king's gate, that he did not stand up or move for him, Haman was filled with anger against Mordecai. **10** Nevertheless Haman refrained himself, and went home; and he sent and fetched his friends and Zeresh his

מָרְדֳּכַי הַיְּהוּדִי יוֹשֵׁב בְּשַׁעַר הַמֶּלֶךְ: יד וַתֹּאמֶר לוֹ זֶרֶשׁ אִשְׁתּוֹ וְכָל־אֹהֲבָיו יַעֲשׂוּ־עֵץ גָּבֹהַּ חֲמִשִּׁים אַמָּה וּבַבֹּקֶר| אֱמֹר לַמֶּלֶךְ וְיִתְלוּ אֶת־מָרְדֳּכַי עָלָיו וּבֹא־עִם־הַמֶּלֶךְ אֶל־הַמִּשְׁתֶּה שָׂמֵחַ וַיִּיטַב הַדָּבָר לִפְנֵי הָמָן וַיַּעַשׂ הָעֵץ: פ

פרק ו'

א בַּלַּיְלָה הַהוּא נָדְדָה שְׁנַת הַמֶּלֶךְ וַיֹּאמֶר לְהָבִיא אֶת־סֵפֶר הַזִּכְרֹנוֹת דִּבְרֵי

נָדְדָה שְׁנַת הַמֶּלֶךְ *the king could not sleep.* Rava teaches (*Megillah* 15b) that Ahashverosh was disturbed by the fact that Esther had invited Haman along to the banquets she had made for her husband. He tossed and turned and wondered, perhaps the two of them, Esther and Haman, are plotting to kill me. Then, continued the king, why is there no man who likes me enough, who is sufficiently loyal to me, to apprise me of this conspiracy and save my life?

Then he said to himself, perhaps there is someone who has done me a good turn but whom I have failed to compensate. Maybe I have been an ingrate, and therefore I have lost the loyalty of my friends. That is why he ordered the chronicles to be read to him. And indeed, he did recall what the good Mordecai had done for him. Ahashverosh's reward to Mordecai signaled the beginning of Israel's salvation.

What we have here is a momentous moral teaching. We become truly moral beings when we take the giant step from blaming others for our misery to searching our own souls and hearts for the source of our troubles; from suspecting conspiring neighbors to analyzing the labyrinthine channels of our own egos. What was truly remarkable was that Ahashverosh could achieve this moral stature. The royal insomnia became a creative challenge. He converted it from a suspicion of plots by others to a discovery of shortcomings within himself; from outer subversion to inner corruption; from scheming courtiers to a seething conscience. The miracle lay in his ability to make the transition from a frightened animal afraid of others to a spiritual human afraid of what he had found within himself.

Do we not all of us have occasions when, in a deeper sense than the merely physical, our sleep is disturbed and we are plagued by all kinds of anxieties, by a vague restlessness and an unhappy lack of serenity?

wife. **11** And Haman recounted for them the glory of his riches, and the multitude of his children, and everything as to how the king had promoted him, and how he had advanced him above the princes and servants of the king. **12** Haman said: "Even, Esther the queen let no man come with the king to the banquet that she had prepared but myself; and tomorrow I am also invited by her together with the king. **13** Yet all this is worth nothing to me, so long as I see Mordecai the Jew sitting at the king's gate." **14** Then said Zeresh his wife and all his friends to him: "Let a gallows of fifty cubits high be made, and in the morning speak to the king that Mordecai may be hanged on it; then go merrily with the king to the banquet." And the thing pleased Haman; and he caused the gallows to be made.

Chapter 6

1 On that night the king could not sleep; and he commanded to bring the book of records of the chronicles, and they were read before the

---

Our restlessness and insomnia lead us to suspect others of nefarious plots, and we see evil and malice all about us. Our first conscious reaction to our own uneasiness is to blame others. The real miracle occurs when we have the moral courage to undertake painful self-criticism. We must learn to find the source of our restlessness not in conspiracies but in our own consciences. On Purim an otherwise undistinguished Persian potentate points the way to spiritual progress, from fear of what others may do to me to a fear of what I may have failed to do for others. This, then, is the meaning of the royal insomnia for us: If modern man suffers a gnawing sleeplessness, it is not so much because of his oppressive outer world as because of his depressed inner life.

לְהָבִיא אֶת סֵפֶר הַזִּכְרֹנוֹת *to bring the book of records.* The *Megillah* reminds us *le-havi et sefer ha-zikhronot,* to reread our individual Books of Memories. What each of us finds there must remain his own private secret. No man has the same *zikhronot* as any other. But upon examining this book of our innermost thoughts and most well kept secrets, we must then be big enough to recognize that we are small, great enough to acknowledge pettiness, and bold enough to move on to a new kind of

הַיָּמִים וַיִּהְיוּ נִקְרָאִים לִפְנֵי הַמֶּלֶךְ: ב וַיִּמָּצֵא כָתוּב אֲשֶׁר הִגִּיד מָרְדֳּכַי עַל־
בִּגְתָנָא וָתֶרֶשׁ שְׁנֵי סָרִיסֵי הַמֶּלֶךְ מִשֹּׁמְרֵי הַסַּף אֲשֶׁר בִּקְשׁוּ לִשְׁלֹחַ יָד
בַּמֶּלֶךְ אֲחַשְׁוֵרוֹשׁ: ג וַיֹּאמֶר הַמֶּלֶךְ מַה־נַּעֲשָׂה יְקָר וּגְדוּלָּה לְמָרְדֳּכַי עַל־
זֶה וַיֹּאמְרוּ נַעֲרֵי הַמֶּלֶךְ מְשָׁרְתָיו לֹא־נַעֲשָׂה עִמּוֹ דָּבָר: ד וַיֹּאמֶר הַמֶּלֶךְ
מִי בֶחָצֵר וְהָמָן בָּא לַחֲצַר בֵּית־הַמֶּלֶךְ הַחִיצוֹנָה לֵאמֹר לַמֶּלֶךְ לִתְלוֹת
אֶת־מָרְדֳּכַי עַל־הָעֵץ אֲשֶׁר־הֵכִין לוֹ: ה וַיֹּאמְרוּ נַעֲרֵי הַמֶּלֶךְ אֵלָיו הִנֵּה
הָמָן עֹמֵד בֶּחָצֵר וַיֹּאמֶר הַמֶּלֶךְ יָבוֹא: ו וַיָּבוֹא הָמָן וַיֹּאמֶר לוֹ הַמֶּלֶךְ מַה־
לַעֲשׂוֹת בָּאִישׁ אֲשֶׁר הַמֶּלֶךְ חָפֵץ בִּיקָרוֹ וַיֹּאמֶר הָמָן בְּלִבּוֹ לְמִי יַחְפֹּץ
הַמֶּלֶךְ לַעֲשׂוֹת יְקָר יוֹתֵר מִמֶּנִּי: ז וַיֹּאמֶר הָמָן אֶל־הַמֶּלֶךְ אִישׁ אֲשֶׁר
הַמֶּלֶךְ חָפֵץ בִּיקָרוֹ: ח יָבִיאוּ לְבוּשׁ מַלְכוּת אֲשֶׁר לָבַשׁ־בּוֹ הַמֶּלֶךְ וְסוּס
אֲשֶׁר רָכַב עָלָיו הַמֶּלֶךְ וַאֲשֶׁר נִתַּן כֶּתֶר מַלְכוּת בְּרֹאשׁוֹ: ט וְנָתוֹן הַלְּבוּשׁ
וְהַסּוּס עַל־יַד־אִישׁ מִשָּׂרֵי הַמֶּלֶךְ הַפַּרְתְּמִים וְהִלְבִּישׁוּ אֶת־הָאִישׁ אֲשֶׁר
הַמֶּלֶךְ חָפֵץ בִּיקָרוֹ וְהִרְכִּיבֻהוּ עַל־הַסּוּס בִּרְחוֹב הָעִיר וְקָרְאוּ לְפָנָיו כָּכָה
יֵעָשֶׂה לָאִישׁ אֲשֶׁר הַמֶּלֶךְ חָפֵץ בִּיקָרוֹ: י וַיֹּאמֶר הַמֶּלֶךְ לְהָמָן מַהֵר קַח

---

life before God: one in which we will rectify past errors and omissions, improve the moral tone and ethical quality of our lives. We must learn to be grateful for what we have, not complain over what we have not; to express our gratitude to those who deserve it; to be helpful to friend and neighbor, appreciative of associates, and loyal to Torah — the word of God. Then, when we have done this, our wandering sleep shall return and be sweet to us, and our rest delicious. Then the Almighty will grant us the blessings of tranquility, the most precious possession of a mature and moral mind.

חָפֵץ בִּיקָרוֹ *wishes to honor*. The need for praise is almost universal; very few people are so secure, so saintly, that they can get along without any approbation at all. A kind word, if merited, is the feedback that makes an individual feel and know that he is on the right track. Even if a person is fishing for a compliment, if his bait is virtuous or beneficial or constructive in any way — bite at it! Give him the compliment he seeks!

Unfortunately, not everyone is so benevolently disposed. I know

king. 2 And it was found written, that Mordecai had told of Bigthana and Teresh, two of the king's chamberlains, the keepers of the door, who had sought to lay hands on the king Ahashverosh. 3 And the king said: "What honor and dignity has been done to Mordecai for this?" Then the king's servants that ministered to him said: "Nothing has been done for him." 4 And the king said: "Who is in the court?" — Now Haman was coming into the outer court of the king's house, to speak to the king to hang Mordecai on the gallows that he had prepared for him. — 5 And the king's servants said to him: "Behold, Haman is standing in the court." And the king said: "Let him come in." 6 And Haman came in. And the king said to him: "What shall be done to the man whom the king wishes to honor?" — Now Haman said in his heart: "Whom would the king wish delight to honor besides myself?" — 7 And Haman said to the king: "For the man whom the king wishes to honor, 8 let royal apparel be brought which the king wears, and the horse that the king rides upon, and on whose head a crown royal is set; 9 and let the apparel and the horse be delivered to the hand of one of the king's most noble princes, that they may array the man whom the king wishes to honor, and lead him on horseback through the street of the city, and proclaim before him: Thus shall it be done to the man whom the king wishes to honor." 10 Then the king said to Haman: "Make haste, and take the apparel and the horse, as

---

husbands and wives who, even if they mean well toward each other, find themselves unable to offer a sincere compliment. Brothers and sisters are often incapable of saying a kind, warm word to each other. I have had men in their mature years who, in my study, break down crying and say of a father or mother that he or she "never had a good word to say to me all my life!" How often, unfortunately, we find employers who are reluctant to offer a compliment to their employees, or colleagues who cannot offer a decent word of praise. Why is that so? Perhaps the answer is envy, or perhaps some people are so insecure that they feel threatened by a competing ego that praise may strengthen.

אֶת־הַלְּבוּשׁ וְאֶת־הַסּוּס כַּאֲשֶׁר דִּבַּרְתָּ וַעֲשֵׂה־כֵן לְמָרְדֳּכַי הַיְּהוּדִי הַיּוֹשֵׁב
בְּשַׁעַר הַמֶּלֶךְ אַל־תַּפֵּל דָּבָר מִכֹּל אֲשֶׁר דִּבַּרְתָּ: יא וַיִּקַּח הָמָן אֶת־הַלְּבוּשׁ
וְאֶת־הַסּוּס וַיַּלְבֵּשׁ אֶת־מָרְדֳּכָי וַיַּרְכִּיבֵהוּ בִּרְחוֹב הָעִיר וַיִּקְרָא לְפָנָיו כָּכָה
יֵעָשֶׂה לָאִישׁ אֲשֶׁר הַמֶּלֶךְ חָפֵץ בִּיקָרוֹ: יב וַיָּשָׁב מָרְדֳּכַי אֶל־שַׁעַר הַמֶּלֶךְ
וְהָמָן נִדְחַף אֶל־בֵּיתוֹ אָבֵל וַחֲפוּי רֹאשׁ: יג וַיְסַפֵּר הָמָן לְזֶרֶשׁ אִשְׁתּוֹ וּלְכָל־
אֹהֲבָיו אֵת כָּל־אֲשֶׁר קָרָהוּ וַיֹּאמְרוּ לוֹ חֲכָמָיו וְזֶרֶשׁ אִשְׁתּוֹ אִם מִזֶּרַע
הַיְּהוּדִים מָרְדֳּכַי אֲשֶׁר הַחִלּוֹתָ לִנְפֹּל לְפָנָיו לֹא־תוּכַל לוֹ כִּי־נָפוֹל תִּפּוֹל

Sometimes people have just not been trained or habituated to express admiration.

Of course this theme is not without its problems. Praise can be extravagant, and therefore hypocritical and phony. Overdo praise and it becomes meaningless. "Praise," said Dr. Samuel Johnson, "like gold and diamonds, owes its value to its scarcity…. He who praises everybody, praises nobody." Often, praise degenerates into simple flattery, and is hence false and merely manipulative. Thus the Rabbis were weary of official eulogizers, and they said (*Berakhot* 62a): "Just as the dead will have to stand in judgment before the Divine Judge, so those who eulogize them will have to answer for their extravagancies." A compliment, to be effective, must be well chosen. It must fit the person and the place and the time. It must speak to his mind and his heart, to his fears and anxieties and insecurities. Just praise is a debt that the rest of us must pay to one who has earned it.

כָּכָה יֵעָשֶׂה לָאִישׁ אֲשֶׁר הַמֶּלֶךְ חָפֵץ בִּיקָרוֹ *Thus shall it be done to the man whom the king wishes to honor.* Liberalism is beginning to suffer from a hardening of the arteries, when its blood coagulates because it reaches too high and falls too low. Consider the rash of comments from some American Jewish liberals concerning Israel There were, for example, cries against Jewry when Israel kidnapped Eichmann and brought him to trial in Israel. We heard liberals implying that Israel was no less guilty in capturing and trying Eichmann than that monster was in destroying six million Jews.

I wonder what these liberals would have said had they lived in the days of King Ahashverosh. No doubt they would have fulminated against

you have said, and do so to Mordecai the Jew, who sits at the king's gate; let nothing fail of all that you have spoken." **11** Then Haman took the apparel and the horse, and arrayed Mordecai, and led him on horseback through the street of the city, and proclaimed before him: "Thus shall it be done to the man whom the king wishes to honor." **12** And Mordecai returned to the king's gate. But Haman hastened to his house, mourning and having his head covered. **13** And Haman recounted to Zeresh his wife and all his friends everything that had befallen him. Then his wise men and Zeresh his wife said to him: "If Mordecai, before whom you have begun to fall, is of the seed of the Jews, then you shall not prevail against him, but you shall surely

---

Mordecai and, on the basis of the principles of liberalism and democracy, demanded freedom (or at least clemency) for Haman. Mordecai, they would have pointed out, had no jurisdiction in Shushan. Haman should be tried not by Jewish judges, but by judges drawn from the one hundred and twenty-seven countries which were under the reins of Ahashverosh. Besides, Mordecai was only a Jewish nationalist and Esther a Zionist lobbyist, applying political pressure on Ahashverosh before election time. Furthermore, did not Haman suffer enough when he was forced to lead his archenemy through the streets announcing, "Thus shall be done to the one whom the king wishes to honor"? And what right does Mordecai have to punish Haman and his gang — they only *planned* to destroy, kill, and eradicate every Jew, young and old, in all of the lands of Ahashverosh; they did not actually do it. Finally, the grandstand trial of Haman and his execution were as heinous and as evil as Haman's designs against the Jewish people.

Look at how a wonderful conception can lead astray! Look at how passionate liberals were in defending the Eichmanns and how silent they are when Jewish causes are in the forefront. Liberalism has become their god.

אִם מִזֶּרַע הַיְּהוּדִים מָרְדְּכַי *If Mordecai is of the seed of the Jews.* There is a marvelous story recorded in the Talmud (*Megillah* 16a): Haman took the royal robes and the king's horse to Mordecai, who was teaching his students. He was in the middle of a *shiur* about how the *kohen*

לְפָנָיו: יד עוֹדָם מְדַבְּרִים עִמּוֹ וְסָרִיסֵי הַמֶּלֶךְ הִגִּיעוּ וַיַּבְהִלוּ לְהָבִיא אֶת־
הָמָן אֶל־הַמִּשְׁתֶּה אֲשֶׁר־עָשְׂתָה אֶסְתֵּר:

פרק ז׳

א וַיָּבֹא הַמֶּלֶךְ וְהָמָן לִשְׁתּוֹת עִם־אֶסְתֵּר הַמַּלְכָּה: ב וַיֹּאמֶר הַמֶּלֶךְ לְאֶסְתֵּר

---

performed *kemitzah*, the taking of a fistful of flour for the *minhah* offering on the altar. When Mordecai saw Haman approaching and leading the horse, he became frightened and said, "This villain is coming to kill me. Get out of his way so that you do not get into trouble with him." Mordecai thereupon drew his robe round him and stood up to recite the *Shemoneh Esrei*. Haman came up and sat down and waited till Mordecai had finished his prayer. He said to him: "What have you been discussing?" He replied: "When the Temple stood, if a man brought a meal-offering he used to offer a handful of fine flour on the altar and his sins would be forgiven." Haman replied, "A mere fistful of your fine flour outweighed and outshone my ten thousand talents of silver that I gave the king to allow me to kill all the Jews!"

How remarkable is the picture presented to us by the Talmud! Despite the danger to his life, Mordecai is not preparing an escape plan, not pulling political strings, not hiding out someplace. He is teaching his students Torah. And not only Torah, but especially a topic which might appear to be irrelevant and impractical — laws relating to the ancient days when there was a Temple and sacrifices and altars and flour offerings. But it was not really impractical at all, because it contained a secret message of Jewish survival: The teaching of Torah outweighs all else and can overcome our most powerful and wealthy enemies.

And that, says Rabbi Meir Shapiro, founder and Rosh Yeshivat Hakhmei Lublin, is what Haman's wife Zeresh meant when she said that if Mordecai wais "of the seed of Judah," Haman would not prevail. If indeed Mordecai was engaged in teaching Torah to the next generation of Jews, and if he was teaching it to the seed of Judah, Jewish children, despite all dangers, then no one in the world can overcome us and we shall be the victors. It is Torah, the study of Torah, the study itself and

fall before him." **14** While they were still talking with him, the king's chamberlains come and brought Haman hurriedly to the banquet that Esther had prepared.

Chapter 7

1 So the king and Haman came to drink with Esther the queen. **2** And

---

for itself and not necessarily because it is "relevant," that make of us an eternal people.

נָפוֹל תִּפּוֹל לְפָנָיו *you shall surely fall before him.* Often we are plunged into a gray mood when we consider our state and even the international situation. The constant attrition, the state of no-war/no-peace, the ever impending threat of greater warfare involving the Great Powers, the increasing isolation of Israel from neutrals and friends — all this is not calculated to encourage great cheer on behalf of those who love Israel. Nevertheless, we must never permit ourselves to lose our sense of balance. We are only humans, and therefore our perspectives are limited. Even we, in our present situation, can begin to appreciate that quite possibly our present situation is the best of all, that the alternatives may be far worse, that what is happening at present may be propaedeutic to something much greater, much nobler, much happier. May God grant that!

And the same holds true for personal life. Life is full of crises. No human being can be spared trauma in his existence. If we lose heart and are discouraged and become crushed, then our pessimism is a self-fulfilling prophecy. We lose sight of opportunities, and we almost wish ourselves into a plunging descent. But if we adopt a more sanguine attitude, then our optimism becomes self-fulfilling as it sensitizes us to the creative possibilities in our dilemma. So let us leave the pessimistic views to the anti-Semites. Recall what Zeresh, wife of Haman, told him when his star began to fail: "If Mordecai, before whom you have begun to fall, is one of the children of the Jews, then you shall not prevail over him but you will fall completely." Jews must take a different attitude. For ourselves we must learn to endure failure as but a temporary setback, as preparation for a greater rise.

גַּם בַּיּוֹם הַשֵּׁנִי בְּמִשְׁתֵּה הַיַּיִן מַה־שְּׁאֵלָתֵךְ אֶסְתֵּר הַמַּלְכָּה וְתִנָּתֵן לָךְ וּמַה־
בַּקָּשָׁתֵךְ עַד־חֲצִי הַמַּלְכוּת וְתֵעָשׂ: ג וַתַּעַן אֶסְתֵּר הַמַּלְכָּה וַתֹּאמַר אִם־
מָצָאתִי חֵן בְּעֵינֶיךָ הַמֶּלֶךְ וְאִם־עַל־הַמֶּלֶךְ טוֹב תִּנָּתֶן־לִי נַפְשִׁי בִּשְׁאֵלָתִי
וְעַמִּי בְּבַקָּשָׁתִי: ד כִּי נִמְכַּרְנוּ אֲנִי וְעַמִּי לְהַשְׁמִיד לַהֲרוֹג וּלְאַבֵּד וְאִלּוּ
לַעֲבָדִים וְלִשְׁפָחוֹת נִמְכַּרְנוּ הֶחֱרַשְׁתִּי כִּי אֵין הַצָּר שֹׁוֶה בְּנֵזֶק הַמֶּלֶךְ: ס
ה וַיֹּאמֶר הַמֶּלֶךְ אֲחַשְׁוֵרוֹשׁ וַיֹּאמֶר לְאֶסְתֵּר הַמַּלְכָּה מִי הוּא זֶה וְאֵי־זֶה הוּא

בְּמִשְׁתֵּה הַיַּיִן *at the wine party*. Ever since the modern era began and the
American Founding Fathers proclaimed man's natural right to the "pursuit of happiness," we have been doing just that — pursuing happiness
breathlessly, relentlessly, almost fanatically. But happiness has proved
to be quite an elusive prize. Let us discuss not what happiness is — that
might take too long — but rather what happiness is not, beginning
with a halakhah codified by Maimonides in his Code of Jewish law:
"When a man eats and drinks and is happy on the festival, let him not
overindulge in wine, and in jesting, and in levity, saying to himself that
whoever does this thereby observes more fully the commandment to
be happy. But drunkenness and jesting and levity are not at all *simhah*
(happiness); they are merely madness and folly" (*Hilkhot Yom Tov* 6:20).

I believe that the words in the second chapter of the Book of Kohelet
are the source of the law codified by Maimonides. Life, Solomon says,
is full of pain and bitter frustration; how then can we be successful in
the pursuit of happiness? "I decided to pamper myself with wine," he
says (Ecclesiastes 2:3). If life seems painful, if existence is filled with
sharp agonies, then perhaps it is best to take to drink and drown one's
sorrows. This is the answer of drunkenness: overwhelming the senses
either by pleasure or immorality or narcotics or liquor, or any other
excess. Solomon tries this technique, but he is not happy with it. It
simply does not work, for after the spirits are spent, the spirit remains
just as low. Sooner or later one must wake up, rise out of the drunken
stupor, and face the sober facts of life; the frustration and pain remain
unchanged even when covered with the haze of alcohol.

Happiness is reserved by the Torah especially for the festivals, and
most especially for the three "pilgrim" festivals, those holidays when

the king said again to Esther on the second day at the wine party: "Whatever you petition, queen Esther, it shall be granted to you; and whatever your request, even to the half of the kingdom, it shall be performed." 3 Then Esther the queen answered and said: "If I have found favor in your eyes, O king, and if it please the king, let my life be spared at my petition, and my people at my request; 4 for we are sold, I and my people, to be destroyed, to be slain, and to perish. But if we had been sold merely for bondmen and bondwomen, I would have held my tongue, for the affliction is not worthy that the king be damaged." 5 Then the king Ahashverosh spoke and said to Esther the queen: "Who is he, and where is he, that presumes in his heart to

---

the Jew in the Holy Land was commanded to make a pilgrimage to the Temple in Jerusalem *lifnei Hashem*, to visit the House of God and there to be happy. This, then, is the road for the proper pursuit of *simhah*. Wherever we are geographically, we must aspire to be spiritually aware of the fact that we are before God, that we live in the face of God.

To be happy, in the Jewish sense, does not mean to ignore life's hardships and pain. Instead, it means the knowledge that we are not alone in our difficulties, that God sympathizes with us, that our pain is not senseless. *Simhah* means that there is hope — or, better, that there is meaning in life. Better pain that is purposeful than pleasure that is pointless. Better a hard life hallowed by a touch of holiness than a soft life in which man sinks into swamps of sensuality and which ultimately drives him insane from solitude.

Happiness is the hope that the Creator of disease will also create for us healing; that He who created pain will create balm; that He who created failure will give us triumph; that He who made frustration will grant us fulfillment; that He who gave us loneliness will bless us with fellowship. Or, in the concluding words of Kohelet himself, he who knew so well what happiness is not: "Fear God and observe His commandments" (Ecclesiastes 12:13). Place yourself *lifnei Hashem*, constantly and ceaselessly in the presence of God, align yourself with His will, for this is the totality of man in his genuine and blessed pursuit of authentic *simhah*.

אֲשֶׁר־מִלְאוֹ לִבּוֹ לַעֲשׂוֹת כֵּן: ו וַתֹּאמֶר־אֶסְתֵּר אִישׁ צַר וְאוֹיֵב הָמָן הָרָע
הַזֶּה וְהָמָן נִבְעַת מִלִּפְנֵי הַמֶּלֶךְ וְהַמַּלְכָּה: ז וְהַמֶּלֶךְ קָם בַּחֲמָתוֹ מִמִּשְׁתֵּה
הַיַּיִן אֶל־גִּנַּת הַבִּיתָן וְהָמָן עָמַד לְבַקֵּשׁ עַל־נַפְשׁוֹ מֵאֶסְתֵּר הַמַּלְכָּה כִּי רָאָה
כִּי־כָלְתָה אֵלָיו הָרָעָה מֵאֵת הַמֶּלֶךְ: ח וְהַמֶּלֶךְ שָׁב מִגִּנַּת הַבִּיתָן אֶל־בֵּית|
מִשְׁתֵּה הַיַּיִן וְהָמָן נֹפֵל עַל־הַמִּטָּה אֲשֶׁר אֶסְתֵּר עָלֶיהָ וַיֹּאמֶר הַמֶּלֶךְ הֲגַם
לִכְבּוֹשׁ אֶת־הַמַּלְכָּה עִמִּי בַּבָּיִת הַדָּבָר יָצָא מִפִּי הַמֶּלֶךְ וּפְנֵי הָמָן חָפוּ: ס
ט וַיֹּאמֶר חַרְבוֹנָה אֶחָד מִן־הַסָּרִיסִים לִפְנֵי הַמֶּלֶךְ גַּם הִנֵּה־הָעֵץ אֲשֶׁר־
עָשָׂה הָמָן לְמָרְדֳּכַי אֲשֶׁר דִּבֶּר־טוֹב עַל־הַמֶּלֶךְ עֹמֵד בְּבֵית הָמָן גָּבֹהַּ
חֲמִשִּׁים אַמָּה וַיֹּאמֶר הַמֶּלֶךְ תְּלֻהוּ עָלָיו: י וַיִּתְלוּ אֶת־הָמָן עַל־הָעֵץ אֲשֶׁר־
הֵכִין לְמָרְדֳּכָי וַחֲמַת הַמֶּלֶךְ שָׁכָכָה: פ

פרק ח'

א בַּיּוֹם הַהוּא נָתַן הַמֶּלֶךְ אֲחַשְׁוֵרוֹשׁ לְאֶסְתֵּר הַמַּלְכָּה אֶת־בֵּית הָמָן צֹרֵר
הַיְּהוּדִים [הַיְּהוּדִיִּים כ'] וּמָרְדֳּכַי בָּא לִפְנֵי הַמֶּלֶךְ כִּי־הִגִּידָה אֶסְתֵּר מַה
הוּא־לָהּ: ב וַיָּסַר הַמֶּלֶךְ אֶת־טַבַּעְתּוֹ אֲשֶׁר הֶעֱבִיר מֵהָמָן וַיִּתְּנָהּ לְמָרְדֳּכָי
וַתָּשֶׂם אֶסְתֵּר אֶת־מָרְדֳּכַי עַל־בֵּית הָמָן: פ ג וַתּוֹסֶף אֶסְתֵּר וַתְּדַבֵּר לִפְנֵי
הַמֶּלֶךְ וַתִּפֹּל לִפְנֵי רַגְלָיו וַתֵּבְךְּ וַתִּתְחַנֶּן־לוֹ לְהַעֲבִיר אֶת־רָעַת הָמָן הָאֲגָגִי

חֲמַת הַמֶּלֶךְ *the king's wrath.* Anger should never become one's master; it is too good a servant. He who nurses a grudge weans his own misery and raises complications which compound a bad situation with one's own irascibility. He who controls his inner emotions controls the bad situation and ameliorates it. The great Koretzer Rebbe once said, "Long ago I conquered my anger and placed it in my pocket. Now, whenever I need it, I simply take it out and use it!"

In a world filled with anger, when men and women get drunk on the wine of the grapes of wrath and bubble over in anger, it is good to relearn this lesson of Jewish law and ethics: With the exception of righteous indignation and instrumental anger, both used for non-egotistic purposes, both used to serve higher and non-selfish ends, there must be no *ka'as* at all.

do so?" **6** And Esther said: "An adversary and an enemy, this wicked Haman." Then Haman was terrified before the king and the queen. **7** And the king arose in his wrath from the banquet of wine and went into the palace garden; but Haman remained to plead for his life to Esther the queen; for he saw that there was evil determined against him by the king. **8** Then the king returned out of the palace garden into the place of the banquet of wine; and Haman was fallen upon the couch where Esther was. And the king said: "Will he even assault the queen in my own presence in the house?" As the word went out of the king's mouth, they covered Haman's face. **9** Then Harbonah, one of the chamberlains that were before the king, said: "Behold also, the gallows fifty cubits high, which Haman made for Mordecai, who spoke good for the king, stands in the house of Haman." And the king said: "Hang him upon it." **10** So they hanged Haman on the gallows that he had prepared for Mordecai. Then the king's wrath was assuaged.

Chapter 8

1 On that day the king Ahashverosh gave the house of Haman the Jews' enemy to Esther the queen. And Mordecai came before the king; for Esther had told what he was to her. **2** And the king took off his ring, which he had taken from Haman, and gave it to Mordecai. And Esther set Mordecai over the house of Haman. **3** And Esther spoke yet again before the king, and fell down at his feet, and pleaded with him with tears to put aside the evil of Haman the Agagite, and his

---

This is a lesson worth putting into practice in our daily lives as we tend to burst into rage because of social crises or professional misery or business worries or domestic irritations. To retain our inner calm at all times is one of the great lessons of Judaism. The Jew may sometimes *use* anger; never must he allow himself to *be used by it.*

It is the study of Torah which can endow us with the ability to control ourselves, to find rather than to lose our even temper. It is the study of Torah which will help us control our *ka'as*, our anger, and which can lead us and all humanity to the blessings of peace.

וְאֵת מַחֲשַׁבְתּוֹ אֲשֶׁר חָשַׁב עַל־הַיְּהוּדִים: ד וַיּוֹשֶׁט הַמֶּלֶךְ לְאֶסְתֵּר אֵת שַׁרְבִט הַזָּהָב וַתָּקָם אֶסְתֵּר וַתַּעֲמֹד לִפְנֵי הַמֶּלֶךְ: ה וַתֹּאמֶר אִם־עַל־הַמֶּלֶךְ טוֹב וְאִם־מָצָאתִי חֵן לְפָנָיו וְכָשֵׁר הַדָּבָר לִפְנֵי הַמֶּלֶךְ וְטוֹבָה אֲנִי בְּעֵינָיו יִכָּתֵב לְהָשִׁיב אֶת־הַסְּפָרִים מַחֲשֶׁבֶת הָמָן בֶּן־הַמְּדָתָא הָאֲגָגִי אֲשֶׁר כָּתַב לְאַבֵּד אֶת־הַיְּהוּדִים אֲשֶׁר בְּכָל־מְדִינוֹת הַמֶּלֶךְ: ו כִּי אֵיכָכָה אוּכַל וְרָאִיתִי בָּרָעָה אֲשֶׁר־יִמְצָא אֶת־עַמִּי וְאֵיכָכָה אוּכַל וְרָאִיתִי בְּאָבְדַן מוֹלַדְתִּי: ס ז וַיֹּאמֶר הַמֶּלֶךְ אֲחַשְׁוֵרֹשׁ לְאֶסְתֵּר הַמַּלְכָּה וּלְמָרְדֳּכַי הַיְּהוּדִי הִנֵּה בֵית־ הָמָן נָתַתִּי לְאֶסְתֵּר וְאֹתוֹ תָּלוּ עַל־הָעֵץ עַל אֲשֶׁר־שָׁלַח יָדוֹ בַּיְּהוּדִים [בַּיְּהוּדִיִּים כ']: ח וְאַתֶּם כִּתְבוּ עַל־הַיְּהוּדִים כַּטּוֹב בְּעֵינֵיכֶם בְּשֵׁם הַמֶּלֶךְ וְחִתְמוּ בְּטַבַּעַת הַמֶּלֶךְ כִּי־כְתָב אֲשֶׁר־נִכְתָּב בְּשֵׁם־הַמֶּלֶךְ וְנַחְתּוֹם בְּטַבַּעַת הַמֶּלֶךְ אֵין לְהָשִׁיב: ט וַיִּקָּרְאוּ סֹפְרֵי־הַמֶּלֶךְ בָּעֵת־הַהִיא בַּחֹדֶשׁ הַשְּׁלִישִׁי הוּא־חֹדֶשׁ סִיוָן בִּשְׁלוֹשָׁה וְעֶשְׂרִים בּוֹ וַיִּכָּתֵב כְּכָל־אֲשֶׁר־צִוָּה מָרְדֳּכַי אֶל־הַיְּהוּדִים וְאֶל הָאֲחַשְׁדַּרְפְּנִים־וְהַפַּחוֹת וְשָׂרֵי הַמְּדִינוֹת אֲשֶׁר| מֵהֹדּוּ וְעַד־כּוּשׁ שֶׁבַע וְעֶשְׂרִים וּמֵאָה מְדִינָה מְדִינָה וּמְדִינָה כִּכְתָבָהּ וְעַם וָעָם כִּלְשֹׁנוֹ וְאֶל־הַיְּהוּדִים כִּכְתָבָם וְכִלְשׁוֹנָם: י וַיִּכְתֹּב בְּשֵׁם הַמֶּלֶךְ אֲחַשְׁוֵרֹשׁ וַיַּחְתֹּם בְּטַבַּעַת הַמֶּלֶךְ וַיִּשְׁלַח סְפָרִים בְּיַד הָרָצִים בַּסּוּסִים רֹכְבֵי הָרֶכֶשׁ הָאֲחַשְׁתְּרָנִים בְּנֵי הָרַמָּכִים: יא אֲשֶׁר נָתַן הַמֶּלֶךְ לַיְּהוּדִים| אֲשֶׁר| בְּכָל־ עִיר־וָעִיר לְהִקָּהֵל וְלַעֲמֹד עַל־נַפְשָׁם לְהַשְׁמִיד וְלַהֲרֹג וּלְאַבֵּד אֶת־כָּל־חֵיל עַם וּמְדִינָה הַצָּרִים אֹתָם טַף וְנָשִׁים וּשְׁלָלָם לָבוֹז: יב בְּיוֹם אֶחָד בְּכָל־ מְדִינוֹת הַמֶּלֶךְ אֲחַשְׁוֵרוֹשׁ בִּשְׁלוֹשָׁה עָשָׂר לְחֹדֶשׁ שְׁנֵים־עָשָׂר הוּא־חֹדֶשׁ אֲדָר: יג פַּתְשֶׁגֶן הַכְּתָב לְהִנָּתֵן דָּת בְּכָל־מְדִינָה וּמְדִינָה גָּלוּי לְכָל־הָעַמִּים וְלִהְיוֹת הַיְּהוּדִים [הַיְּהוּדִיִּים כ'] עֲתִידִים [עֲתוּדִים כ'] לַיּוֹם הַזֶּה לְהִנָּקֵם מֵאֹיְבֵיהֶם: יד הָרָצִים רֹכְבֵי הָרֶכֶשׁ הָאֲחַשְׁתְּרָנִים יָצְאוּ מְבֹהָלִים וּדְחוּפִים בִּדְבַר הַמֶּלֶךְ וְהַדָּת נִתְּנָה בְּשׁוּשַׁן הַבִּירָה: פ טו וּמָרְדֳּכַי יָצָא| מִלִּפְנֵי הַמֶּלֶךְ בִּלְבוּשׁ מַלְכוּת תְּכֵלֶת וָחוּר וַעֲטֶרֶת זָהָב גְּדוֹלָה וְתַכְרִיךְ בּוּץ וְאַרְגָּמָן וְהָעִיר שׁוּשָׁן צָהֲלָה וְשָׂמֵחָה: טז לַיְּהוּדִים הָיְתָה אוֹרָה וְשִׂמְחָה וְשָׂשֹׂן וִיקָר: יז וּבְכָל־מְדִינָה וּמְדִינָה וּבְכָל־עִיר וָעִיר מְקוֹם אֲשֶׁר דְּבַר הַמֶּלֶךְ

scheme that he had devised against the Jews. **4** Then the king held out to Esther the golden scepter. So Esther arose, and stood before the king. **5** And she said: "If it please the king, and if I have found favor in his eyes, and the thing seem right before the king, and I be pleasing in his eyes, let it be written to reverse the letters devised by Haman the son of Hammedatha the Agagite, which he wrote to destroy the Jews that are in all the king's provinces; **6** for how can I endure to see the evil that shall come upon my people? or how can I endure to see the destruction of my kindred?" **7** Then the king Ahashverosh said to Esther the queen and to Mordecai the Jew: "Behold, I have given Esther the house of Haman, and they have hanged him upon the gallows, because he laid his hand upon the Jews. **8** Write also as you please concerning the Jews, in the king's name, and seal it with the king's ring; for the writing which is already written in the king's name, and sealed with the king's ring, cannot be revoked." **9** Then the king's scribes were called at that time, in the third month, which is the month Sivan, on the twenty-third day thereof; and it was written according to all that Mordecai commanded concerning the Jews, to the satraps, and the governors and princes of the provinces which are from India to Ethiopia, a hundred twenty and seven provinces, to every province according to the writing thereof, and to every people according to their language, and to the Jews according to their writing, and according to their language. **10** And they wrote in the name of king Ahashverosh, and sealed it with the king's ring, and sent letters by couriers on horseback, riding on swift horses that were used in the king's service, bred from the stud mares; **11** that the king had granted the Jews that were in every city to gather themselves together, and to stand for their life, to destroy, and to slay, and to cause to perish, all the forces of the people and province that would assault them, their children and women, and plunder their goods, **12** upon one day in all the provinces of king Ahashverosh, namely, upon the thirteenth day of the twelfth month, which is the month Adar. **13** The copy of the writing, to be given out for a decree in every province, was to be published to all the peoples, and that the Jews should be ready against that day to avenge themselves on their enemies. **14** So the couriers

וְדָתוֹ מַגִּיעַ שִׂמְחָה וְשָׂשׂוֹן לַיְּהוּדִים מִשְׁתֶּה וְיוֹם טוֹב וְרַבִּים מֵעַמֵּי הָאָרֶץ מִתְיַהֲדִים כִּי־נָפַל פַּחַד־הַיְּהוּדִים עֲלֵיהֶם:

פרק ט'

א וּבִשְׁנֵים עָשָׂר חֹדֶשׁ הוּא־חֹדֶשׁ אֲדָר בִּשְׁלוֹשָׁה עָשָׂר יוֹם בּוֹ אֲשֶׁר הִגִּיעַ דְּבַר־הַמֶּלֶךְ וְדָתוֹ לְהֵעָשׂוֹת בַּיּוֹם אֲשֶׁר שִׂבְּרוּ אֹיְבֵי הַיְּהוּדִים לִשְׁלוֹט בָּהֶם וְנַהֲפוֹךְ הוּא אֲשֶׁר יִשְׁלְטוּ הַיְּהוּדִים הֵמָּה בְּשֹׂנְאֵיהֶם: ב נִקְהֲלוּ הַיְּהוּדִים בְּעָרֵיהֶם בְּכָל־מְדִינוֹת הַמֶּלֶךְ אֲחַשְׁוֵרוֹשׁ לִשְׁלֹחַ יָד בִּמְבַקְשֵׁי רָעָתָם וְאִישׁ לֹא־עָמַד לִפְנֵיהֶם כִּי־נָפַל פַּחְדָּם עַל־כָּל־הָעַמִּים: ג וְכָל־שָׂרֵי הַמְּדִינוֹת וְהָאֲחַשְׁדַּרְפְּנִים וְהַפַּחוֹת וְעֹשֵׂי הַמְּלָאכָה אֲשֶׁר לַמֶּלֶךְ מְנַשְּׂאִים אֶת־הַיְּהוּדִים כִּי־נָפַל פַּחַד־מָרְדֳּכַי עֲלֵיהֶם: ד כִּי־גָדוֹל מָרְדֳּכַי בְּבֵית הַמֶּלֶךְ וְשָׁמְעוֹ הוֹלֵךְ בְּכָל־הַמְּדִינוֹת כִּי־הָאִישׁ מָרְדֳּכַי הוֹלֵךְ וְגָדוֹל: פ ה וַיַּכּוּ הַיְּהוּדִים בְּכָל־אֹיְבֵיהֶם מַכַּת־חֶרֶב וְהֶרֶג וְאַבְדָן וַיַּעֲשׂוּ בְשֹׂנְאֵיהֶם כִּרְצוֹנָם: ו וּבְשׁוּשַׁן הַבִּירָה הָרְגוּ הַיְּהוּדִים וְאַבֵּד חֲמֵשׁ מֵאוֹת אִישׁ:

ז	וְאֵת
פַּרְשַׁנְדָּתָא	וְאֵת
דַּלְפוֹן	וְאֵת

פַּרְשַׁנְדָּתָא *Parshandatha.* Effective leadership depends not so much upon the leader as upon his followers. No leader can be effective and inspired if his followers do not show the proper spirit of fellowship and brotherliness and fraternity. True, an inspired leader can help cement relationships among his people. Religion wields no Big Stick. Leadership and success of any religious venture depend primarily upon the fraternal feelings of the members of that religion. The Talmud, discussing the laws relating to the reading of the *Shema* in the morning, says that one is not permitted to read the *Shema* in early morning until it is so light that a man can see his friend from a distance (*Berakhot* 9b). One cannot start to say *Shema Yisrael*, one cannot hope to express love for God, until he can see his friend from the distance, until he can love and feel sympathetic toward him. A person who cannot see his friend, a person

that rode upon swift horses that were used in the king's service went out, being hastened and pressed on by the king's commandment; and the decree was given out in Shushan the capital. **15** And Mordecai went forth from the presence of the king in royal apparel of blue and white, and with a great crown of gold, and with a robe of fine linen and purple; and the city of Shushan shouted and was glad. **16** The Jews had light and gladness, and joy and honor. **17** And in every province, and in every city, wherever the king's commandment and his decree came, the Jews had gladness and joy, a feast and a good day. And many from among the peoples of the land became Jews; for the fear of the Jews had fallen upon them.

Chapter 9

1 Now in the twelfth month, which is the month Adar, on the thirteenth day of the same, when the king's commandment and his decree drew near to be put in execution, in the day that the enemies of the Jews hoped to have power over them; whereas it was turned to the contrary, that the Jews had power over those that hated them; **2** the Jews gathered together in their cities throughout all the provinces of the king Ahashverosh, to lay hand on such as sought their hurt; and no man could withstand them; for the fear of them had fallen upon all the peoples. **3** And all the princes of the provinces, and the satraps, and the governors, and they that did the king's business, helped the Jews; because the fear of Mordecai had fallen upon them. **4** For Mordecai was great in the king's house, and his fame went forth throughout all the provinces; for the man Mordecai grew greater and greater. **5** And the Jews smote all their enemies with the stroke of the sword, and with slaughter and destruction, and did as they pleased to those that hated them. **6** And in Shushan the capital the Jews slew and destroyed five hundred men. **7** And Parshandatha, and Dalphon, and

---

who is blind to the fate of his fellows, who never sees the break of day in his religious life, can never say *Shema* in concert with others.

Perhaps our Sages of the Midrash had both these ideas in mind when

וְאֵת | ח אַסְפָּתָא:

וְאֵת | פּוֹרָתָא

וְאֵת | אֲדַלְיָא

וְאֵת | ט אֲרִידָתָא:

וְאֵת | פַּרְמַשְׁתָּא

וְאֵת | אֲרִיסַי

וְאֵת | אֲרִדַי

עֲשֶׂרֶת | י וַיְזָתָא:

בְּנֵי הָמָן בֶּן־הַמְּדָתָא צֹרֵר הַיְּהוּדִים הָרָגוּ וּבַבִּזָּה לֹא שָׁלְחוּ אֶת־יָדָם: יא בַּיּוֹם הַהוּא בָּא מִסְפַּר הַהֲרוּגִים בְּשׁוּשַׁן הַבִּירָה לִפְנֵי הַמֶּלֶךְ: ס יב וַיֹּאמֶר הַמֶּלֶךְ לְאֶסְתֵּר הַמַּלְכָּה בְּשׁוּשַׁן הַבִּירָה הָרְגוּ הַיְּהוּדִים וְאַבֵּד חֲמֵשׁ מֵאוֹת אִישׁ וְאֵת עֲשֶׂרֶת בְּנֵי־הָמָן בִּשְׁאָר מְדִינוֹת הַמֶּלֶךְ מֶה עָשׂוּ וּמַה־שְׁאֵלָתֵךְ וְיִנָּתֵן לָךְ וּמַה־בַּקָּשָׁתֵךְ עוֹד וְתֵעָשׂ: יג וַתֹּאמֶר אֶסְתֵּר אִם־עַל־הַמֶּלֶךְ טוֹב יִנָּתֵן גַּם־מָחָר לַיְּהוּדִים אֲשֶׁר בְּשׁוּשָׁן לַעֲשׂוֹת כְּדָת הַיּוֹם וְאֵת עֲשֶׂרֶת בְּנֵי־הָמָן יִתְלוּ עַל־הָעֵץ: יד וַיֹּאמֶר הַמֶּלֶךְ לְהֵעָשׂוֹת כֵּן וַתִּנָּתֵן דָּת בְּשׁוּשָׁן וְאֵת עֲשֶׂרֶת בְּנֵי־הָמָן תָּלוּ: טו וַיִּקָּהֲלוּ הַיְּהוּדִים [הַיְּהוּדִיִּים כ'] אֲשֶׁר־בְּשׁוּשָׁן גַּם בְּיוֹם אַרְבָּעָה עָשָׂר לְחֹדֶשׁ אֲדָר וַיַּהַרְגוּ בְשׁוּשָׁן שְׁלֹשׁ מֵאוֹת אִישׁ וּבַבִּזָּה לֹא שָׁלְחוּ אֶת־יָדָם: טז וּשְׁאָר הַיְּהוּדִים אֲשֶׁר בִּמְדִינוֹת הַמֶּלֶךְ נִקְהֲלוּ| וְעָמֹד עַל־נַפְשָׁם וְנוֹחַ מֵאֹיְבֵיהֶם וְהָרֹג בְּשֹׂנְאֵיהֶם חֲמִשָּׁה וְשִׁבְעִים אָלֶף וּבַבִּזָּה לֹא שָׁלְחוּ אֶת־יָדָם: יז בְּיוֹם־שְׁלֹשָׁה עָשָׂר לְחֹדֶשׁ

---

they relate, in extraordinarily symbolic language, the legend that when Haman wanted to hang Mordecai, it was Haman's son Parshandatha who took upon himself to prepare the gallows and set the time of execution (*Yalkut Shimoni, Be-Shallah 256*). The anti-Semites wanted to strike the Jew in his weak points. And so Parshandatha built the gallows from a plank of the Ark of Noah and said, "Tomorrow, at the time of the reading of the *Shema* in the morning, I will hang Mordecai on it." By telling us of the plans of these enemies, the Midrash summarizes for

Aspatha, **8** and Poratha, and Adalia, and Aridatha, **9** and Parmashta, and Arisai, and Aridai, and Vaizatha, **10** the ten sons of Haman the son of Hammedatha, the Jews' enemy, they slew; but they did not lay their hand on the plunder. **11** On that day the number of those that were slain in Shushan the capital was brought before the king. **12** And the king said to Esther the queen: "The Jews have slain and destroyed five hundred men in Shushan the capital, and the ten sons of Haman; what then have they done in the rest of the king's provinces! Now whatever your petition, it shall be granted you; and whatever you request further, it shall be done." **13** Then Esther said: "If it please the king, let it be granted to the Jews that are in Shushan to do tomorrow also according to this day's decree, and let Haman's ten sons be hanged upon the gallows." **14** And the king commanded it to be done; and a decree was given out in Shushan; and they hanged Haman's ten sons. **15** And the Jews that were in Shushan gathered together on the fourteenth day also of the month Adar, and slew three hundred men in Shushan; but they did not lay their hand on the plunder. **16** And the other Jews that were in the king's provinces gathered together, and stood up for their lives, and had rest from their enemies, and slew of their foes seventy-five thousand — but did not lay their hand on the plunder — **17** on the thirteenth day of the month Adar, and on the

---

us two elements of good leadership. Haman and his son thought that the Jews were vulnerable because their leaders were ineffective. They thought that the Jewish leaders in Persia were like Noah of old, the Noah whose symbol of failure was the Ark he built for himself alone. They suspected also that the Jewish masses were weak as followers, that they were ripped apart by inner conflicts and controversies. And so they planned the execution for the time of the morning *Shema*, the time when a Jew is bidden to see his fellow from a distance, to see him and feel for him and be with him.

Fortunately, Mordecai was a real leader and they were good followers. Haman's plans were frustrated and Israel was saved.

אֲדָר וְנֹוֹחַ בְּאַרְבָּעָה עָשָׂר בֹּו וְעָשֹׁה אֹתֹו יֹום מִשְׁתֶּה וְשִׂמְחָה: יח וְהַיְּהוּדִים
[וְהַיְּהוּדִיים כ'] אֲשֶׁר־בְּשׁוּשָׁן נִקְהֲלוּ בִּשְׁלֹשָׁה עָשָׂר בֹּו וּבְאַרְבָּעָה עָשָׂר
בֹּו וְנֹוֹחַ בַּחֲמִשָּׁה עָשָׂר בֹּו וְעָשֹׁה אֹתֹו יֹום מִשְׁתֶּה וְשִׂמְחָה: יט עַל־כֵּן
הַיְּהוּדִים הַפְּרָזִים [הַפְּרוֹזִים כ'] הַיֹּשְׁבִים בְּעָרֵי הַפְּרָזֹות עֹשִׂים אֵת יֹום
אַרְבָּעָה עָשָׂר לְחֹדֶשׁ אֲדָר שִׂמְחָה וּמִשְׁתֶּה וְיֹום טֹוב וּמִשְׁלֹוֹחַ מָנֹות אִישׁ
לְרֵעֵהוּ: פ כ וַיִּכְתֹּב מָרְדֳּכַי אֶת־הַדְּבָרִים הָאֵלֶּה וַיִּשְׁלַח סְפָרִים אֶל־כָּל־
הַיְּהוּדִים אֲשֶׁר בְּכָל־מְדִינֹות הַמֶּלֶךְ אֲחַשְׁוֵרֹושׁ הַקְּרֹובִים וְהָרְחֹוקִים: כא
לְקַיֵּם עֲלֵיהֶם לִהְיֹות עֹשִׂים אֵת יֹום אַרְבָּעָה עָשָׂר לְחֹדֶשׁ אֲדָר וְאֵת יֹום־
חֲמִשָּׁה עָשָׂר בֹּו בְּכָל־שָׁנָה וְשָׁנָה: כב כַּיָּמִים אֲשֶׁר־נָחוּ בָהֶם הַיְּהוּדִים

וּמִשְׁתֶּה וְיֹום טֹוב וּמִשְׁלֹחַ מָנֹות *gladness and feasting, and a holiday, and of sending choice portions.* Chronologically and in order of value, the mitzvah of Purim is the *se'udah*, to eat, and drink; but prior to that come the commandments of sending gifts to friends and charity to the poor. And, according to some Talmudists (the Rama as opposed to *Peri Hadash*), the commandment of giving gifts is fulfilled as long as one gives, even if his or her friend refuses to receive the gift! (*Orah Hayyim 695:4*).

To give rather than to receive, to turn rising expectations on myself rather than on others — that is the teaching of Purim. Haman fell because he always demanded of others to satisfy him and his wants and his expectations. Mordecai succeeded because he devoted his life not to himself and his appetites, but to his niece and then to his people and to his God. Mordecai was a Jew in that he was great not for himself, but for others. He sought the welfare not of himself and his own glory, but of his people. He sought peace for his children and his posterity after him.

לִהְיֹות עֹשִׂים אֵת יֹום אַרְבָּעָה עָשָׂר לְחֹדֶשׁ אֲדָר *that they should keep the fourteenth day of the month Adar.* Our tradition teaches: "*mi-she-nikhnas Adar marbin be-simhah*, when the month of Adar arrives, one must increase his happiness or joy" — a beautiful idea (*Ta'anit 29a*). However, what if I feel miserable? How can one command a person to be happy? The answer of the Jewish tradition, accumulated in the course of 3,500 years, is that happiness or joy is a state of mind which can be inspired from

fourteenth day of the same they rested, and made it a day of feasting and gladness. **18** But the Jews that were in Shushan assembled together on the thirteenth day thereof, and on the fourteenth thereof; and on the fifteenth day of the same they rested, and made it a day of feasting and gladness. **19** Therefore do the Jews of the villages, that dwell in the unwalled towns, make the fourteenth day of the month Adar a day of gladness and feasting, and a holiday, and of sending choice portions portions one to another. **20** And Mordecai wrote these things, and sent letters to all the Jews that were in all the provinces of the king Ahashverosh, both near and far, **21** to enjoin them that they should keep the fourteenth day of the month Adar, and the fifteenth day of the same, each year, **22** the days on which the Jews rested from their

---

without as well as aroused from within. If one acts happy, one eventually emerges from under the burden of sadness.

Hasidim made a great principle of this idea. They drank and they sang in the synagogue and even danced, declared that sadness is a sin, and tried to inspire happiness even artificially — and they succeeded. In a continent and in an age when European Jewry was seized with despair because of false messiahs, because of massacres and political persecutions, because of economic and cultural deprivation, Hasidism was able to inspire the idea of *acting* happy, and then *being* happy — by a process of *tokho ke-varo!* Create a greater image than that which is your reality, and then change over your reality to conform to the image. To demand, as some deluded people sometimes do, that we become *baro ke-tokho*, that we remake our outer life to conform to our inner life, is to condemn people to the lowest station of humanity and to deny them hope. However, to urge them toward *tokho ke-varo* is to hold forth a realizable ideal in the finest tradition of Jewish ethical optimism.

One of the greatest commandments in the Torah is to "love the Lord your God" (Deuteronomy 6:5). But how many of us can experience such love? What does one do if he feels that his inner resources have dried up, that he is incapable of any deep experience or feeling? Rabbi Shneur Zalman of Ladi, founder of the Habad movement of Hasidism, recommends a solution: Act *as if* you are possessed of *ahavat Hashem*,

מֵאוֹיְבֵיהֶם וְהַחֹדֶשׁ אֲשֶׁר נֶהְפַּךְ לָהֶם מִיָּגוֹן לְשִׂמְחָה וּמֵאֵבֶל לְיוֹם טוֹב לַעֲשׂוֹת אוֹתָם יְמֵי מִשְׁתֶּה וְשִׂמְחָה וּמִשְׁלוֹחַ מָנוֹת אִישׁ לְרֵעֵהוּ וּמַתָּנוֹת לָאֶבְיוֹנִים: כג וְקִבֵּל הַיְּהוּדִים אֵת אֲשֶׁר־הֵחֵלּוּ לַעֲשׂוֹת וְאֵת אֲשֶׁר־כָּתַב מָרְדֳּכַי אֲלֵיהֶם: כד כִּי הָמָן בֶּן־הַמְּדָתָא הָאֲגָגִי צֹרֵר כָּל־הַיְּהוּדִים חָשַׁב עַל־הַיְּהוּדִים לְאַבְּדָם וְהִפִּיל פּוּר הוּא הַגּוֹרָל לְהֻמָּם וּלְאַבְּדָם: כה וּבְבֹאָהּ לִפְנֵי הַמֶּלֶךְ אָמַר עִם־הַסֵּפֶר יָשׁוּב מַחֲשַׁבְתּוֹ הָרָעָה אֲשֶׁר־חָשַׁב עַל־ הַיְּהוּדִים עַל־רֹאשׁוֹ וְתָלוּ אֹתוֹ וְאֶת־בָּנָיו עַל־הָעֵץ: כו עַל־כֵּן קָרְאוּ לַיָּמִים הָאֵלֶּה פוּרִים עַל־שֵׁם הַפּוּר עַל־כֵּן עַל־כָּל־דִּבְרֵי הָאִגֶּרֶת הַזֹּאת וּמָה־רָאוּ עַל־כָּכָה וּמָה הִגִּיעַ אֲלֵיהֶם: כז קִיְּמוּ וְקִבְּלוּ [וְקִבֵּל כ'] הַיְּהוּדִים| עֲלֵיהֶם|

not in the eyes of others but in the eyes of your own self. Live as if you were possessed of a passionate love of God — and sooner or later the outer appearance will evoke an inner love, the image will create the reality, and by the process of *tokho ke-varo* you will indeed arrive at a level of genuine love. Otherwise, we are left only with despair and never can make any progress.

The same is true of one's social relations. Just as we are commanded to love God, so do we have a commandment to love our neighbor or fellow man. Yet this commandment is much easier to advocate than to practice, for what if one has unlovable neighbors? What if one does not have the ability to love his fellow men as he thinks he ought to? An insight to the solution is provided by Rabbi Samson Raphael Hirsch, who points to the peculiar grammatical construction of this commandment. The Torah says, "*ve-ahavta le-reiakha ka-mokha*, You shall love your neighbor as yourself" (Leviticus 19:18). Actually, the normal Hebrew should be *et reiakha* rather than *le-reiakha*. The way it is written, the verse should be literally translated as, "You shall love to your neighbor as yourself." Genuine love of one's neighbor must come later; first, one must love toward him, one must act in a loving manner to him, one must play the role of the loving fellow man — and then ultimately one will indeed come to love him. First we build up the image, and then, by the process of *tokho ke-varo*, we come to achieve a new inner transformation.

enemies, and the month which was turned for them from sorrow to gladness, and from mourning into a holiday; that they should make them days of feasting and gladness, and of sending choice portions one to another, and gifts to the poor. **23** And the Jews took upon them to do as they had begun, and as Mordecai had written to them; **24** because Haman the son of Hammedatha, the Agagite, the enemy of all the Jews, had schemed against the Jews to destroy them, and had cast pur, that is, the lot, to consume them, and to destroy them; **25** but when she came before the king, he gave written orders that his wicked scheme, which he had devised against the Jews, should return upon his own head; and that he and his sons should be hanged on the gallows. **26** Therefore they called these days Purim, after the name of pur. Therefore because of all the words of this letter, and of that which they had seen concerning this matter, and that which had come to them, **27** the Jews ordained, and took upon them, and upon their

---

יְמֵי מִשְׁתֶּה *days of feasting*. A famous Talmudic statement concerning Purim is that one ought to drink more than his usual standard of sobriety. It permits one to drink so that he does not distinguish between accursed Haman and blessed Mordecai (*Megillah* 7b). This does not mean, assuredly, that one must intoxicate himself to the point where he loses his capacity for analytic distinctions. Rather, it means that one must drink only slightly more than usual so as, on the contrary, he gains greater spiritual insight. This spiritual insight will show that, indeed, there is truly no difference at all between "accursed Haman" and "blessed is Mordecai." The nefarious incriminations of Haman, in and of and by themselves, are the tokens of Mordecai's blessing! It is the accusations which come from Haman's accursed hatred that are the testimony of Mordecai's blessed virtues. It is when the anti-Semite accuses us of fostering the unity of Israel, the differentness of Judaism, and the resistance to idolatry that is part of our national character, that we can rise to our fullest stature as being loyal to our spiritual destiny and vocation. There is, and there should be, no difference between Haman's curse and Mordecai's blessing. Haman's indictment is a "true bill," it points to the source of our strength and our blessing.

וְעַל־זַרְעָם וְעַל כָּל־ הַנִּלְוִים עֲלֵיהֶם וְלֹא יַעֲבוֹר לִהְיוֹת עֹשִׂים אֵת שְׁנֵי
הַיָּמִים הָאֵלֶּה כִּכְתָבָם וְכִזְמַנָּם בְּכָל־שָׁנָה וְשָׁנָה: כּח וְהַיָּמִים הָאֵלֶּה נִזְכָּרִים
וְנַעֲשִׂים בְּכָל־דּוֹר וָדוֹר מִשְׁפָּחָה וּמִשְׁפָּחָה מְדִינָה וּמְדִינָה וְעִיר וָעִיר וִימֵי
הַפּוּרִים הָאֵלֶּה לֹא יַעַבְרוּ מִתּוֹךְ הַיְּהוּדִים וְזִכְרָם לֹא־יָסוּף מִזַּרְעָם: ס כּט
וַתִּכְתֹּב אֶסְתֵּר הַמַּלְכָּה בַת־אֲבִיחַיִל וּמָרְדֳּכַי הַיְּהוּדִי אֶת־כָּל־תֹּקֶף לְקַיֵּם
אֵת אִגֶּרֶת הַפֻּרִים הַזֹּאת הַשֵּׁנִית: ל וַיִּשְׁלַח סְפָרִים אֶל־כָּל־הַיְּהוּדִים
אֶל־שֶׁבַע וְעֶשְׂרִים וּמֵאָה מְדִינָה מַלְכוּת אֲחַשְׁוֵרוֹשׁ דִּבְרֵי שָׁלוֹם וֶאֱמֶת:

דִּבְרֵי שָׁלוֹם וֶאֱמֶת *words of peace and truth.* The victory of the Jews over
Haman and the frustration of his nefarious plot was a surprising triumph and showed that God had not abandoned us. But neither were
there any overt miracles, any clear and indisputable proof that God was
present and responsible for our victory. That is why the Book of Esther
is included in the Bible, and yet it is the only book in which the Name
of God is not mentioned. That is why the Rabbis maintain that the
very name "Esther" is indicative of the hiding of God, the lack of His
full revelation and presence (*Hullin* 139b). "Esther" sounds like *hesther,*
which means "hiddenness."

The *Megillah* itself is described in the Book of Esther as "*divrei shalom
ve-emet,* words of peace and truth." By *emet,* truth, is meant the action
of God directing the forces of history. Intelligent and wise people reading the *Megillah,* or experiencing it during that generation, know that
all that has occurred is the result of the actions of God "Whose seal is
Truth." All these improbable events leading to the redemption of Israel
were obviously the providential design of the God of Israel. But it was
just as possible for one less endowed with spiritual insight to interpret
all the events as *shalom,* peace — that is, as a result of fortuitous events
helped by the stupidity of the Persian king, the arrogance of Haman,
and the wisdom of Mordecai: a diplomatic exploitation of unusually
happy circumstances. Thus, the astounding victory was natural enough;
there was no supernatural intervention in the affairs of the Jews of
Persia. So Jews were free, authentically free, to interpret the events of
that historical episode as they wished.

This lesson should not be lost on us in our individual lives. It is often

seed, and upon all such as joined themselves to them, without fail, that they would keep these two days according to the writing thereof, and according to the appointed time thereof, every year; **28** and that these days should be remembered and kept throughout every generation, every family, every province, and every city; and that these days of Purim should not fail from among the Jews, nor the memorial of them perish from their seed. **29** Then Esther the queen, the daughter of Abihail, and Mordecai the Jew, wrote down most emphatically, to confirm this second letter of Purim. **30** And he sent letters to all the Jews, to the hundred twenty and seven provinces of the kingdom of Ahashverosh, with words of peace and truth, **31** to confirm these days

---

said that in crisis, in the extraordinary moments of life, we can test the true character of a man. I do not believe that this is true, except if his reaction is contrary to expectations. If a man, for instance, responds heroically at a time of tragedy, he may be commended. But if he falls apart in extreme adversity, he cannot be condemned; he simply was not free to do otherwise. The same holds true in reverse situations. One who is friendly and charitable as a result of the miraculous recovery of a sick child, may not yet be considered a man of nobility and generosity. He has almost been forced into charm and sweetness by his overwhelming sense of relief and gratitude. When, then, can we tell what a man is really like? When may he be held morally accountable for his acts, and considered either guilty or praiseworthy? When he is free — he is free when things are neither here nor there, when he is subject neither to elation nor depression, neither to the distress of adversity nor to the uplift of felicity.

It is in the Purims of life, when we have no clear proof that God is with us or against us, that there is a special virtue to accepting the Torah. Those who come to the synagogue and pray only during occasions of *simhah*, or when reciting the *Kaddish*, are doing the right thing. But the real test comes after the *simhah* or the eleven months of *Kaddish* are over — then, when things are neither here nor there, is the religious fiber of a personality tested. And not only is it tested, but at that time the decisions are more meaningful and more enduring.

לֹא לְקַיֵּם אֵת־יְמֵי הַפֻּרִים הָאֵלֶּה בִּזְמַנֵּיהֶם כַּאֲשֶׁר קִיַּם עֲלֵיהֶם מָרְדֳּכַי הַיְּהוּדִי וְאֶסְתֵּר הַמַּלְכָּה וְכַאֲשֶׁר קִיְּמוּ עַל־נַפְשָׁם וְעַל־זַרְעָם דִּבְרֵי הַצֹּמוֹת וְזַעֲקָתָם: לב וּמַאֲמַר אֶסְתֵּר קִיַּם דִּבְרֵי הַפֻּרִים הָאֵלֶּה וְנִכְתָּב בַּסֵּפֶר: פ

פרק י'

א וַיָּשֶׂם הַמֶּלֶךְ אֲחַשְׁוֵרוֹשׁ [אֲחַשְׁרֵשׁ כ'] מַס עַל־הָאָרֶץ וְאִיֵּי הַיָּם: ב וְכָל־ מַעֲשֵׂה תׇקְפּוֹ וּגְבוּרָתוֹ וּפָרָשַׁת גְּדֻלַּת מׇרְדֳּכַי אֲשֶׁר גִּדְּלוֹ הַמֶּלֶךְ הֲלוֹא־הֵם כְּתוּבִים עַל־סֵפֶר דִּבְרֵי הַיָּמִים לְמַלְכֵי מָדַי וּפָרָס: ג כִּי מׇרְדֳּכַי הַיְּהוּדִי מִשְׁנֶה לַמֶּלֶךְ אֲחַשְׁוֵרוֹשׁ וְגָדוֹל לַיְּהוּדִים וְרָצוּי לְרֹב אֶחָיו דֹּרֵשׁ טוֹב לְעַמּוֹ וְדֹבֵר שָׁלוֹם לְכָל־זַרְעוֹ:

לְרֹב אֶחָיו *the multitude of his brethren.* True leadership does not mean agreeing with everybody. If a leader is to achieve his purpose, he must sometimes oppose certain of those who follow him. That, in fact is the very essence of leadership. This intangible but very real quality must be divested of yes-manship and showmanship and flattery. The leader, be he president or prophet, rabbi or teacher, must at times cut through to the heart of a problem even if it hurts some of those he wants to help. Medicine sometimes tastes bitter. And real preaching must sometimes lash as well as soothe. Mordecai, whose exemplary leadership Jews all over the world hail on Purim, was a person who did not try to please everybody. In fact, among the very last words of the *Megillah*, the document which is a testimonial to his courageous leadership, is the statement which can be translated as: "Mordecai was accepted by most of his brethren, *rov ehav*" — accepted by *most*, but *not by all.* Mordecai, the archetype of the great Jewish leader, knew that if he is to set the people back on their feet, he must of necessity step on the toes of some of them. Effective Jewish leadership requires that both leader and followers must realize that leadership demands boldness and courage, at times contrary to the wishes and better judgment of many of the followers. That is how

of Purim in their appointed times, according as Mordecai the Jew and Esther the queen had enjoined them, and as they had ordained for themselves and for their seed, regarding the fasts and their prayers. **32** And the commandment of Esther confirmed these matters of Purim; and it was written in the book.

Chapter 10

1 And the king Ahashverosh laid a tribute upon the land, and upon the isles of the sea. **2** And all the acts of his power and of his might, and the full account of the greatness of Mordecai, how the king advanced him, they are surely written in the book of the chronicles of the kings of Media and Persia. **3** For Mordecai the Jew was viceroy to king Ahashverosh, and great among the Jews, and accepted of the multitude of his brethren; seeking the good of his people and speaking peace to all his seed.

Mordecai became a promoter of good will to his people, and a speaker of peace to *all* its children.

דֹּרֵשׁ טוֹב לְעַמּוֹ וְדֹבֵר שָׁלוֹם לְכָל זַרְעוֹ *seeking the good of his people and speaking peace to all his seed.* In the closing words of the Book of Esther, we learn how "Mordecai the Jew was next unto King Ahashverosh, and accepted by most of his brethren, seeking — *doresh* — the good of his people and speaking peace to all his seed." Mordecai did not throw away his yarmulke and try his best to look and sound like a Persian WASP. He remained a *gadol*, a genuinely great Jew, even while he was second in command to the king himself, and traveling in the highest circles of the Persian government. With all this, he was also one who sought the welfare, the good, for his people. But the word *doresh* means not only to *seek*, but also to *demand!* Mordecai demanded of his people that they act according to the highest principles of Torah, of that which is good and right. And in that manner he assured *shalom*, as both peace and wholesomeness, for his people and their children after them.

אחר קריאת המגילה מברך הקורא:

בָּרוּךְ אַתָּה יְיָ אֱלֹהֵינוּ מֶלֶךְ הָעוֹלָם, הָרָב אֶת רִיבֵנוּ, וְהַדָּן אֶת דִּינֵנוּ, וְהַנּוֹקֵם אֶת נִקְמָתֵנוּ, וְהַמְשַׁלֵּם גְּמוּל לְכָל אֹיְבֵי נַפְשֵׁנוּ, וְהַנִּפְרָע לָנוּ מִצָּרֵינוּ. בָּרוּךְ אַתָּה יְיָ הַנִּפְרָע לְעַמּוֹ יִשְׂרָאֵל מִכָּל צָרֵיהֶם, הָאֵל הַמּוֹשִׁיעַ.

אומרים אשר הניא רק אחר קריאת המגילה בלילה:

אֲשֶׁר הֵנִיא עֲצַת גּוֹיִם וַיָּפֶר מַחְשְׁבוֹת עֲרוּמִים, בְּקוּם עָלֵינוּ אָדָם רָשָׁע, נֵצֶר זָדוֹן מִזֶּרַע עֲמָלֵק. גָּאָה בְּעָשְׁרוֹ וְכָרָה לוֹ בּוֹר, וּגְדֻלָּתוֹ יָקְשָׁה לּוֹ לָכֶד. דִּמָּה בְנַפְשׁוֹ לִלְכֹּד וְנִלְכָּד, בִּקֵּשׁ לְהַשְׁמִיד וְנִשְׁמַד מְהֵרָה. הָמָן הוֹדִיעַ אֵיבַת אֲבוֹתָיו וְעוֹרֵר שִׂנְאַת אַחִים לַבָּנִים, וְלֹא זָכַר רַחֲמֵי שָׁאוּל, כִּי בְחֶמְלָתוֹ עַל אֲגַג נוֹלַד אוֹיֵב. זָמַם רָשָׁע לְהַכְרִית צַדִּיק, וְנִלְכַּד טָמֵא בִּידֵי טָהוֹר. חֶסֶד גָּבַר עַל שִׁגְגַת אָב, וְרָשָׁע הוֹסִיף חֵטְא עַל חֲטָאָיו. טָמַן בְּלִבּוֹ מַחְשְׁבוֹת עֲרוּמָיו, וַיִּתְמַכֵּר לַעֲשׂוֹת רָעָה. יָדוֹ שָׁלַח בִּקְדוֹשֵׁי אֵל, כַּסְפּוֹ נָתַן לְהַכְרִית זִכְרָם. כִּרְאוֹת מָרְדְּכַי כִּי יָצָא קֶצֶף וְדָתֵי הָמָן נִתְּנוּ בְשׁוּשָׁן, לָבַשׁ שַׂק וְקָשַׁר מִסְפֵּד וְגָזַר צוֹם וַיֵּשֶׁב עַל הָאֵפֶר. מִי זֶה יַעֲמֹד לְכַפֵּר שְׁגָגָה וְלִמְחֹל חַטַּאת עֲוֹן אֲבוֹתֵינוּ. נֵץ פָּרַח מִלּוּלָב, הֵן הֲדַסָּה עָמְדָה לְעוֹרֵר יְשֵׁנִים. סָרִיסֶיהָ הִבְהִילוּ לְהָמָן לְהַשְׁקוֹתוֹ יֵין חֲמַת תַּנִּינִים. עָמַד בְּעָשְׁרוֹ וְנָפַל בְּרִשְׁעוֹ, עָשָׂה לוֹ עֵץ וְנִתְלָה עָלָיו. פִּיהֶם פָּתְחוּ כָּל יוֹשְׁבֵי תֵבֵל, כִּי פוּר הָמָן נֶהְפַּךְ לְפוּרֵנוּ. צַדִּיק נֶחֱלַץ מִיַּד רָשָׁע, אוֹיֵב נִתַּן תַּחַת נַפְשׁוֹ. קִימוּ עֲלֵיהֶם לַעֲשׂוֹת פוּרִים וְלִשְׂמֹחַ בְּכָל שָׁנָה וְשָׁנָה. רָאִיתָ אֶת תְּפִלַּת מָרְדְּכַי וְאֶסְתֵּר, הָמָן וּבָנָיו עַל הָעֵץ תָּלִיתָ.

After the reading of the Megillah with a minyan,
the reader recites the following blessing:

Blessed are You, O Lord our God, King of the Universe, Who pleads our cause, judges our claim, and avenges our wrong; Who brings retribution upon all enemies of our soul, and exacts punishment on our behalf from our adversaries. Blessed are You, O Lord, Who on behalf of His people Israel exacts punishment from all their adversaries, O God, the Savior.

The paragraph "Who thwarted" is said only after the Megillah reading at night:

Who thwarted the counsel of the nations, and annulled the designs of the crafty, when a wicked man, an arrogant offshoot of the seed of Amalek, rose up against us. Insolent in his riches, he dug himself a pit, and his own greatness became his own trap. In his mind he thought to entrap, but was himself entrapped; he sought to destroy, but was speedily destroyed. Haman displayed his ancestors' hatred, and stirred up against the children the ancient enmity of the brothers (Esau and Jacob). He did not remember the mercy of Saul, through whose compassion for Agag the enemy was born. The wicked plotted to cut off the righteous, but the impure [one] was caught in the hands of the pure [one]. (Mordecai's) loving-kindness (to Esther) prevailed over the father's (Saul's) error, but the wicked (Haman) piled sin upon sin. In his heart he hid his cunning designs, and sold himself to do wickedness. He stretched forth his hand against God's holy ones; he spent his silver to destroy every remembrance of them. When Mordecai saw that wrath had gone forth, and that the decrees of Haman were issued in Shushan, he put on sackcloth and wrapped himself in mourning, decreed a fast and sat upon ashes: "Who will rise up to atone for error, and obtain pardon for the sin and iniquity of our ancestors?" A flower blossomed from the palm tree: Behold! Hadassah arose to awaken those who slumber. Her servants hastened Haman, to make him drink the wine of the serpent's venom. He rose through his riches, but fell

שׁוֹשַׁנַּת יַעֲקֹב צָהֲלָה וְשָׂמֵחָה בִּרְאוֹתָם יַחַד תְּכֵלֶת מָרְדֳּכָי, תְּשׁוּעָתָם הָיִיתָ לָנֶצַח, וְתִקְוָתָם בְּכָל דּוֹר וָדוֹר. לְהוֹדִיעַ שֶׁכָּל קֹוֶיךָ לֹא יֵבשׁוּ, וְלֹא יִכָּלְמוּ לָנֶצַח כָּל הַחוֹסִים בָּךְ. אָרוּר הָמָן אֲשֶׁר בִּקֵּשׁ לְאַבְּדִי, בָּרוּךְ מָרְדֳּכַי הַיְּהוּדִי. אֲרוּרָה זֶרֶשׁ אֵשֶׁת מַפְחִידִי, בְּרוּכָה אֶסְתֵּר בַּעֲדִי, וְגַם חַרְבוֹנָה זָכוּר לַטּוֹב.

through his wickedness; he built the gallows on which he was hanged. All the inhabitants of the world opened their mouths [in amazement], when Haman's lot became our Purim. When the righteous was saved from the hand of the wicked, and the enemy was substituted for him, the Jews undertook for themselves to celebrate Purim, and to rejoice on it every year. You regarded the prayer of Mordecai and Esther: Haman and his sons You hanged upon the gallows.

The rose of Jacob rejoiced and was glad, when, together, they saw Mordecai garbed in royal blue. You have always been their salvation, and their hope in every generation, to make known that all who hope in You shall not be ashamed, neither shall any who put their trust in You ever be humiliated. Accursed be Haman who sought to destroy me; blessed be Mordecai the Jew. Accursed be Zeresh, the wife of him that terrified me; blessed be Esther [who sacrificed herself] on my behalf. And may Harbonah also be remembered for good.

—◈—

למוצאי שבת:

וִיהִי נֹעַם אֲדֹנָי אֱלֹהֵינוּ עָלֵינוּ, וּמַעֲשֵׂה יָדֵינוּ כּוֹנְנָה עָלֵינוּ, וּמַעֲשֵׂה יָדֵינוּ כּוֹנְנֵהוּ.

יֹשֵׁב בְּסֵתֶר עֶלְיוֹן, בְּצֵל שַׁדַּי יִתְלוֹנָן. אֹמַר לַיָי, מַחְסִי וּמְצוּדָתִי, אֱלֹהַי אֶבְטַח בּוֹ. כִּי הוּא יַצִּילְךָ מִפַּח יָקוּשׁ, מִדֶּבֶר הַוּוֹת. בְּאֶבְרָתוֹ יָסֶךְ לָךְ, וְתַחַת כְּנָפָיו תֶּחְסֶה, צִנָּה וְסֹחֵרָה אֲמִתּוֹ. לֹא תִירָא מִפַּחַד לָיְלָה, מֵחֵץ יָעוּף יוֹמָם. מִדֶּבֶר בָּאֹפֶל יַהֲלֹךְ, מִקֶּטֶב יָשׁוּד צָהֳרָיִם. יִפֹּל מִצִּדְּךָ אֶלֶף, וּרְבָבָה מִימִינֶךָ, אֵלֶיךָ לֹא יִגָּשׁ. רַק בְּעֵינֶיךָ תַבִּיט, וְשִׁלֻּמַת רְשָׁעִים תִּרְאֶה. כִּי אַתָּה יְיָ מַחְסִי, עֶלְיוֹן שַׂמְתָּ מְעוֹנֶךָ. לֹא תְאֻנֶּה אֵלֶיךָ רָעָה, וְנֶגַע לֹא יִקְרַב בְּאָהֳלֶךָ. כִּי מַלְאָכָיו יְצַוֶּה לָּךְ, לִשְׁמָרְךָ בְּכָל דְּרָכֶיךָ. עַל כַּפַּיִם יִשָּׂאוּנְךָ, פֶּן תִּגֹּף בָּאֶבֶן רַגְלֶךָ. עַל שַׁחַל וָפֶתֶן תִּדְרֹךְ, תִּרְמֹס כְּפִיר וְתַנִּין. כִּי בִי חָשַׁק וַאֲפַלְּטֵהוּ, אֲשַׂגְּבֵהוּ, כִּי יָדַע שְׁמִי. יִקְרָאֵנִי וְאֶעֱנֵהוּ, עִמּוֹ אָנֹכִי בְצָרָה, אֲחַלְּצֵהוּ וַאֲכַבְּדֵהוּ. אֹרֶךְ יָמִים אַשְׂבִּיעֵהוּ, וְאַרְאֵהוּ בִּישׁוּעָתִי. אֹרֶךְ יָמִים אַשְׂבִּיעֵהוּ, וְאַרְאֵהוּ בִּישׁוּעָתִי.

—◈—

וְאַתָּה קָדוֹשׁ, יוֹשֵׁב תְּהִלּוֹת יִשְׂרָאֵל: וְקָרָא זֶה אֶל זֶה וְאָמַר, קָדוֹשׁ קָדוֹשׁ קָדוֹשׁ יְיָ צְבָאוֹת, מְלֹא כָל הָאָרֶץ כְּבוֹדוֹ: וּמְקַבְּלִין דֵּין מִן דֵּין,

---

קָדוֹשׁ *Holy. Kavod* (honor) is an external or social act. When we give *kavod* or honor to someone, we perform an act of courtesy and acknowledgment; but we do not imply acceptance of his principles or love or participation or involvement. It is a gesture, possibly very sincere, but it does not touch our depths. *Kedushah* (holiness), however, represents an inner transformation, a total commitment, a dedication of the entire personality to a transcendent goal. It is an existential, not a social act. We can give *kavod* without being changed. When we strive for *kedushah* we must risk a profound metamorphosis. *Kavod* is something of

—◦—

At the conclusion of the Sabbath, add:

And let the pleasantness of the Lord our God be upon us: and establish for us the work of our hands; O, establish the work of our hands.

He who dwells in the shelter of the Most High abides under the shadow of the Almighty. I say of the Lord, He is my Refuge and my Fortress; my God in Whom I trust. — For He will deliver you from the snare of the fowler, and from the deadly pestilence. He will cover you with His wings, and under His wings you will take refuge: His truth shall be a protective shield. You shall not be afraid of the terror by night, nor of the arrow that flies by day; not of the pestilence that walks in darkness, nor of the plague that ravages at noon day. A thousand may fall at your side, and ten thousand at your right hand; but it will not come near you. Only with your eyes shall you look on, and see the retribution of the wicked. For [you said,] "You, O Lord, are my Refuge." — You have made the Most High your dwelling place; there no evil shall befall you, neither shall any scourge come near your tent. For He will command His angels regarding you, to guard you in all your ways. They will bear you upon their hands, lest you strike your foot against a stone. You will tread upon the lion and the viper: you will trample upon the young lion and the serpent. — "Because he loves Me, therefore I will deliver him: I will set him on high, because he knows My Name. When he calls upon Me, I will answer him; I will be with him in trouble: I will deliver him and honor him. With long life I will satisfy him, and will let him see My salvation. With long life I will satisfy him, and will let him see My salvation."

—◦—

But You are the Holy One, O You Who dwells upon the praises of Israel. And one [angel] cried to another, and said, Holy, holy,

וְאָמְרִין קַדִּישׁ, בִּשְׁמֵי מְרוֹמָא עִלָּאָה בֵּית שְׁכִינְתֵּהּ, קַדִּישׁ עַל אַרְעָא
עוֹבַד גְּבוּרְתֵּהּ, קַדִּישׁ לְעָלַם וּלְעָלְמֵי עָלְמַיָּא, יְיָ צְבָאוֹת מַלְיָא כָל אַרְעָא
זִיו יְקָרֵהּ: וַתִּשָּׂאֵנִי רוּחַ, וָאֶשְׁמַע אַחֲרַי קוֹל רַעַשׁ גָּדוֹל, בָּרוּךְ כְּבוֹד יְיָ
מִמְּקוֹמוֹ: וּנְטָלַתְנִי רוּחָא, וְשִׁמְעֵת בַּתְרַי קָל זִיעַ סַגִּיא, דִּמְשַׁבְּחִין וְאָמְרִין,
בְּרִיךְ יְקָרָא דַיְיָ מֵאֲתַר בֵּית שְׁכִינְתֵּהּ: יְיָ יִמְלֹךְ לְעֹלָם וָעֶד: יְיָ מַלְכוּתֵהּ

---

which the masses are capable. But kedushah is something to which only the elite and the initiated are obligated. Isaiah calls out, in his famous "seraphic song," "Holy, holy, holy is the Lord of Hosts, all the world is full of His glory (kavod)" (Isaiah 6:3). God Himself is the highest expression of kedushah, but "all the world" perceives nothing more than His kavod. Kavod is noble and necessary, but it is antiseptic and alienated. Kedushah is higher and deeper and a more faithful commitment. For those who are close to God, kavod is insufficient; only the surpassing goal of kedushah is appropriate.

Too many Jews are willing to respect the synagogue — but never enter it; to respect the service if they attend — but not to participate in it in any meaningful way. Jews respect Torah and Judaism, they respect scholars and rabbis and observant Jews — and the respect and kavod therefore mean that the object of their honor is alien to them, it remains externalized and superficial and meaningless. Our community has almost choked with respectability and kavod. But respect and respectability are only the first baby-steps toward the great goal — which is holiness, kedushah. The goal must be the culmination of meaningfulness in life, to rise, to transcend oneself, to come close to God. Judaism demands kedushah — passion and involvement and risk, and courage even unto death. The synagogue must certainly possess kavod — but only on its way to kedushah. For the goal of a synagogue must not be to become a place of respectability, not even to teach children to respect their parents and all of them to curtsy to the ancestral faith, to respect the honored but obsolete tradition, The ideal of a synagogue, of a Jewish community, is to become a kehillah kedoshah, a "holy community." This means that services were not meant to be enjoyed but to inspire; that words of Torah spoken from the pulpit were meant not to please or tickle the intellect, but to upset and to criticize the status quo.

holy is the Lord of Hosts: the whole world is full of His glory. And they receive permission from one another, and say, "Holy in the highest heavens, the place of His divine abode; holy on earth, the work of His might; holy forever and to all eternity is the Lord of Hosts; the whole earth is full of the radiance of His glory." Then a wind lifted me up, and I heard behind me the sound of a great noise (saying), Blessed be the glory of the Lord from His place. Then a wind lifted me up, and I heard behind me the sound of a great rushing, of those who uttered praises, and said, "Blessed be the glory of the Lord from the region of His divine abode." The Lord shall reign forever and ever. The kingdom of the Lord

---

The State of Israel also suffers today from an inner tension which I would describe as a contest between *kavod* and *kedushah*. Almost all Israelis, with the exception of an unimportant fringe element, agree that Israel must be a Jewish state. It is the result of three and a half thousand years of Jewish history, and it therefore must bear a Jewish character. The great question is: How? In what way? What form shall it take, and to what degree shall it be Jewish? Some Israelis, perhaps most, are satisfied that the Jewishness of the state should be expressed in the form of *kavod*. Israel must honor its Jewish past; and so Saturday is an official day of rest, all the holidays are officially observed, and the Holy Tongue is the spoken language of the state. Others, however, maintain that *Medinat Israel* must really strive to become *Eretz Israel*, and *Eretz Israel* is, for us, *artzenu ha-kedoshah*, our Holy Land. And *kedushah* implies not just a gesture toward the Sabbath, but a real Sabbath, as it was historically observed, and not as we see it in the streets of Tel Aviv. *Kedushah* means a higher moral tone in the community of Israel, not to continue importing the decadent hedonism that has corrupted the Western world and especially America. *Kedushah* means that Jewish law must return to the Jewish state, which must not be satisfied with a patchwork of English, common, and Ottoman law.

One can never tell how and when the courtesy of *kavod* will culminate in a career of *kedushah*. But we hope it will come soon.

קָאָם לְעָלַם וּלְעָלְמֵי עָלְמַיָּא: יְיָ אֱלֹהֵי אַבְרָהָם יִצְחָק וְיִשְׂרָאֵל אֲבוֹתֵינוּ, שָׁמְרָה זֹּאת לְעוֹלָם, לְיֵצֶר מַחְשְׁבוֹת לְבַב עַמֶּךָ, וְהָכֵן לְבָבָם אֵלֶיךָ: וְהוּא רַחוּם, יְכַפֵּר עָוֹן וְלֹא יַשְׁחִית, וְהִרְבָּה לְהָשִׁיב אַפּוֹ וְלֹא יָעִיר כָּל חֲמָתוֹ: כִּי אַתָּה אֲדֹנָי טוֹב וְסַלָּח, וְרַב חֶסֶד, לְכָל קוֹרְאֶיךָ: צִדְקָתְךָ צֶדֶק לְעוֹלָם, וְתוֹרָתְךָ אֱמֶת: תִּתֵּן אֱמֶת לְיַעֲקֹב, חֶסֶד לְאַבְרָהָם אֲשֶׁר נִשְׁבַּעְתָּ לַאֲבוֹתֵינוּ מִימֵי קֶדֶם: בָּרוּךְ אֲדֹנָי, יוֹם יוֹם יַעֲמָס לָנוּ, הָאֵל יְשׁוּעָתֵנוּ סֶלָה: יְיָ צְבָאוֹת עִמָּנוּ, מִשְׂגָּב לָנוּ, אֱלֹהֵי יַעֲקֹב סֶלָה: יְיָ צְבָאוֹת, אַשְׁרֵי אָדָם בֹּטֵחַ בָּךְ: יְיָ הוֹשִׁיעָה, הַמֶּלֶךְ יַעֲנֵנוּ בְיוֹם קָרְאֵנוּ: בָּרוּךְ הוּא אֱלֹהֵינוּ, שֶׁבְּרָאָנוּ לִכְבוֹדוֹ, וְהִבְדִּילָנוּ מִן הַתּוֹעִים, וְנָתַן לָנוּ תּוֹרַת אֱמֶת, וְחַיֵּי עוֹלָם נָטַע בְּתוֹכֵנוּ, הוּא יִפְתַּח לִבֵּנוּ בְּתוֹרָתוֹ וְיָשֵׂם בְּלִבֵּנוּ אַהֲבָתוֹ וְיִרְאָתוֹ, וְלַעֲשׂוֹת רְצוֹנוֹ וּלְעָבְדוֹ בְּלֵבָב שָׁלֵם, לְמַעַן לֹא נִיגַע לָרִיק, וְלֹא נֵלֵד לַבֶּהָלָה: יְהִי רָצוֹן מִלְּפָנֶיךָ, יְיָ אֱלֹהֵינוּ וֵאלֹהֵי אֲבוֹתֵינוּ, שֶׁנִּשְׁמֹר חֻקֶּיךָ בָּעוֹלָם הַזֶּה, וְנִזְכֶּה וְנִחְיֶה וְנִרְאֶה, וְנִירַשׁ טוֹבָה וּבְרָכָה, לִשְׁנֵי יְמוֹת הַמָּשִׁיחַ, וּלְחַיֵּי הָעוֹלָם הַבָּא: לְמַעַן יְזַמֶּרְךָ כָבוֹד וְלֹא יִדֹּם, יְיָ אֱלֹהַי לְעוֹלָם אוֹדֶךָ: בָּרוּךְ הַגֶּבֶר אֲשֶׁר יִבְטַח בַּיְיָ, וְהָיָה יְיָ מִבְטַחוֹ: בִּטְחוּ בַיְיָ עֲדֵי עַד, כִּי בְּיָהּ יְיָ צוּר עוֹלָמִים: וְיִבְטְחוּ בְךָ יוֹדְעֵי שְׁמֶךָ, כִּי לֹא עָזַבְתָּ דֹרְשֶׁיךָ יְיָ: יְיָ חָפֵץ לְמַעַן צִדְקוֹ, יַגְדִּיל תּוֹרָה וְיַאְדִּיר.

endures forever and to all eternity. O Lord, God of Abraham, of Isaac, and of Israel, our forefathers, keep this forever in the imagination of the thoughts of the heart of Your people, and direct their heart to You. And He, being merciful, forgives iniquity, and does not destroy. Many a time He turns His anger away, and does not stir up all His wrath. For You, O Lord, are good and forgiving, and abounding in loving kindness to all those who call on You. Your righteousness is an everlasting righteousness, and Your Torah is truth. You will show truth to Jacob and loving-kindness to Abraham, as You swore to our forefathers from the days of old. Blessed be the Lord for, day after day, He burdens us with His blessings; God is our salvation, Selah! The Lord of Hosts is with us; the God of Jacob is our stronghold, Selah! O Lord of Hosts, happy is the one who trusts in You. Save, Lord! May the King answer us on the day when we call. Blessed is our God, Who has created us for His glory, and has separated us from them who go astray, and has given us the Torah of truth and planted everlasting life in our midst. May He open our heart to His Torah, and place love and awe of Him within our hearts, that we may do His will and serve Him with a perfect heart, that we may not labor in vain, nor produce for confusion. May it be Your will, O Lord our God and God of our ancestors, that we may keep Your statutes in This World, and be worthy to live to witness and inherit happiness and blessing in the days of the Messiah and in the life of the World to Come. So that my soul may sing praise to You, and not be silent: O Lord my God, I will give thanks to You forever. Blessed is the man who trusts in the Lord; the Lord will be his security. Trust in the Lord forever; for God the Lord is an everlasting Rock. And those who know Your Name will put their trust in You; for You, Lord, have not forsaken those who seek You. It pleased the Lord, for the sake of Israel's righteousness, to make the Torah great and glorious.

קדיש

ש״ץ: יִתְגַּדַּל וְיִתְקַדַּשׁ שְׁמֵהּ רַבָּא. בְּעָלְמָא דִּי בְרָא כִרְעוּתֵהּ, וְיַמְלִיךְ מַלְכוּתֵהּ בְּחַיֵּיכוֹן וּבְיוֹמֵיכוֹן וּבְחַיֵּי דְכָל בֵּית יִשְׂרָאֵל. בַּעֲגָלָא וּבִזְמַן קָרִיב וְאִמְרוּ אָמֵן:

קהל וש״ץ: יְהֵא שְׁמֵהּ רַבָּא מְבָרַךְ לְעָלַם וּלְעָלְמֵי עָלְמַיָּא:

ש״ץ: יִתְבָּרַךְ וְיִשְׁתַּבַּח, וְיִתְפָּאַר וְיִתְרוֹמַם וְיִתְנַשֵּׂא וְיִתְהַדָּר וְיִתְעַלֶּה וְיִתְהַלָּל שְׁמֵהּ דְּקֻדְשָׁא בְּרִיךְ הוּא. לְעֵלָּא מִן כָּל בִּרְכָתָא וְשִׁירָתָא, תֻּשְׁבְּחָתָא וְנֶחֱמָתָא, דַּאֲמִירָן בְּעָלְמָא, וְאִמְרוּ אָמֵן:

יְהֵא שְׁלָמָא רַבָּא מִן שְׁמַיָּא וְחַיִּים עָלֵינוּ וְעַל כָּל יִשְׂרָאֵל, וְאִמְרוּ אָמֵן: עֹשֶׂה שָׁלוֹם בִּמְרוֹמָיו הוּא יַעֲשֶׂה שָׁלוֹם עָלֵינוּ וְעַל כָּל יִשְׂרָאֵל, וְאִמְרוּ אָמֵן:

בְּעָלְמָא דִּי בְרָא כִרְעוּתֵהּ *in the world which He has created according to His will.* We seek the sanctification of God's Name not only in another world, in another arena, but here and now, *be-alma divera khirutei,* in this world whose existence You willed. Give us, here in this world, a society and a community which will actualize ever-more the visions of peace and justice. Restore it to full human harmony, so that "Nation shall not lift up sword against nation, and they will learn war no more" (Isaiah 2:4). Give us a society and a community in which children will not perish from hunger by the thousands while their elders debate the politics of civil war; a world in which young university students and women and children in supermarkets will not be subject to the terrorist's bomb; a civilization in which the best of our youth will not be shipped off to distant lands to fight wars for purposes of which they are ignorant.

KADDISH

Leader: Magnified and sanctified may His great Name be, in the world which He has created according to His will. May He establish His kingdom during your life and during your days, and during the life of all the house of Israel, even speedily and at a near time, and say, Amen.

Cong. and Leader: May His great Name be blessed forever and to all eternity.

Leader: Blessed, praised, glorified, exalted, extolled, honored, magnified, and lauded be the Name of the Holy One, Blessed be He, beyond all the blessings and hymns, praises and consolations, which are uttered in the world; and say, Amen.

May there be abundant peace from Heaven, and life for us and for all Israel; and say, Amen.

He Who makes peace in His high places, may He make peace for us and for all Israel; and say, Amen.

וְיַמְלִיךְ מַלְכוּתֵהּ *May He establish His kingdom.* May the reign of disharmony and hatred come to an end, and the Kingdom of God come to the world, the kingdom of justice and of peace and of truth. *Yehei shemei rabba mevarakh.* May God's Name be great and sanctified and complete forever and ever. But we are only human; we cannot wait until that "forever and ever and ever." We ask of God to begin now, right now: *be-hayekhon u-ve'yimekhon*, in Your lifetime and in Your days — right now. O God, whose Name we care for more than all else: Protect Your Great Name, cease to cause your children to suffer the presence of premature death, to tolerate evil, to countenance hunger and misery and loneliness and unrequited love. For Your own Name, do not permit evil to dominate. For God's sake, do something, O God!

─── ◆ ───

למוצאי שבת:

וְיִתֶּן לְךָ הָאֱלֹהִים מִטַּל הַשָּׁמַיִם וּמִשְׁמַנֵּי הָאָרֶץ, וְרֹב דָּגָן וְתִירֹשׁ: יַעַבְדוּךָ עַמִּים וְיִשְׁתַּחֲווּ לְךָ לְאֻמִּים, הֱוֵה גְבִיר לְאַחֶיךָ וְיִשְׁתַּחֲווּ לְךָ בְּנֵי אִמֶּךָ, אֹרְרֶיךָ אָרוּר, וּמְבָרֲכֶיךָ בָּרוּךְ: וְאֵל שַׁדַּי יְבָרֵךְ אֹתְךָ וְיַפְרְךָ וְיַרְבֶּךָ, וְהָיִיתָ לִקְהַל עַמִּים: וְיִתֶּן לְךָ אֶת בִּרְכַּת אַבְרָהָם לְךָ וּלְזַרְעֲךָ אִתָּךְ, לְרִשְׁתְּךָ אֶת אֶרֶץ מְגֻרֶיךָ אֲשֶׁר נָתַן אֱלֹהִים לְאַבְרָהָם: מֵאֵל אָבִיךָ וְיַעְזְרֶךָּ וְאֵת שַׁדַּי וִיבָרֲכֶךָּ, בִּרְכֹת שָׁמַיִם מֵעָל, בִּרְכֹת תְּהוֹם רֹבֶצֶת תָּחַת בִּרְכֹת שָׁדַיִם וָרָחַם: בִּרְכֹת אָבִיךָ גָּבְרוּ עַל בִּרְכֹת הוֹרַי, עַד תַּאֲוַת גִּבְעֹת עוֹלָם, תִּהְיֶיןָ לְרֹאשׁ יוֹסֵף וּלְקָדְקֹד נְזִיר אֶחָיו: וַאֲהֵבְךָ וּבֵרַכְךָ וְהִרְבֶּךָ, וּבֵרַךְ פְּרִי בִטְנְךָ וּפְרִי אַדְמָתֶךָ דְּגָנְךָ וְתִירֹשְׁךָ וְיִצְהָרֶךָ, שְׁגַר אֲלָפֶיךָ וְעַשְׁתְּרֹת צֹאנֶךָ, עַל הָאֲדָמָה, אֲשֶׁר נִשְׁבַּע לַאֲבֹתֶיךָ לָתֶת לָךְ: בָּרוּךְ תִּהְיֶה מִכָּל הָעַמִּים, לֹא יִהְיֶה בְךָ עָקָר וַעֲקָרָה וּבִבְהֶמְתֶּךָ: וְהֵסִיר יְיָ מִמְּךָ כָּל חֹלִי, וְכָל מַדְוֵי מִצְרַיִם הָרָעִים אֲשֶׁר יָדַעְתָּ, לֹא יְשִׂימָם בָּךְ, וּנְתָנָם בְּכָל שֹׂנְאֶיךָ:

הַמַּלְאָךְ הַגֹּאֵל אֹתִי מִכָּל רָע, יְבָרֵךְ אֶת הַנְּעָרִים, וְיִקָּרֵא בָהֶם שְׁמִי, וְשֵׁם אֲבֹתַי אַבְרָהָם וְיִצְחָק, וְיִדְגּוּ לָרֹב בְּקֶרֶב הָאָרֶץ: יְיָ אֱלֹהֵיכֶם הִרְבָּה אֶתְכֶם, וְהִנְּכֶם הַיּוֹם כְּכוֹכְבֵי הַשָּׁמַיִם לָרֹב: יְיָ אֱלֹהֵי אֲבוֹתֵיכֶם, יֹסֵף עֲלֵיכֶם כָּכֶם, אֶלֶף פְּעָמִים, וִיבָרֵךְ אֶתְכֶם, כַּאֲשֶׁר דִּבֶּר לָכֶם:

—◦•◦—

At the conclusion of the Sabbath, add:

And may God give you of the dew of heaven, and of the fatness of the earth, and plenty of corn and wine: may peoples serve you, and nations bow down to you: be lord over your brothers, and may your mother's sons bow down to you: cursed be everyone who curses you, and blessed be everyone who blesses you. And may God Almighty bless you, and make you fruitful, and multiply you, that you may be a congregation of peoples; and may He give you the blessing of Abraham, to you and to your descendants with you; that you may inherit the land of your sojournings, which God gave to Abraham. From the God of your father — may He help you — and from the Almighty — may He bless you with blessings of the heaven above, blessings of the deep that crouches below, blessings of the bosom and the womb. The blessings of your father have surpassed the blessings of my fathers to the utmost bound of the everlasting hills: may they be on the head of Joseph, and on the brow of the head of him who is prince among his brothers. And He will love you, and bless you, and multiply you: He will bless the fruit of your womb and the fruit of your land, your corn, your wine, and your oil, the offspring of your cattle and the young of your flocks, in the land which He swore to your fathers to give you. You shall be blessed above all peoples: there shall not be among you a barren man or woman, nor among your cattle. And the Lord will take away from you all sickness; and He will put none of the evil diseases of Egypt, which you knew, upon you, but will inflict them upon all those who hate you.

May the angel who redeems me from all evil bless the lads; and may my name be pronounced on them, and the names of my forefathers Abraham and Isaac; and may they grow into a multitude within the land. The Lord your God has multiplied you, and behold, you are this day as the stars of heaven in abundance. May the Lord, the God of your forefathers, increase you a thousand-fold, and bless you, as He promised you.

בָּרוּךְ אַתָּה בָּעִיר, וּבָרוּךְ אַתָּה בַּשָּׂדֶה: בָּרוּךְ טַנְאֲךָ וּמִשְׁאַרְתֶּךָ: בָּרוּךְ פְּרִי
בִטְנְךָ וּפְרִי אַדְמָתְךָ וּפְרִי בְהֶמְתֶּךָ, שְׁגַר אֲלָפֶיךָ וְעַשְׁתְּרוֹת צֹאנֶךָ: בָּרוּךְ
אַתָּה בְּבֹאֶךָ, וּבָרוּךְ אַתָּה בְּצֵאתֶךָ: יְצַו יְיָ אִתְּךָ אֶת הַבְּרָכָה בַּאֲסָמֶיךָ וּבְכֹל
מִשְׁלַח יָדֶךָ, וּבֵרַכְךָ בָּאָרֶץ, אֲשֶׁר יְיָ אֱלֹהֶיךָ נֹתֵן לָךְ: יִפְתַּח יְיָ לְךָ אֶת אוֹצָרוֹ
הַטּוֹב אֶת הַשָּׁמַיִם לָתֵת מְטַר אַרְצְךָ בְּעִתּוֹ, וּלְבָרֵךְ אֵת כָּל מַעֲשֵׂה יָדֶךָ,
וְהִלְוִיתָ גּוֹיִם רַבִּים, וְאַתָּה לֹא תִלְוֶה: כִּי יְיָ אֱלֹהֶיךָ בֵּרַכְךָ, כַּאֲשֶׁר דִּבֶּר לָךְ,
וְהַעֲבַטְתָּ גּוֹיִם רַבִּים, וְאַתָּה לֹא תַעֲבֹט, וּמָשַׁלְתָּ בְּגוֹיִם רַבִּים, וּבְךָ לֹא
יִמְשֹׁלוּ: אַשְׁרֶיךָ יִשְׂרָאֵל מִי כָמוֹךָ, עַם, נוֹשַׁע בַּיְיָ, מָגֵן עֶזְרֶךָ, וַאֲשֶׁר חֶרֶב
גַּאֲוָתֶךָ, וְיִכָּחֲשׁוּ אֹיְבֶיךָ לָךְ, וְאַתָּה עַל בָּמוֹתֵימוֹ תִדְרֹךְ:

מָחִיתִי כָעָב פְּשָׁעֶיךָ וְכֶעָנָן חַטֹּאתֶיךָ, שׁוּבָה אֵלַי כִּי גְאַלְתִּיךָ: רָנּוּ שָׁמַיִם כִּי
עָשָׂה יְיָ, הָרִיעוּ תַּחְתִּיּוֹת אָרֶץ, פִּצְחוּ הָרִים רִנָּה, יַעַר וְכָל עֵץ בּוֹ, כִּי גָאַל יְיָ
יַעֲקֹב וּבְיִשְׂרָאֵל יִתְפָּאָר: גְּאָלֵנוּ יְיָ צְבָאוֹת שְׁמוֹ, קְדוֹשׁ יִשְׂרָאֵל:

יִשְׂרָאֵל נוֹשַׁע בַּיְיָ תְּשׁוּעַת עוֹלָמִים, לֹא תֵבֹשׁוּ וְלֹא תִכָּלְמוּ עַד עוֹלְמֵי עַד:
וַאֲכַלְתֶּם אָכוֹל וְשָׂבוֹעַ, וְהִלַּלְתֶּם אֶת שֵׁם יְיָ אֱלֹהֵיכֶם אֲשֶׁר עָשָׂה עִמָּכֶם
לְהַפְלִיא, וְלֹא יֵבֹשׁוּ עַמִּי לְעוֹלָם: וִידַעְתֶּם כִּי בְקֶרֶב יִשְׂרָאֵל אָנִי, וַאֲנִי יְיָ
אֱלֹהֵיכֶם וְאֵין עוֹד, וְלֹא יֵבֹשׁוּ עַמִּי לְעוֹלָם: כִּי בְשִׂמְחָה תֵצֵאוּ וּבְשָׁלוֹם
תּוּבָלוּן, הֶהָרִים וְהַגְּבָעוֹת יִפְצְחוּ לִפְנֵיכֶם רִנָּה וְכָל עֲצֵי הַשָּׂדֶה יִמְחֲאוּ כָף:

You will be blessed in the city, and you will be blessed in the field. You will be blessed when you come in, and you will be blessed when you go out. Your basket and your kneading-trough will be blessed. The fruit of your womb will be blessed, and the fruit of your land, and the fruit of your cattle, the offspring of your cattle, and the young of your flocks. The Lord will command the blessing upon you in your barns, and wherever you put your hand; and He will bless you in the land which the Lord your God gives you. The Lord will open for you His good treasury, the heaven, to give rain on your land in its season, and to bless all the work of your hands: and you will lend to many nations, but you will not borrow. For the Lord your God will bless you, as He promised you: and you will lend to many nations, but you will not borrow; and you will rule over many nations, but they will not rule over you. Happy are you, O Israel: who is like you, a people saved by the Lord, Who is the Shield of your help, and Who is the Sword of your majesty! And your enemies shall be false with you; and you will tread upon their high places.

I have blotted out, as a cloud, your transgressions, and, as a mist, your sins; return to Me, for I have redeemed you. Sing joyfully, O heavens, for the Lord has done so; shout, O nethermost depths of the earth; break out into singing, O mountains, and forests and every tree within it; for the Lord has redeemed Jacob, and will glorify Himself in Israel. Our Redeemer, the Lord of Hosts is His Name, the Holy One of Israel.

Israel is saved by the Lord with an everlasting salvation: you will not be ashamed nor confounded forever and ever. And you will eat and be satisfied, and will praise the Name of the Lord your God, Who has dealt wondrously with you: and My people will never be ashamed. And you will know that I am in the midst of Israel, and that I am the Lord your God, and there is none else: and My people will never be ashamed. For you will go out with joy, and be led out with peace: the mountains and the hills will break out before you into singing, and all the trees of the field will

הִנֵּה אֵל יְשׁוּעָתִי, אֶבְטַח וְלֹא אֶפְחָד, כִּי עָזִּי וְזִמְרָת יָהּ יְיָ, וַיְהִי לִי לִישׁוּעָה: וּשְׁאַבְתֶּם מַיִם בְּשָׂשׂוֹן, מִמַּעַיְנֵי הַיְשׁוּעָה: וַאֲמַרְתֶּם בַּיּוֹם הַהוּא, הוֹדוּ לַיְיָ קִרְאוּ בִשְׁמוֹ הוֹדִיעוּ בָעַמִּים עֲלִילֹתָיו, הַזְכִּירוּ כִּי נִשְׂגָּב שְׁמוֹ: זַמְּרוּ יְיָ כִּי גֵאוּת עָשָׂה, מוּדַעַת זֹאת בְּכָל הָאָרֶץ: צַהֲלִי וָרֹנִּי יוֹשֶׁבֶת צִיּוֹן, כִּי גָדוֹל בְּקִרְבֵּךְ קְדוֹשׁ יִשְׂרָאֵל: וְאָמַר בַּיּוֹם הַהוּא, הִנֵּה אֱלֹהֵינוּ זֶה קִוִּינוּ לוֹ וְיוֹשִׁיעֵנוּ, זֶה יְיָ קִוִּינוּ לוֹ, נָגִילָה וְנִשְׂמְחָה בִּישׁוּעָתוֹ:

בֵּית יַעֲקֹב, לְכוּ וְנֵלְכָה בְּאוֹר יְיָ: וְהָיָה אֱמוּנַת עִתֶּיךָ חֹסֶן יְשׁוּעֹת חָכְמַת וָדָעַת, יִרְאַת יְיָ הִיא אוֹצָרוֹ: וַיְהִי דָוִד לְכָל דְּרָכָיו מַשְׂכִּיל וַיְיָ עִמּוֹ: פָּדָה בְשָׁלוֹם נַפְשִׁי מִקְּרָב לִי כִּי בְרַבִּים הָיוּ עִמָּדִי: וַיֹּאמֶר הָעָם אֶל שָׁאוּל, הֲיוֹנָתָן יָמוּת אֲשֶׁר עָשָׂה הַיְשׁוּעָה הַגְּדוֹלָה הַזֹּאת בְּיִשְׂרָאֵל, חָלִילָה, חַי יְיָ אִם יִפֹּל מִשַּׂעֲרַת רֹאשׁוֹ אַרְצָה, כִּי עִם אֱלֹהִים עָשָׂה הַיּוֹם הַזֶּה, וַיִּפְדּוּ הָעָם אֶת יוֹנָתָן וְלֹא מֵת: וּפְדוּיֵי יְיָ יְשֻׁבוּן וּבָאוּ צִיּוֹן בְּרִנָּה, וְשִׂמְחַת עוֹלָם עַל רֹאשָׁם, שָׂשׂוֹן וְשִׂמְחָה יַשִּׂיגוּ, נָסוּ יָגוֹן וַאֲנָחָה: הָפַכְתָּ מִסְפְּדִי לְמָחוֹל לִי, פִּתַּחְתָּ שַׂקִּי וַתְּאַזְּרֵנִי שִׂמְחָה: וְלֹא אָבָה יְיָ אֱלֹהֶיךָ לִשְׁמֹעַ אֶל בִּלְעָם, וַיַּהֲפֹךְ יְיָ אֱלֹהֶיךָ לְּךָ אֶת הַקְּלָלָה לִבְרָכָה, כִּי אֲהֵבְךָ יְיָ אֱלֹהֶיךָ: אָז תִּשְׂמַח בְּתוּלָה בְּמָחוֹל וּבַחוּרִים וּזְקֵנִים יַחְדָּו, וְהָפַכְתִּי אֶבְלָם לְשָׂשׂוֹן, וְנִחַמְתִּים, וְשִׂמַּחְתִּים מִיגוֹנָם:

clap their hands. Behold, God is my salvation; I will trust, and will not be afraid: for God the Lord is my strength and song; and He has become my salvation. Therefore, with joy you will draw water out of the springs of salvation. And on that day you will say, "Give thanks to the Lord, proclaim His Name, declare His deeds among the peoples"; remind that His Name is exalted. Sing to the Lord; for He has done glorious things: this is known throughout the earth. Shout aloud and sing joyfully, you inhabitant of Zion: for great is the Holy One of Israel in your midst. And one shall say on that day, "Behold! This is our God; we have hoped for Him that He should save us: this is the Lord; we have hoped for Him, let us be glad and rejoice in His salvation."

O house of Jacob, come, and let us walk in the light of the Lord. He will be the steadfastness of your times, a rich store of salvation, wisdom, and knowledge: the fear of the Lord is a person's treasure. And David prospered in all his ways; and the Lord was with him. He redeemed my soul in peace from the battle waged against me, for the sake of the many who were with me. And the people said to Saul, "Shall Jonathan die, who has performed this great salvation for Israel? Heaven forbid! As surely as the Lord lives, not one hair of his head shall fall to the ground; for he did this with God's help this day." So the people rescued Jonathan and he did not die. And those redeemed by the Lord will return; they will come to Zion with song; and everlasting joy will crown their heads: they will attain gladness and joy, and sorrow and sighing will flee away. You have turned for me my sorrow into dancing; You removed my sackcloth and clothed me with gladness. And the Lord your God did not want to listen to Balaam; and the Lord your God turned the curse into a blessing, because the Lord your God loves you. Then the maiden will rejoice in a dance, and the young men and the old together; for I will turn their mourning into joy, and will comfort them, and make them rejoice from their sorrow.

בּוֹרֵא נִיב שְׂפָתָיִם, שָׁלוֹם שָׁלוֹם לָרָחוֹק וְלַקָּרוֹב אָמַר יְיָ וּרְפָאתִיו: וְרוּחַ
לָבְשָׁה אֶת עֲמָשַׂי רֹאשׁ הַשָּׁלִישִׁים, לְךָ דָוִיד וְעִמְּךָ בֶן יִשַׁי, שָׁלוֹם שָׁלוֹם
לְךָ וְשָׁלוֹם לְעֹזְרֶךָ, כִּי עֲזָרְךָ אֱלֹהֶיךָ, וַיְקַבְּלֵם דָּוִיד וַיִּתְּנֵם בְּרָאשֵׁי הַגְּדוּד:
וַאֲמַרְתֶּם כֹּה לֶחָי, וְאַתָּה שָׁלוֹם וּבֵיתְךָ שָׁלוֹם וְכֹל אֲשֶׁר לְךָ שָׁלוֹם: יְיָ עֹז
לְעַמּוֹ יִתֵּן, יְיָ יְבָרֵךְ אֶת עַמּוֹ בַשָּׁלוֹם:

אָמַר רַבִּי יוֹחָנָן, בְּכָל מָקוֹם שֶׁאַתָּה מוֹצֵא גְּדֻלָּתוֹ שֶׁל הַקָּדוֹשׁ בָּרוּךְ
הוּא, שָׁם אַתָּה מוֹצֵא עַנְוְתָנוּתוֹ. דָּבָר זֶה כָּתוּב בַּתּוֹרָה, וְשָׁנוּי בַּנְּבִיאִים,
וּמְשֻׁלָּשׁ בַּכְּתוּבִים: כָּתוּב בַּתּוֹרָה, כִּי יְיָ אֱלֹהֵיכֶם הוּא אֱלֹהֵי הָאֱלֹהִים
וַאֲדֹנֵי הָאֲדֹנִים, הָאֵל הַגָּדוֹל הַגִּבּוֹר וְהַנּוֹרָא, אֲשֶׁר לֹא יִשָּׂא פָנִים וְלֹא יִקַּח
שֹׁחַד: וּכְתִיב בַּתְרֵהּ, עֹשֶׂה מִשְׁפַּט יָתוֹם וְאַלְמָנָה, וְאֹהֵב גֵּר לָתֶת לוֹ
לֶחֶם וְשִׂמְלָה: שָׁנוּי בַּנְּבִיאִים, דִּכְתִיב, כִּי כֹה אָמַר רָם וְנִשָּׂא שֹׁכֵן עַד
וְקָדוֹשׁ שְׁמוֹ, מָרוֹם וְקָדוֹשׁ אֶשְׁכּוֹן, וְאֶת דַּכָּא וּשְׁפַל רוּחַ, לְהַחֲיוֹת רוּחַ
שְׁפָלִים וּלְהַחֲיוֹת לֵב נִדְכָּאִים: מְשֻׁלָּשׁ בַּכְּתוּבִים, דִּכְתִיב, שִׁירוּ לֵאלֹהִים,
זַמְּרוּ שְׁמוֹ, סֹלּוּ לָרֹכֵב בָּעֲרָבוֹת בְּיָהּ שְׁמוֹ וְעִלְזוּ לְפָנָיו: וּכְתִיב בַּתְרֵהּ, אֲבִי
יְתוֹמִים וְדַיַּן אַלְמָנוֹת, אֱלֹהִים בִּמְעוֹן קָדְשׁוֹ: יְהִי יְיָ אֱלֹהֵינוּ עִמָּנוּ כַּאֲשֶׁר
הָיָה עִם אֲבֹתֵינוּ אַל יַעַזְבֵנוּ וְאַל יִטְּשֵׁנוּ: וְאַתֶּם הַדְּבֵקִים בַּיְיָ אֱלֹהֵיכֶם,
חַיִּים כֻּלְּכֶם הַיּוֹם: כִּי נִחַם יְיָ צִיּוֹן נִחַם כָּל חָרְבֹתֶיהָ, וַיָּשֶׂם מִדְבָּרָהּ כְּעֵדֶן
וְעַרְבָתָהּ כְּגַן יְיָ, שָׂשׂוֹן וְשִׂמְחָה יִמָּצֵא בָהּ, תּוֹדָה וְקוֹל זִמְרָה: יְיָ חָפֵץ לְמַעַן
צִדְקוֹ, יַגְדִּיל תּוֹרָה וְיַאְדִּיר:

I create the fruit of the lips: "Peace, peace to him who is far off and to him who is near," says the Lord, "and I will heal him." Then the spirit came upon Amasai, who was chief of the captains, [and he said], "For your sake, David, and on your side, O son of Jesse; peace, peace to you, and peace to him who helps you; for your God has helped you." Then David received them, and made them leaders of his troop. And you will say, "To life! Peace be to you, and peace be to your household, and peace be to all that you have." The Lord will give strength to His people; the Lord will bless His people with peace.

Rabbi Yochanan said, In every passage where you find the greatness of God mentioned, there you also find His humility. This is written in the Torah, repeated in the Prophets, and stated a third time in the Writings. It is written in the Torah: "For the Lord your God, He is God of gods, and Lord of lords, the great, mighty, and revered God, Who shows no favoritism and accepts no bribe." And afterwards it is written, "He performs justice for the orphan and widow, and loves the stranger, giving him food and clothing." It is repeated in the Prophets, as it is written, "For thus says the High and Exalted One, Who lives forever, and Whose Name is holy, 'I dwell in the high and holy place, but also with the contrite and humble in spirit, to revive the spirit of the humble, and to revive the heart of the contrite ones.'" It is a third time stated in the Writings, "Sing to God, sing praises to His Name: extol Him Who rides upon the heavens, with His Name — God — and rejoice before Him." And it is written afterwards, "Father of the orphans, and Judge of the widows, is God in His holy habitation." May the Lord our God be with us, as He was with our ancestors: may He never leave us, nor forsake us. And you who cleave to the Lord your God are alive, every one of you, this day. For the Lord comforts Zion: He comforts all her ruins, and will make her wilderness like Eden, and her desert like the garden of the Lord; joy and gladness will be found there, thanksgiving and the sound of music. It pleased the Lord, for the sake of Israel's righteousness, to make the Torah great and glorious.

שִׁיר הַמַּעֲלוֹת, אַשְׁרֵי כָּל יְרֵא יְיָ, הַהֹלֵךְ בִּדְרָכָיו: יְגִיעַ כַּפֶּיךָ כִּי תֹאכֵל,
אַשְׁרֶיךָ וְטוֹב לָךְ: אֶשְׁתְּךָ כְּגֶפֶן פֹּרִיָּה בְּיַרְכְּתֵי בֵיתֶךָ, בָּנֶיךָ כִּשְׁתִלֵי זֵיתִים
סָבִיב לְשֻׁלְחָנֶךָ: הִנֵּה כִי כֵן יְבֹרַךְ גָּבֶר יְרֵא יְיָ: יְבָרֶכְךָ יְיָ מִצִּיּוֹן, וּרְאֵה בְּטוּב
יְרוּשָׁלָיִם כֹּל יְמֵי חַיֶּיךָ: וּרְאֵה בָנִים לְבָנֶיךָ, שָׁלוֹם עַל יִשְׂרָאֵל:

נוטל כוס יין בימינו ואומר:

סַבְרִי מָרָנָן וְרַבָּנָן וְרַבּוֹתַי:

בָּרוּךְ אַתָּה יְיָ, אֱלֹהֵינוּ מֶלֶךְ הָעוֹלָם, בּוֹרֵא פְּרִי הַגָּפֶן:

על הבשמים:

בָּרוּךְ אַתָּה יְיָ, אֱלֹהֵינוּ מֶלֶךְ הָעוֹלָם, בּוֹרֵא מִינֵי בְשָׂמִים:

על הנר:

בָּרוּךְ אַתָּה יְיָ, אֱלֹהֵינוּ מֶלֶךְ הָעוֹלָם, בּוֹרֵא מְאוֹרֵי הָאֵשׁ:

בָּרוּךְ אַתָּה יְיָ, אֱלֹהֵינוּ מֶלֶךְ הָעוֹלָם, הַמַּבְדִּיל בֵּין קֹדֶשׁ לְחוֹל, בֵּין אוֹר
לְחשֶׁךְ, בֵּין יִשְׂרָאֵל לָעַמִּים, בֵּין יוֹם הַשְּׁבִיעִי לְשֵׁשֶׁת יְמֵי הַמַּעֲשֶׂה. בָּרוּךְ
אַתָּה יְיָ, הַמַּבְדִּיל בֵּין קֹדֶשׁ לְחוֹל:

———◆———

עָלֵינוּ לְשַׁבֵּחַ לַאֲדוֹן הַכֹּל, לָתֵת גְּדֻלָּה לְיוֹצֵר בְּרֵאשִׁית, שֶׁלֹּא עָשָׂנוּ
כְּגוֹיֵי הָאֲרָצוֹת, וְלֹא שָׂמָנוּ כְּמִשְׁפְּחוֹת הָאֲדָמָה, שֶׁלֹּא שָׂם חֶלְקֵנוּ כָּהֶם,
וְגֹרָלֵנוּ כְּכָל הֲמוֹנָם (שֶׁהֵם מִשְׁתַּחֲוִים לְהֶבֶל וָרִיק וּמִתְפַּלְלִים אֶל אֵל לֹא

A Song of Ascents. Happy is every person who fears the Lord, who walks in His ways. When you eat the fruit of your labor, you will be happy, and it will be well with you. Your wife will be like a fruitful vine, in the inner chambers of your house: your children like olive plants, round about your table. Behold, so shall the man who fears the Lord be blessed. May the Lord bless you from Zion: may you see the good of Jerusalem all the days of your life, and may you see your children's children. Peace be upon Israel!

A cup of wine is taken in the right hand, and the following is said:

With your permission, my masters and teachers:

Blessed are You, O Lord our God, King of the Universe Who creates the fruit of the vine.

Blessing on spices:

Blessed are You, O Lord our God, King of the Universe Who creates diverse kinds of spices.

Blessing on fire:

Blessed are You, O Lord our God, King of the Universe, Who creates the lights of the fire.

Blessed are You, O Lord our God, King of the Universe, Who makes a distinction between holy and secular, between light and darkness, between Israel and other nations, between the seventh day and the six working days. Blessed are You, O Lord, Who makes a distinction between holy and secular.

It is our duty to praise the Lord of all things, to ascribe greatness to Him Who formed the world in the beginning, since He has not made us like the nations of other lands, and has not placed us like other families of the earth, since He has not assigned to us a portion as to them, nor a lot as to all their multitudes. (For they bow to vanity and emptiness, and pray to a god which does

יוֹשִׁיעַ) וַאֲנַחְנוּ כּוֹרְעִים וּמִשְׁתַּחֲוִים וּמוֹדִים, לִפְנֵי מֶלֶךְ, מַלְכֵי הַמְּלָכִים, הַקָּדוֹשׁ בָּרוּךְ הוּא. שֶׁהוּא נוֹטֶה שָׁמַיִם וְיֹסֵד אָרֶץ, וּמוֹשַׁב יְקָרוֹ בַּשָּׁמַיִם מִמַּעַל, וּשְׁכִינַת עֻזּוֹ בְּגָבְהֵי מְרוֹמִים, הוּא אֱלֹהֵינוּ אֵין עוֹד. אֱמֶת מַלְכֵּנוּ אֶפֶס זוּלָתוֹ, כַּכָּתוּב בְּתוֹרָתוֹ: וְיָדַעְתָּ הַיּוֹם וַהֲשֵׁבֹתָ אֶל לְבָבֶךָ, כִּי יְיָ הוּא הָאֱלֹהִים בַּשָּׁמַיִם מִמַּעַל, וְעַל הָאָרֶץ מִתָּחַת, אֵין עוֹד:

עַל כֵּן נְקַוֶּה לְךָ יְיָ אֱלֹהֵינוּ, לִרְאוֹת מְהֵרָה בְּתִפְאֶרֶת עֻזֶּךָ, לְהַעֲבִיר גִּלּוּלִים מִן הָאָרֶץ וְהָאֱלִילִים כָּרוֹת יִכָּרֵתוּן לְתַקֵּן עוֹלָם בְּמַלְכוּת שַׁדַּי, וְכָל בְּנֵי בָשָׂר יִקְרְאוּ בִשְׁמֶךָ. לְהַפְנוֹת אֵלֶיךָ כָּל רִשְׁעֵי אָרֶץ. יַכִּירוּ וְיֵדְעוּ כָּל יוֹשְׁבֵי תֵבֵל, כִּי לְךָ תִּכְרַע כָּל בֶּרֶךְ, תִּשָּׁבַע כָּל לָשׁוֹן: לְפָנֶיךָ יְיָ אֱלֹהֵינוּ יִכְרְעוּ וְיִפֹּלוּ. וְלִכְבוֹד שִׁמְךָ יְקָר יִתֵּנוּ. וִיקַבְּלוּ כֻלָּם אֶת עוֹל מַלְכוּתֶךָ. וְתִמְלֹךְ עֲלֵיהֶם מְהֵרָה לְעוֹלָם וָעֶד. כִּי הַמַּלְכוּת שֶׁלְּךָ הִיא, וּלְעוֹלְמֵי עַד תִּמְלוֹךְ בְּכָבוֹד: כַּכָּתוּב בְּתוֹרָתֶךָ, יְיָ יִמְלֹךְ לְעוֹלָם וָעֶד: וְנֶאֱמַר, וְהָיָה יְיָ לְמֶלֶךְ עַל כָּל הָאָרֶץ, בַּיּוֹם הַהוּא יִהְיֶה יְיָ אֶחָד, וּשְׁמוֹ אֶחָד:

בַּיּוֹם הַהוּא יִהְיֶה ה' אֶחָד וּשְׁמוֹ אֶחָד *in that day shall the Lord be One, and His Name One.* A famous story is related in the Talmud (*Sanhedrin* 39b): At the time the Egyptians were drowned in the Red Sea, the angels sought to sing praises to God, but the Almighty stopped them, saying, "How can you think of song when the work of My hands is drowning in the sea?" This is a beautiful aggadah. But should it not occur to us to ask why, if this is wrong, did not God stop the Israelites from singing *their* song of praise, the *Az yashir.* Should not the same principle apply? The answer is simple. The angels had no right to sing. *They* were not in exile. *They* did not suffer. *Their* children were not thrown into the mortar and cemented into the pyramids. *They* did not waste away in the labor camps, torn away from their wives and families. They, therefore, must contain themselves. They needed no release, no safety valve. Angels should not sing when humans are dying.

The Jews were different. It was they who had experienced the anguish and the pain. It was they who had tasted the *maror,* the bitterness. It was their backs that were lashed by the whip of the cruel taskmaster, and their hearts that were pierced by the cries of their suffering

not save,) But we bend the knee and offer worship and thanks before the supreme King of kings, the Holy One, blessed be He, Who stretches forth the heavens and establishes the foundations of the earth, the seat of Whose glory is in the heavens above, and the abode of Whose might is in the loftiest heights. He is our God; there is none else: in truth He is our King; there is none besides Him; as it is written in His Torah, "And You shall know this day, and lay it to your heart, that the Lord He is God in heaven above and upon the earth beneath: there is none else."

We therefore hope in You, O Lord our God, that we may speedily behold the glory of Your might, when You will remove the abominations from the earth and the idols will be utterly cut off, when the world will be perfected under the kingdom of the Almighty and all humanity will call upon Your Name, to turn all the wicked of the earth to You. All the inhabitants of the world will perceive and know that to You every knee must bow, every tongue must swear loyalty. Before You, O Lord our God, they will bow and fall; and to Your glorious Name they will give honor; they will all accept the yoke of Your kingdom, and You will reign over them speedily, and forever and ever. For the kingdom is Yours, and to all eternity You will reign in glory; as it is written in Your Torah, "The Lord shall reign forever and ever." And it is said, "The Lord shall be King over all the earth: on that day shall the Lord be One, and His Name One."

---

children. They, therefore, *must* sing out a victory in full voice; not that this was their right, but that only thus could they rid themselves of their resentment, so that years later they could react benignly when God proclaimed to them, through His prophet, that even the Egyptians were their brothers.

We who are distant in time from the Egyptian bondage skip part of the *Hallel* on the last six days of Passover, out of sympathy with our defeated enemies. But we nevertheless recite the major part of *Hallel*, for we still suffer much from the spiritual heirs of Pharaoh. We must

קדיש יתום

ש״ץ: יִתְגַּדַּל וְיִתְקַדַּשׁ שְׁמֵהּ רַבָּא. בְּעָלְמָא דִּי בְרָא כִרְעוּתֵהּ, וְיַמְלִיךְ
מַלְכוּתֵהּ בְּחַיֵּיכוֹן וּבְיוֹמֵיכוֹן וּבְחַיֵּי דְכָל בֵּית יִשְׂרָאֵל. בַּעֲגָלָא וּבִזְמַן
קָרִיב וְאִמְרוּ אָמֵן:

קהל וש״ץ: יְהֵא שְׁמֵהּ רַבָּא מְבָרַךְ לְעָלַם וּלְעָלְמֵי עָלְמַיָּא:

ש״ץ: יִתְבָּרַךְ וְיִשְׁתַּבַּח, וְיִתְפָּאַר וְיִתְרוֹמַם וְיִתְנַשֵּׂא וְיִתְהַדָּר וְיִתְעַלֶּה
וְיִתְהַלָּל שְׁמֵהּ דְּקֻדְשָׁא בְּרִיךְ הוּא. לְעֵלָּא מִן כָּל בִּרְכָתָא וְשִׁירָתָא,
תֻּשְׁבְּחָתָא וְנֶחֱמָתָא, דַּאֲמִירָן בְּעָלְמָא, וְאִמְרוּ אָמֵן:

---

hate hatred and berate brutality until (as Beruriah, the wife of Rabbi Meir, read the words of the *Tehillim*), *"yitamu hataim min ha-aretz*, until sin vanishes from the face of the earth" (Psalms 104:35), until mankind learns the principles of mercy and love and compassion. "On that day shall the Lord be One and His Name One" (Zechariah 14:9).

קדיש יתום *Mourner's Kaddish.* What relation is there between death and the *Kaddish*? A touching and illuminating explanation was offered by the great Hebrew writer and Israel's Nobel laureate, Shmuel Yosef Agnon, in a brief eulogy for the martyrs of the Holy Land many years ago. There is a difference, says Agnon, between a mortal, human king and the divine King of the whole world. When an ordinary, mortal king goes into battle, he sends forth his soldiers as a group and does not consider them as individuals. If one soldier falls, another can take his place. It makes little difference to the king who the individual soldiers are, what are their needs or loves or fears or aspirations. Not so the Almighty, the King of kings, the Holy One, blessed be He! Every one of God's troops is unique. With Him, all the king's men are each ineffably precious. The Lord does not deal with His children as statistics, but as wholly unique individuals. Therefore, when one of the soldiers in God's army dies — and we are all His soldiers, all the king's men — that place remains empty forever, and no one else can ever replace him. When a person passes away, therefore, not only does his earthly family grieve,

MOURNER'S KADDISH

Mourner. — Magnified and sanctified may His great Name be, in the world which He has created according to His will. May He establish His kingdom during your life and during your days, and during the life of all the house of Israel, even speedily and at a near time, and say, Amen.

Cong. and Mourner: May His great Name be blessed forever and to all eternity.

Mourner: Blessed, praised, glorified, exalted, extolled, honored, magnified, and lauded be the Name of the Holy One, Blessed be He, beyond all the blessings and hymns, praises and consolations, which are uttered in the world; and say, Amen.

---

but God, too, as it were, grieves for him, and God too must be consoled, for He suffers with us.

And so we offer the divine Father our condolences for His grievous and irreparable loss: *Yitgadal ve-'yitkadash shemeih rabba*, May Your great Name be magnified and sanctified. When one of Your children dies — and they are so few and so precious! — Your great Name is diminished and it is desecrated, it is a *hillul Hashem*. So we pray: May Your great Name *yitgadal*, may it be magnified and restored to its previous greatness, and *yitkadash*, may it again be sanctified after its dreadful desecration. God's kingdom has suffered; His soldier has fallen. There is a void, an emptiness, in His realm. So we say to Him: "*ve-yamlikh malkhutei*, may His kingdom too be restored."

What a consoling thought — to know that we are not alone in our grief. What a powerful and sensitive and beautiful way of enunciating this principle of man's individual greatness. If a human being is so precious to God that He must be consoled at a human's loss, then He, the Almighty, has invested something of Himself in each of His human creatures. That something is the source of man's religious potentialities, his moral greatness, and his spiritual attainments. It is because of this that we must never despair of any man at any time.

יְהֵא שְׁלָמָא רַבָּא מִן שְׁמַיָּא וְחַיִּים עָלֵינוּ וְעַל כָּל יִשְׂרָאֵל, וְאִמְרוּ אָמֵן:
עֹשֶׂה שָׁלוֹם בִּמְרוֹמָיו הוּא יַעֲשֶׂה שָׁלוֹם עָלֵינוּ וְעַל כָּל יִשְׂרָאֵל, וְאִמְרוּ
אָמֵן:

May there be abundant peace from heaven, and life for us and for all Israel; and say, Amen.

He Who makes peace in His high places, may He make peace for us and for all Israel; and say, Amen.

Derashot on Days of Salvation and Thanksgiving

Hanukkah

The Progressive Candles:
A Commentary on Jewish Life

Perhaps the most significant aspect of the most important feature of Hanukkah — the Hanukkah candles — is the increase in the number of candles from day to day. The lighting of the candles is progressive; that is, we proceed from least to most. The first night we light one candle, the second night two candles, the third night three candles, and so until the eighth night, when the candelabrum is ablaze with all eight candles. What we have is growth and increase and progress. It was the House of Hillel which gave this order its legal form when it

said that *mosif ve-holekh*, the number of candles is to be increased each night, because *ma'alin be-kodesh*, because one must rise, increase, or progress in holiness.

In a sense, this idea of increase, of addition, of the progressive candles, is a very deep and incisive commentary on Jewish life and what it should be. The Hanukkah candles represent more than merely the military victory of the Jewish Maccabeans over the Greek Antiochus. They symbolize as well the clash of cultures, the war of world-views. There was the Greek world, steeped in its oriental idolatry, pitted against a Jewish minority stubbornly proud of its pure belief in one God.

One should not dismiss the Greek world lightly. The world's greatest philosophers were nursed in the cradle of Greek culture. But the great difference between Hellenism, as the Greek culture is known, and Judaism, lies in this: The Greek world glorified contemplation, the Jewish world glorified behavior, mitzvot. The Greeks stressed creed, while we insisted upon deed. The Greeks were inclined to inactivity — the perfection of form, while the

Jew insisted upon activity. The Greeks had many philosophers but few saints; many thinkers but few doers. With the Jews this was reversed. Our world was not one of cold thought, but one of warm action. And this Jewish attitude is best represented by the progressive candles — increase, growth, action, progress. I have no doubt that if the Greeks had won the war, and decided to celebrate it by the lighting of candles, they would have constructed one gigantic, beautiful candle in front of the statue of Zeus, or a thousand smaller ones all around him — but it would have remained that way. With us Jews, however, Hanukkah is celebrated by progressive candles. *Ma'alin be-kodesh.*

In human terms, we could call the Greeks sitters or standers; that is, in their cold inactivity they confined themselves, insofar as ethics and good deeds are concerned, to one place and there stagnated. They were sitters or standers who rarely chose to help a fellow man. And if the Greeks were sitters and standers, we Jews were walkers and goers. And when one of us decided to "sit it out," and not participate actively in the good life, then our Rabbis were merciless in their criticism.

The Torah tells us, "*Va-yeshev Ya'akov ba-aretz megurei aviv*," which is usually translated as, "and Jacob dwelt in the land of his father's residence," but which literally means, "and Jacob *sat* in the land of his father's residence" (Genesis 37:1). Even Jacob — who was all his life a great and dynamic "doer" and "goer" — was at times a "sitter." And listen to the Rabbis' biting remark: "Wherever man sits, Satan jumps; wherever man becomes inactive, Satan raises his ugly head and becomes active" (*Bereishit Rabbah, Va-Yeshev* 84). Here was Jacob, an old man who was tired and weary of a life of wandering and running away. He felt that his energies were spent in wrestling with angels, in warding off Laban, and in protecting himself from Esau. He now had twelve children and he was ready to retire. "Enough done in one lifetime," he thought. "Now is the time to get a little *nahat*, the time to sit back and relax."

And so Jacob *sat back* and relaxed where his father had once lived. And what happens? Satan becomes active. Once a Jacob sits, jealousy invades his home, and his sons begin a struggle with each other over a mere colored shirt. Once a Jacob sits, then one son speaks evil of another. Once a Jacob sits, then he finds that his son Joseph, as the Rabbis relate, spends more time combing his hair in front of a mirror than in poring over his schoolbooks, and he soon begins to dream high-handed dreams of conquest and royalty. Indeed, once a Jacob sits, then his family is torn apart and some sons sell other sons down the river and into slavery.

And sitting, in this sense of inactivity, leads not only to family dissension, but also to downright immorality. Here was Israel, a "holy nation and a kingdom of priests" (Exodus 19:6), wandering in the desert, and suddenly "Israel *sat* in the plains of Moab" (Exodus 22:1). What happens when a nation sits? The children of Israel entered into immoral relationships with the daughters of Moab. So sitting leads to immorality as well. Indeed, once stagnation sets in, once there is only sitting or standing but no going or progress, then Satan jumps and becomes ferociously hyperactive.

What is the Jewish way? Certainly not sitting or standing, but going and walking. In the great vision that Abraham beheld, God's command was clear and to the point: "Walk before me and be perfect" (Genesis 17:1). When a man walks, not sits, then he has a chance of becoming perfect. When Joshua the high priest stands before Almighty God, and Satan is at his right hand, God promises Joshua the ultimate redemption of Israel and tells him, "If you will walk in my ways, then I will give you places to walk among those that stand" (Zechariah 3:7). Yes, the world is full of sitters and standers, those who in their inactivity and stagnation invite the company of Satan. But the Abrahams and the Joshuas are committed to a policy of walking and going, of constant activity and positive, helpful deeds. For such is the active policy of Jews in all ages, an activation symbolized by the progressive candles of the Hanukkah menorah. *Ma'alin be-kodesh.*

How unfortunate, therefore, that so many of our modern Jews, while lighting the candles, forget their meaning. How often a rabbi hears the following remarks: "You see, Rabbi, it's true I am not an Orthodox Jew, I don't put on *tefillin*, I don't observe Shabbat, I don't observe the dietary laws; but, Rabbi, let me tell you that I have a good heart; it's all in here." And this is followed by a thumping of his chest.

Of course, that is precisely what Rabbis are afraid of — that it's all in here, that the good heart is something which lies buried between the ribs and behind the diaphragm, and whose warm heartbeats cannot be heard without the aid of artificial instruments. The "good heart" is the excuse of the sitter or the stander. The "good heart" excuse is in the tradition of Greece, and not Israel. I am very wary, indeed, when all a person has to offer is a good heart; whose good intentions cannot be reflected in good limbs and good pockets and good deeds. Imagine what would happen if we would translate that "good heart" idea into actual medical terms. If all the blood were to be drained from your body, from the fingertips to the tips of your toes, and concentrated in your heart, it would certainly be a good heart because it would contain all the blood in your body. But such a situation can only lead to death, because a good heart is not enough; we must have a heart which can circulate this goodness all over the body.

Good intentions without good deeds and good actions are characteristic of the Greeks and not of the Jews. I feel sure, for example, that our synagogues were not built by good intentions or good hearts alone, but by good deeds and good actions. The UJA and Yeshiva University were not built by good hearts alone. They required sturdy hands and sharp heads and noble actions.

With this in mind, we can understand part of the special *Al ha-Nissim* prayer. In the course of that prayer we praise God and thank Him for assuring us of victory over the Greeks, who, we say, wanted to cause us to forget the Torah and to transgress God's commandments. This statement is, seemingly, not true from a historical point of view. We know that Antiochus promulgated only three harsh laws against the Jews: He forbade the observance of Shabbat, the festival of Rosh Hodesh, and the rite of circumcision. But nowhere do we find that this mad emperor prohibited the study of Torah.

The answer, however, lies in the idea we have been trying to convey; that is, if the Jew is forbidden to observe the practical commandments, the *hukkei retzonekha*, if the study of the Torah cannot lead to resolute action, then it is the same as if he were prohibited from even thinking about the Torah — and it must lead to forgetting the Torah. Of what use is Torah if it does not lead to concrete action and noble deeds? If Antiochus did not allow the Jews to observe their commandments, then he stands accused in the eyes of history of destroying their study of the Torah. For the Jew, study without implementation is of slight value. Creed must give birth to deed; contemplation must result in behavior; thought must end in action. *Ma'alin be-kodesh.*

The light of the progressive candles is, therefore, for us, an enlightening commentary on what Jewish life should be. They inspire us to better behavior, challenge us to greater deeds, and urge us on to new and broader horizons, with that ever-valid commandment, "Rise in holiness."

Yom ha-Atzma'ut

Our Dependence Upon Israel's Independence

The anniversary of the independence of the State of Israel, which we shall soon celebrate, affords us the occasion to reexamine our own attitudes and orientations toward the State. I do not in all honesty believe that full justice can be done to such a significant theme in the confines of a single sermon. Let us, therefore, merely outline some general principles which ought to guide such considerations.

This introspection is most characterized, above all, by a radical frankness and an honesty which may prove painful. In the past, economic exigencies, organizational bias, and the normal desire to avoid confronting unpleasant dilemmas have usually deterred us from a self-analysis. Indeed, such a searching self-examination will probably leave many of us perplexed, and even deeply disturbed. But it is a blessed perplexity that takes the place of the pedestrian platitudes that have so long substituted for thinking.

The fact is that American Jews of all persuasions are in a state of crisis concerning their position and orientation toward the State of Israel. We are beset by certain paradoxes and contradictions. If I be permitted to paraphrase the section from *Pirkei Avot* which we often read: "The world stands on three things: on Torah, on *avodah* [which means prayer or the sacrificial service], and on charitable endeavors" (*Avot* 1:2). So may it be said of the American Jewish world with regard to Israel, that it consists of three groups. First is "Torah": the Orthodox Jew, whose love for Israel and devotion to the State is part of the larger context of his commitment to Torah and Judaism. The second is *avodah* — literally the word means "work," and here I include those who are devoted organizational workers for the various Zionist groups.

The third, *gemillat hassadim,* comprises those many people whose major expression of interest in Israel is through financial support, such as the UJA. and Bonds for Israel.

American Jews whose orientation to Israel is expressed as *avodah,* that is, political Zionists, and especially secular Zionists, are in a state of deep crisis. Their dilemma is well known — they have, paradoxically, been defeated by success. Their stated purpose was the creation of an independent state. They succeeded in this goal; because it has been fulfilled, they are left without a purpose. It is fairly apparent to all objective observers that if not for institutional inertia, these organizations would have disappeared with the emergence of the State of Israel in 1948.

Gemillat hassadim as an expression of loyalty to Israel is very important. Israel needs our financial assistance. But all of us hope that the time is not far off when the State will achieve economic independence from us as well as peace with its neighbors. What then? When we no longer have to contribute financially or politically to the State of Israel, how shall we relate to it? Is it conceivable that American Jews will be left with no special relationship toward Israel?

We Orthodox Jews, whose position in Israel is expressed by the word "Torah," have been spared, largely, the crises of the other two. Our love for Israel is independent either of political or economical conditions. Our program is not merely one of supporting an economy or creating a governmental machinery. Our purpose depends neither upon votes nor upon funds, though it may include both. Therefore, neither independence nor peace nor security constitutes a threat to our relationship to Israel, for these do not represent the fulfillment of our goals. Our end is nothing less than the Messianic vision of the *ge'ulah sheleimah,* the complete redemption, a term which includes a spiritual renaissance of the Land of Israel and the People of Israel according to the Torah of Israel, and, ultimately, the spiritual regeneration of all mankind in universal peace and justice.

Yet, American Orthodox Jews do face a problem that they

cannot continue to avoid indefinitely. Our critics in Israel, both those who are Orthodox and those who are not, have pressed this problem upon us, and we ought to consider it seriously and coura-geously, not — as we have done — polemically. That is, that *yishuv Eretz Yisrael*, the act of settling in the Land of Israel, is one of the 613 commandments. In a remarkable passage, Rav Kook points out that, surprisingly, Maimonides does not include in his Sefer ha-Mitzvot as detailed commandments those precepts which are fundamental to the whole of Torah; therefore *yishuv Eretz Yisrael* is not reckoned by him as an individual commandment because it is an underlying principle of the whole of Judaism. It is too important to be regarded as just a mitzvah.

In the past, our people did not emigrate to the Land of Israel en masse because of the extremely difficult conditions that pre-vailed: hostile government, harsh and forbidding environment, the absence of a community large enough and stable enough to absorb immigrants. But today Israel is a free and independent state, and is even blessed with a measure of prosperity. Hence, the question is asked: Why not practice and stress the great precept of *aliyah?* And we ought honestly to ask the same question of our-selves: indeed, why not *aliyah?* How can we square our religious conscience and intellectual integrity with our apparent noncon-cern with *aliyah?* There are of course a number of objections to *aliyah* that are offered as an excuse for our neglect of this great principle of Jewish life. Upon reflection, most of them are not worth taking seriously. Let us, for the sake of analysis, consider them briefly.

We are told by some people that American Jews are not in exile, in *galut*, and that therefore *aliyah* is not obligatory upon us. Some of those who propose this comparatively novel thesis are motivated by an exaggerated Americanism. They fear that the assertion of our exilehood is an act of disloyalty to the United States. Historically, this is false. There were amongst our ancestors some who lived in countries of the Diaspora that were blessed with benign governments and allowed full freedom to Jews and

Judaism. Yet they never doubted that they were in exile, and never were aware of any conflict between their loyalty to their government and their desire for redemption. Only a totalitarian government insists upon the total loyalty of its citizens. A democratic government asks only that its citizens perform their civic duties and affirm their allegiance to the constitution; it does not forbid them to cherish ancient dreams, present prayers, and visions of a future redemption.

It is odd that those who protest loudest against the idea that we are in exile in this country, do so largely because they are afraid of the impression that will be made upon other Americans if American Jews appear to consider themselves in exile. What greater exile is there than this?

Indeed, we are in *galut!* To deny this is to abandon our hopes for *ge'ulah* for redemption, to scuttle our belief in the Messiah, to make a shambles of our Torah, to invalidate all of our Jewish past and its sublime dreams for the future, and to reduce our prayers — including many of those we recite today — to a kind of sanctified hypocrisy. Ours may be a comfortable *galut,* a *galut* in which we have a large measure of freedom; but even a convenient *galut* remains a *galut!*

The Baal Shem Tov taught this principle in one of his inimitable comments. We read in Isaiah a verse with which we are familiar because we recite it on Rosh Hashanah: "On that day [the day of the redemption] a great *shofar* will be sounded, and those who are lost in the land of Ashur [Assyria] and those who are dispersed in the Land of Egypt will return to the Holy Land" (Isaiah 27:13). But, asks the Baal Shem Tov, are Assyria and Egypt the only countries from which the exiles will return in the future?

He replies that these two countries represent two types of exile. He explains these symbols by rearranging the vowels. *Mitzrayim* (Egypt) can be rearranged to read *metzarim* (narrow straits, difficulty, oppression). *Ashur* (Assyria) can be read as *osher* (happiness, prosperity, plenty). In other words, there are two types of exile: One of them, symbolized by Egypt, is the classical form of *galut,* that of oppression and hatred and bigotry, in which our people are persecuted and dispersed. But there is also another kind of exile which is just the reverse. It is the one symbolized by Assyria. It is the exile of Jews in *osher,* or luxury, in which we are lost, because our sublime aims and lofty goals have been deflected as a result of the abundance of convenience and comfort and plenty and prosperity.

Indeed, the greatest exile — as a great Jew once said — occurs when we do not know that we are in exile. The more we forget our exilehood, the deeper we are caught in it. And what is our condition in America if not exile, when we read of the increasing assimilation and growing intermarriage, when non-Jews nationally proclaim that we are the "vanishing Jews of America"? One need not be a pessimist about the future survival of our people in this country to admit that we are suffering a terrible attrition. *Galut* indeed! The argument against *aliyah* because we American Jews are not in exile is a spurious one, and does not deserve to be taken seriously.

Then there are those who turn the argument around, and would discourage *aliyah,* or excuse our neglect of it, because of faults they find in the State of Israel. Israel, they tell us, is itself not exactly a completely religious state; not all of its citizens are totally observant. The Israelis too are in *galut* in Israel! Perhaps conditions in Israel are less than ideal, but this argument is only a semantic trick. One need not equate the State of Israel with the complete redemption and the ultimate Messianic state in order to promote the idea of *aliyah*. The fact is that there is more *Yiddishkeit* and opportunity for the practice of Judaism in Israel than anyplace else in the world — Brooklyn and Manhattan included.

It is true that to the untrained eye of a tourist, it sometimes seems as if Judaism is in exile in the Holy Land. However, it requires a special insight, an extraordinary gift, in order to be able to see the truth: that Judaism is much more vibrant, much more prevalent, much more real in Israel than it is anyplace in the world. A great rabbi once explained, with regard to this special insight, one of the prayers in the *Amidah*. We pray thrice daily "May our eyes behold when You return to Zion in love." Why, he asks, do we pray that our eyes behold that God returns to Zion; why do we not simply pray that God return to Zion? The answer is that even if God returned to Zion, we might not notice it. Sometimes He is there in His full holiness and glory — only we fail to see it! We are blind to the great and secret realities of God's presence in the Holy Land. Therefore we implore Him: Almighty God, allow our eyes to see what already is a fact — that You have indeed returned to Zion!

The only real objection to *aliyah* is not theoretical but practical. We have made our lives here in this country. We have settled here, raised our families, struck our roots, built our businesses, advanced our careers and professions. *Aliyah* proves very difficult for us, no matter how genuine our commitment to it. This is a more honest position than to attempt to argue away our responsibility and justify our failure. It is a frank admission of a practical failure, and not an attempt to rationalize our inadequacy by discarding the ideal as such.

Nevertheless, we must never remain satisfied with merely abstract ideals, for that which is unrealizable is essentially unreal. *Aliyah* must be not only an ideal but a principle. It must govern behavior and conduct. Therefore, if we ourselves, for very practical reasons, cannot emigrate to the Holy Land, we should encourage and assist those who can. But that too is insufficient. Such an approach might well lead us into the classical position of the two Zionists who express their Zionism by deciding that a third must go on *aliyah* to Israel. If we are honest about our reasons for not emigrating — that they are practical, not theoretical — then we must at least see to it that our children will go. We must prepare our children for *aliyah* before they have settled here. If not all our children, at least each family must decide that the one child most fit for emigration ought to be prepared for it. We must decide to train at least one child in the kind of career or profession or business which will enable him to go on *aliyah*. We must imbue him with the spirit of Israel, and create in him that idealism which will help him fulfill the destiny which all of Israel must ultimately share.

No parent regards it as a tragedy if his child becomes a lawyer in California or marries an engineer in South America, or goes into business in Alaska. The world is smaller today than it ever was before. It will be smaller yet ten years from now. We should regard it as a blessing if a child of ours fulfills our dreams, our duties, our highest spiritual and national vocation, by directing him to settle in the Holy Land, on *aliyah,* and live a full, vibrant Jewish life.

Our religious integrity requires it. Israel needs *olim* from the United States. And America needs it! The American Jewish community will be able the better to survive if it sends some of the cream of its youth to the Holy Land. American Jewish youth has begun to look elsewhere for outlets for its native idealism. We must redirect our children and their idealism to the State of Israel. These precious *olim* will be the permanent human bond between Israeli and American Jewry. For indeed, if we will not be *olim,* we will be *yordim.* If we will not "go up," we may, heaven forbid, go down!

The solution is not overly difficult, and is not too easy. Facing this issue is no easier for me than for anyone else. But we ignore it at the peril of our own souls and our own integrity. Now that Israel is independent, we must consider *aliyah* as an opportunity. The future of American Jewry itself will be enhanced by such *aliyah.* We are, in a large measure, dependent upon Israel's independence.

As seen in this perspective, the question of *aliyah* is not a problem but a prospect, not a perplexity but an opportunity. Let us never lose sight of our attachment to that Land. Let us never substitute for our real loyalty to it a mere financial commitment or political interest or sentimental association. For the Land is indeed very, very good. Through our loyalty to it, may it continue to be very, very good for us, for our children, for all Israel, and ultimately for all mankind.

Israel Independence Day

The conjunction of the *sidrot* of *Tazria* and *Metzora* is remarkable. The first speaks of birth, the second of a kind of death: "*metzora harei hu ke-met*, a leper is considered as partially dead." *Tazria* describes the joyous acceptance into the fold of a new Jew by means of *berit milah*, circumcision, while *Metzora* tells of the expulsion of the leper from the community. Yet, these two portions are often read on the same Shabbat with no interruption between them. The tension between these two opposites, this dialectic between birth and death, between pleasure and plague, between rejoicing and rejecting, speaks to us about the human condition as such and the existence of the Jew specifically.

Even more, this tension contains fundamental teachings of Judaism that are relevant to the problems of the State of Israel, whose eighteenth birthday we shall be celebrating this Monday. After delineating the laws of childbirth, the Torah in the first *sidrah* gives us the laws of circumcision. The *Midrash Tanhuma* relates a fascinating conversation concerning this Jewish law (*Tanhuma, Tazria* 5). We are told that Turnus Rufus, a particularly vicious Roman commander during the Hadrianic persecutions in Palestine, spoke to Rabbi Akiva, the revered leader of our people. He asked Rabbi Akiva: "Which is more beautiful: the work of God or the work of man?" Rabbi Akiva answered: "The work of man." Turnus Rufus was visibly shocked by the answer.

He continued: "Why do you circumcise your children?" Rabbi Akiva said: "My first reply serves as an answer to this question as well." Whereupon Rabbi Akiva brought before the Roman commander *shibbolim* and *gluskaʾot*, stalks of wheat and loaves of good white bread. He said to the Roman: "Behold, these are the works of God, and these are the works of man. Are not the works of man more beautiful and useful?" Said the Roman to Rabbi Akiva: "But if God wants people to be circumcised, why are they not born circumcised?" Rabbi Akiva replied: "God gave the mitzvot to Israel, to temper or purify His people thereby."

Here is the triumphant Roman commander, activist, arrogant, proud, and power-drunk. In an attitude of contempt, he faces the aged Jewish leader of this conquered people, a man who proclaims that the greatest principle of life is the study of Torah. What can these otherworldly mystics know about the world, about reality, about life? So he taunts the old rabbi: How come you circumcise your children? Do you not believe that man, as God's creation, is already born perfect? But the Roman pagan is amazed by the response: *No!* All of Judaism — its philosophy, its Torah, its mitzvot — is based upon the premise that God withheld perfection from His creation, that He only began the task and left it to man, His *tzelem*, His "image," to complete.

In Genesis, we are taught that God rested from creating the world "*asher bara Elohim la-asot,* which God created to do" (Genesis 2:3). Rabbi Samson Raphael Hirsch interpreted this to mean that God created the world for man "to do." Therefore, Rabbi Akiva shows Turnus Rufus the wheat stalks and the white bread, to teach him that God has created wheat because He wants man to do something with it. It is God's will that man make the created world more beautiful and more perfect. No wonder that in the Jewish view science and technology play such a positive role. No wonder that religious Jewry has contributed so mightily, throughout the ages and today as well, to the advancement of science and the control of nature. Therefore, too, the mitzvot, and especially circumcision, were revealed to Israel to teach that man must act by himself in order to perfect his self and his world, and in the process, *le-tzaref ba-hen,* to purify himself and fulfill all his sublime potentialities.

Indeed, Rabbi Akiva himself exemplified this great principle. He was, on the one hand, one of the saintliest spirits in all our history. The Talmud, in imaginative grasp of the truth, tells us that when Moses ascended Mount Sinai to receive the Torah and he saw the sacred soul of Rabbi Akiva, he protested to God that

Akiva was more worthy to be the bearer of Torah than he. And yet, on the other hand, it was the same Rabbi Akiva who did not isolate himself in the academy, but became the sponsor of Bar Kochba, the great Jewish general who led the revolt against Rome.

This, then, is what *milah* teaches us: "*ma'aseh basar va-dam na'im*, the work of flesh and blood is beautiful" indeed. The world is an uncompleted creation; man's fate and destiny is to finish it. It is the principle of activism. The State of Israel was built by people who perceived this Jewish principle. They were the ones who refused to stand aside, outside of the stream of history, but who actively took it upon themselves to rebuild Jewish statehood. Their activity was in full keeping with the Jewish tradition as taught by the law of *milah*. More than enough Jewish blood was spilled in the effort, and the sweat and tears invested in the State shall never be forgotten.

Yet, this is only half the story. There is an opposite danger. If man is indeed a creator, then there is the peril that he will become intoxicated with power and self-delusions, that he will begin boasting and bragging and proclaiming bombastically: "*kohi ve-otzem yadi*, my own power and my own strength" have performed all this. When he circumcises his child, he tends to forget that a healthy child is the gift of God. When he bakes his bread, he does not always realize that the wheat came from God's earth. When he builds his state, he ignores the fact that without the divine promise to Abraham and divine guidance throughout the ages there would be no Jews to build the Jewish state. When he is self-completing, he tends to become, in his imagination, self-creating. He is self-finishing and thinks that he is therefore self-made; and God spare us from self-made men!

To help us avoid this dangerous delusion, we have the teachings of *Metzora*. Just as *Tazria* and *milah* warn us to avoid the passivism that issues from a misunderstanding of faith, so *Metzora* and the law of *shilu'ah ha-mahaneh*, the banishing of the leper outside the camp, teach us to avoid the fatal illusion that issues from faithlessness. Just as one *sidrah* tells us to circumcise the flesh and assert our manhood, so the second tells us to circumcise the heart and serve our God.

The great medieval scholar Rabbi Elazar of Worms explains the law of the *metzora* and his banishment outside the camp by means of a comment on a famous verse in the Psalms: "*ve-adam bi-yekar bal yalin nimshal ka-behemot nidmu,* man does not abide in his glory, he is compared to the animals" (Psalms 49:13). Man, says Rabbi Elazar, is born naked and ignorant, without understanding and intelligence. But God puts him on his feet, grants him wisdom and insight, feeds him and clothes him and makes him great. But then man forgets and does not understand that all this glory came to him from his God. Therefore, he becomes like a *behemah,* a mere animal. An animal is not kept at home, but sent out to pasture; he is unfit to live in a truly human community. So man who forgets God is a *metzora,* he is morally sick, and must be sent outside the camp of his peers. The leper symbolizes the man who acquired self-confidence at the cost of fidelity to God, and he therefore is reduced to the role of a beast.

Man, then, must be a co-creator with God. *Tazria* teaches that man must imitate his Maker; *Metzora* reminds him not to impersonate his God, not to be an impostor. One *sidrah* stresses the virtue of human commission; the other — the virtue of human submission to God.

Indeed, in an insight brimming with tremendous significance, the eminent Italian-Jewish thinker Rabbi Mosheh of Trani finds this second principle in the commandment of *milah* itself. Just as circumcision teaches that man must act, so its particular designation for the eighth day teaches that his actions must not lead to the mere amassing of power and self-importance. Rather, man must acknowledge and reach out to the Creator of all the world. The number seven, Rabbi Mosheh teaches, is the symbol of Nature. Seven is the number of days in the week, the unit of time which establishes the rhythm of our lives. The earth itself agriculturally follows a seven-year cycle in Judaism — that of the *Shemittah.* The number seven, therefore, stands for this world in its fullness.

The number eight, however, is beyond seven: It teaches that you transcend what seven symbolizes; you must go beyond Nature and reach out for the supernatural, for God, He who creates Nature. Were *milah* on the seventh day, then the duty of man would be to correct the imperfections of Nature, but forever to stay within it as nothing more than a clever animal. But *milah* was commanded for the eighth day, to teach that the purpose of all man's activity, the purpose of his work on Nature, is to elevate himself beyond the perfection of body and mind, beyond the conquest of the world, beyond technology. When man controls his environment, he fulfills the number seven; when he controls his instincts, he reaches number eight. His technology is symbolized by the number seven; his theology by eight, *Milah* on the eighth day teaches that man must not only complete himself but must grow beyond himself; he must yearn for and aspire to something higher. It signifies not only *milah* but *berit*; not only a surgical cut, but the sign of the covenant, a contract with God sealed in blood. It means that if a human being does not strive to be more than human, he will become less than human, an animal, *nimshal ka-behemot nidmu*. Then man becomes a *metzora*, and like an animal must be sent out *hutz la-mahaneh*, outside the camp of human beings.

Indeed, this is the crucial problem concerning the character of the State of Israel. Is it to be the symbol of seven, or the symbol of eight? Will it be just a natural state, or something higher, something nobler? If Israel will only be natural, a state like all others, a small sliver of real estate on the shores of the Mediterranean, considered nothing more than the creation of the Haganah and sabra ingenuity, then it has no special claim on Jewish communities throughout the world — no more than its population warrants. It has no right to Messianic pretenses. Such a conception places it *hutz la-mahaneh*, outside the purview of authentic Jewish history, an aberration. It is then in defiance of the covenant; it is the way of *tumah*, impurity. Only by fulfilling the symbol of eight, of loyalty to the covenant of God, of Torah, lies the way of *taharah*, of purity and rebirth, of joyous fulfillment of the historic dreams and prayers and prophecies of our history.

This, then, is the real problem on this eve of the eighteenth birthday of the State of Israel: Will it be *milah* or *berit?* Surgery or covenant? *Tazria* or *Metzora? Taharah* or *tumah?* Striving to be more than a natural human political entity, or falling to a mere natural group which, under the impress of secular nationalism often becomes beastly; *nimshal ka-behemot nidmu?*

Such decisions are never made all at once. They involve long processes measured in historical time, certainly more than eighteen years. Many facts will determine the answer, and not the least of them will be the spiritual leadership in the state under the resolute stewardship of our distinguished and revered guest, His Eminence, Chief Rabbi Unterman, may he live and be well. Their enormously difficult task is to be both responsive to their fellow Israelis and responsible to our Heavenly Father. Like the *kohanim* in our *sidrah*, they must confront all Jews, the perfectly pure and the perilously impure. Sometimes it is their unhappy and tragic task to say to a man: *tamei*, impure, you must go out! Yet their greater and nobler task is to teach this same *tamei* to return, to bring Jews back into the historic community of Israel, to train all Jews in the way of the Torah's *taharah*. It is by no means a simple duty; it is, in fact, unenviable and difficult. Our hopes and good wishes and our prayers for divine guidance and blessings go to Chief Rabbi Unterman and his distinguished colleagues in this historic mission.

We have spoken of *berit milah* in relation to the State of Israel. The eighteenth birthday also has another significance: *shemoneh esreh le-huppah*, the eighteenth year is traditionally the year of marriage. Let us conclude, then, by extending our wishes to Israel in a manner appropriate to both events. Let us all wish the State of Israel the divine blessings: *le-Torah, le-huppah u-le-maʾasim tovim*. May it be a future of Torah — in which Israel will accept the divine word and turn to its Father in heaven. May it be the time of *huppah*, the marriage of hearts between Israel and Jews throughout the world. And then, having returned to God and to Jews throughout the world, may Israel become the shining beacon of *maasim tovim*, of good deeds and noble living, throughout the world and for all mankind. *Le-Torah, le-huppah u-le-maʾasim tovim*. Amen.

Yom Yerushalayim

In This Hour of Crisis
(May 27, 1967)

This is an hour of crisis, not only for Israel as a state but for Israel as a people. Our destiny, and the destiny of our children and children's children after us, is being forged by the soldiers of Israel on lonely outposts in the Gaza Strip and on the heights overlooking the Gulf of Aqaba. No Jew can afford to look upon the tense situation as an outsider. As Mordecai the Jew said to Queen Esther, highly placed in non-Jewish society and politics, "*al tedami be-nafshekh le-himalet beit ha-melekh* — do not imagine that you will find safety whilst danger befalls the rest of the House of Israel" (Esther 4:14).

The Arab guns aimed at the heart of the State are aimed at our hearts. The stranglehold on the Gulf of Aqaba, the lifeline of the *medinah*, is a stranglehold on our throats. And the Russian contempt for the State of Israel bespeaks the old, traditional Russian contempt for all of us as Jews. How ought we react in this grave hour? How have Jews always and should Jews now react?

The archetypical and symbolic confrontation between Israel and its enemies was that between Jacob and Esau. When Jacob, surrounded by his wives and children and his retinue, heard that the armed columns of Esau were marching toward him with vengeance in their hearts, the Rabbis tell us, he prepared a threefold strategy: *le-tefillah, le-doron, u-le-milhamah*; he prepared himself for prayer, for gifts, and for war (*Tanhuma* [Buber], *Va-Yishlah* 6). It is this threefold approach that must become the pattern for our attitude as well.

The *doron*, or gift, that Jacob presented to his brother was a form of legitimate appeasement of a bloodthirsty aggressor, in an attempt to turn his hatred into goodwill. Indeed, it happened to work with Jacob. But it cannot work for Israel today. First, you cannot placate an enemy who is implacable. Those of us who saw King Faisal on television two days ago heard him declare his avowed intention of exterminating Israel, and President Nasser said the same thing yesterday. Nothing less than that would satisfy our enemies. Moreover, Israel has nothing left to give. It has given all but the bare skeletal structure necessary for the survival of a modern country. Hence, our *doron* must be the gift that we American Jews are going to give to the Jews and the government of the State of Israel; in other words, our accelerated participation in that great and historic venture known as the UJA. No Jew who fails to give, and to significantly increase his pledge over the past, has a moral right to be proud that he is a Jew. This year Israel faces unusual economic difficulty; the present fall-off in tourism, together with the stupendous military expenditures that it must undertake, make the situation and the need grave indeed. Those who will therefore give this year far in excess of what they gave in the past, and far in excess of what they are able to give, will be performing an invaluable service. Those who do not do so are, for all their talk, valueless to Israel. Their talk, their worry, their advice, their concern, their pride, their keeping their ears glued to the radio — all this is meaningless! The Jewish Center family will have an opportunity on June 7th to demonstrate the extent of its commitment. I should like to see an enthusiastic response like never before. It behooves us to give our *doron* before we are solicited, and to prepare a gift that will tell Israel that we have not faltered, and all the world that Israel does not stand alone.

The second part of that strategy is *milhamah*, war. Can we participate in *milhamah* if it should be necessary? Yes we can, and yes it is necessary. There are many ways to fight a war, many fronts, and many weapons. Our contribution, though not military, must not be underestimated. For one thing, we must undertake an indefatigable political campaign. As members of a subculture in this great democracy, it is entirely proper that we make our opinion felt where opinions carry weight. We must undertake to inform our president, by letter and telegram, that we support his support of Israel, and to tell him as well as our senators and representatives that it was at the urging of an American secretary of state that Israel gave up much of its precious victory in Sinai, and that the United States has treaty obligations to Israel. This is one campaign in which we can participate immediately after the Sabbath is over.

Another way of making our political influence felt, in a more social manner, will come tomorrow morning when we shall participate physically in demonstrating our support for the State of Israel. We must all take our families and be present at the Salute to Israel parade. Even more directly, our young people can volunteer to help in Israel. Let them be encouraged. American law forbids military service on behalf of a foreign power. But there is much urgent work to be done, taking the places of Israel's men and women who have been pressed into military service. People are urgently needed, and young people should by all means participate in the Summer Work in Israel program, which has now been expanded, and in the *Sherut Le-umi*, which offers one or two years of service in Israel. The medical services and all other specialties are urgently needed; but Israel even needs people just to dig trenches and build shelters. So far, it is good to report that the results have been most encouraging. Let no one henceforth speak flippantly of "the vanishing Jews of America"! The volunteer offers have been extremely heartening. I am told that only yesterday a surgeon called from San Francisco to New York to offer his services provided that his two sons could come with him. Of particular interest to this congregation is the fact that a brief notice pinned on the bulletin board at Yeshiva University produced, in thirty-six hours, more than three hundred volunteers! I myself have been on the phone with a number of students, including a number of young ladies, from Yavneh, the religious Jewish students association, who have asked my intercession with their families to permit them to go forthwith to Israel. There is something ineffably precious about the Jewish soul which allows it to express its idealism so immediately and so openly. Each in his own way, therefore, can participate in this great *milhamah*.

We are an irenic, peace-loving people. Our hopes and prayers are for peace not only for us but for the entire world. The author of *Or ha-Hayyim* made this comment in a beautiful interpretation of a verse in today's *sidrah*. We read "*vi-yeshavtem la-vetah be-artzekhem*, and you shall dwell securely in your land" (Leviticus 26:5), followed by "*ve-natati shalom ba-aretz*, and I shall give peace to the land" (Leviticus 26:6). But, asks the *Or ha-Hayyim*, if we already are told that God will let us dwell securely in our land, surely that includes peace; why then repeat the promise that God will give peace to the land?

In his answer he distinguishes between *artzekhem* and *eretz*: the first verse refers to security in "*artzekhem*, your land," which means the Land of Israel. The second verse, however, refers to the granting of peace in *eretz*, which should be translated not as "the land," but as "the world." In addition to our own national security, we are committed to the great hope and striving for peace throughout the world.

However, when duty and destiny call upon us to work so that others might bear arms on behalf of Israel, or even, if need be, that we do so ourselves, we shall not be found hesitating or faltering! If we were a nation like unto other nations, this fight would still be noble, but natural. Our existence is at stake, and we shall not submit to the murderous ambitions of that Hitler of the Nile, to those hysterical pygmies of Damascus, or to that venal and obnoxious monarch of the desert kingdom of slave traders.

But Israel is more than that. The creation of the State of Israel was the minimum act by the powers of the world by which they salvaged the barest trace of human dignity left to them. Israel is a state conceived in the ghettos of Europe, born in the death camps of Auschwitz and Treblinka, delivered in the detention camps of Cyprus, and swaddled in the rags by which the Western powers blindfolded themselves to our agony and stuffed their ears not to hear our cry of anguish. Israel is a penance paid by Russia for Babi Yar, by England for the *Struma*, by the United States for its refusal to hear the cry of the refugees in time, by the Catholic countries for the silence of the pope, by each and every country for its own public and private crimes against the people of the Lord.

When we shall, therefore, act in defense of Israel, we will be fighting not only for Israel's and our existence, but, in effect, for the honor of Russia and England and America and France and all of mankind, whether they know it or not, realize or not, care or not, appreciate it or not, even whether they want it or not. For we shall ever remain, as Yehudah Halevi called us, the heart of the nations and their conscience.

Tani be-shem Rab Elazar, "*Ha-sayaf ve-ha-sefer nitnu mekor-akhin min ha-shamayim*, the sword and the book were given wrapped together from Heaven" (*Va-Yikra Rabbah* 35). We have given the world its *sefer*, its Book. We shall, if need be, now defend that *sefer*, and the *am ha-sefer*, the People of the Book, with a *sayaf*, a sword of courage and honor. For that charge and that mission is *min ha-shamayim*, decreed from Heaven!

Finally, the third element in this Jewish strategy first taught by Jacob is *tefillah*, prayer. We can perform that by keeping the present situation in mind every time we speak, in our *tefillot*, of Jerusalem and Zion. In addition, we shall at the conclusion of services today recite special prayers for the welfare of the State of Israel. But wedded to prayer is the concept of hope. Our prayer and our outlook must always be hopeful, never desperate.

I would like to commend to your attention an insight which speaks not only of hope but offers a perspective that goes far beyond the parochial limits of power politics. Our *sidrah*, in enumerating the blessings God promises us, says: "*u-faniti ale-khem*, and I shall turn to you, *ve-hifreti etkhem ve-hirbeti etkhem*, and I shall increase you, and make you fruitful, and keep My covenant with you" (Leviticus 26:9). On the words "I shall turn to you," Rashi quotes the Sages: "I shall turn away from all My other preoccupations in order to grant you your reward." What a strange remark! Are we really to take it so anthropomorphically, so primitively? Is God "busy" with other matters so that He has to take "time off" in order to pay loving attention to us?

An answer is provided to us by Rabbi Mordecai Rogov of Chicago, in his work *Ateret Mordecai*. He points to the midrash which states in the name of Rabbi Samuel ben Nachman, that God says: "I know the thoughts of all men." Applying this to the story of Joseph and his brothers, the midrash tells us that the brothers were preoccupied with the selling of Joseph, Joseph was busy bemoaning his own bitter fate, Judah was involved in looking for a wife — but all this while, God was preoccupied with the light of the Messiah! (*Bereishit Rabbah* 85).

Each of the actors in the great drama thought that he knew the whole story. The brothers saw it as an act of vengeance, Joseph as a bitter tragedy that had reached its nadir, Judah was altogether distracted by an extraneous matter. None of them really saw the entire episode in its true, ultimate perspective. None of them realized that God was not "busy" moving affairs as he individually saw them, but that the Almighty was simply making preparations for the ultimate development of Jewish history, leading to the final redemption.

The Joseph story, even more than others, reveals how human intention and divine design can sometimes be utterly different and yet mesh with each other, and how the divine plan often uses humans who do not even appreciate the role that they play.

Man, by virtue of his natural human limitations, can see only a segment of reality and experience. But if man is wise, he recognizes this, and he understands that beyond his own comprehension there is a God Whose own designs defy our pitiful human attempts at probing His mysteries. We are all actors who play significant roles in a great drama; but few of us ever have any inkling of the extent and direction of the plot. So it is with the current episode.

Today the Arabs are thinking of a quick victory. Russia sees the entire incident as a chance to dislodge the United States from

Vietnam. Israel views it as one great crisis that must be overcome. The United States considers it an added complication forcing it to juggle both Near Eastern and Far Eastern commitments. The United Nations regards it as a need to make up for U Thant's blunder, the biggest in the history of diplomacy. But our hope and our confidence is that God will take "time out" from these individual considerations of the protagonists of the drama and ultimately reveal to us His true preoccupation: *ve-ha-Kadosh barukh Hu hayah asuk be-oro shel Mashia*h, that Almighty God is weaving all these political and military strands into the garment of light that the Messiah will wear, into the intricate designs by which there will come to Israel and all the world the *ge'ulah sheleimah*, the complete redemption.

May, indeed, all our heartache and anxiety, all our worry and preparation for war, be transcended by the *yeshuah*, by the great victory and salvation which will come, speedily in our day, *ve-shalom al Yisrael* — and may peace arrive for Israel and all mankind.

מגילת אסתר

Three Long Lessons
from One Short War
(June 10, 1967)

The difference in mood and temperament of all our people
between last Saturday and this one can best be summed up in one
verse of King David's Psalms that we recite in our *Hallel*: "From
the straits I called out to the Lord, and the Lord answered me with
enlargement" (Psalms 118:5). Last week we called out in anguish,
hemmed in by enemies on all sides, encircled by adversaries seeking to destroy us utterly. By this Shabbat, the Lord has given us
His blessing, He has enlarged us; we are now able to breathe more
safely and securely, having broken out of the ring of death that
surrounded us only a few days ago.

What does this sudden deliverance mean? Of course, it is vain
to attempt to see the events that have occurred this week in their
proper perspective. This chapter in history is hardly over; we are
still very much involved in its consequences. Yet, time in our days
has become condensed, communications are incredibly rapid,
and even wars are fought and decided in three or four days; hence,
our understanding must keep pace and our evaluation must be
accelerated. We do this although we appreciate how complicated
our problem is — especially considering events which can be
described as nothing less than *nissim*, miracles. Indeed, they are
not the garden variety of miracles, the *nissim nistarim*, hidden
miracles, but quite obviously they are in the category of *nissim
geluyim*, evident and open miracles which only a blind man can
fail to see and only one who is obtuse can fail to appreciate.

The victory of Israel was totally unexpected by the victor, by
the conqueror, or by the observers. The extent of what has happened staggers the imagination. This is the week that Jews for the
first time in twenty years visited the grave of Rachel in Bethlehem,

and that for the first time in the memory of any person alive today, a Jew entered the *me'arat ha-makhpelah*, the burial grounds of the Patriarchs of Israel. Above all else, this is the week that Jews once again danced in the streets of Jerusalem, a city united. Jerusalem is one; no longer two Jerusalems! This is the week that Jews once again prayed at the Western Wall, shedding tears not of anguish but of joy and reunion. So it is difficult, but necessary, to take the long look, to attempt to recapitulate some of the important lessons of this short war.

The first one was stated quite clearly and simply by King David: "You shall not trust in the princes" (Psalms 146:3). You shall not place your ultimate faith in presidents or prime ministers, in generals or commanders, in treaties or alliances. It is still too early to tell to what extent the president of the United States and the prime minister of England stood by us, and how extensive was their support for us, given the possibility of nuclear confrontation with Russia. For whatever genuine help we did receive, we are eternally grateful. Yet it is clear that, in essence, Israel fought alone — and probably will remain mostly alone in the diplomatic battles that are yet to come. The supposed best friend of Israel stood aloof when the crisis came, remotely neutral. Others, bound to Israel by treaty, waited for other maritime powers to join it before honoring that treaty; it waited and waited and, when no one came, made no move on its own. Our State Department ignored American commitments — in thought, word, and deed.

All this — and, I fear, what lies ahead in the days to come — recalls the old adage: "May God protect me from my friends, I will take care of my enemies myself." We must realize that in an ultimate sense we are, as a gentile prophet noticed with great perception, "*am levadad yishkon*, a people that dwells alone" (Numbers 23:9). Of course, Israel needs and should seek alliances, just as individuals need and should seek out friends. But after all is said and done, we are a lonely people. It is that loneliness which is our greatest weakness and our greatest strength, a source of our deepest anguish and our highest joy.

In the first of the threefold blessing of the *kohanim* as given to us in today's *sidrah*, we read "*yevarekhekha Hashem*, the Lord bless you, *ve-yishmerekha*, and keep you" (Numbers 6:24). Our tradition has explained this last word as *yishmerekha min ha-mazikin*, may the Lord keep you from those who would injure you. *Mazikin* generally is translated as "demons, injurious spirits." The Aramaic translator *Targum Jonathan* identifies two groups of *mazikin*. He refers to them as *bnei tiharerei*, the sons of dusk, and *bnei tzafrirei*, the sons of dawn. There are two kinds of demons — those who appear in their true colors, black as night, and those who disguise themselves in the brightness of dawn. Some *mazikin* show their blackness openly; Russia and the Arabs are a good example. Others appear as sweet as dawn. India, for example, has always postured as a paragon of peace and piety. Yet, when it comes to Israel, she is nothing more or less than a *mazik*, a malevolent spirit. Close friends of Israel, such as the French government, have proved that underneath the exterior of *bnei tzafrirei* they are yet *mazikin*, ready to injure us. And even closer friends who are well intentioned and would genuinely want to remain "the sons of dawn" found themselves ready to abandon us before our strength showed.

The second of the three lessons has to do with the performance of our religious youth. It was amazing how all people of goodwill rallied to our side: non-Jews in all walks of life demonstrated friendship, and almost all Jews — with the exception of a sick and psychotic minority which does not deserve to be dignified by mention — were united in their enthusiasm. But the noblest example of all was provided by those many young people who were ready to give not only their substance but themselves, their own lives, placing themselves at the disposal of Israel wherever they might be needed in that war-torn country. It is a source of profound pride to us that the first to volunteer — when the situation was still dark and dismal — and in numbers highly disproportionate to our percentage of the population, were students from Yeshiva University and other yeshivot, young people who had a day school background, some Jewish education, some anchorage in a life of Torah. I am told that at the beginning of the crisis crowds of young people gathered at the Jewish Agency building to volunteer their services for Israel, and that a leading secular Zionist ideologist opened the door to the office, observed the young people, and turned to an Orthodox member of the Jewish Agency staff, asking, "I wonder where the boys without the *kippot* are!" Certainly we have noticed the presence of young religious Jews in the pictures that appeared in the press, and in the rally in Washington, D.C. We have always known of the greatness of Torah; rarely have we had this God-given opportunity to observe the graciousness of Torah! What a *kiddush Hashem!*

The second of the threefold blessing reads "*ya'er Hashem panav elekha,* may the Lord cause His countenance to shine upon you, *ve-hunekha,* and be gracious unto you" (Numbers 6:25). Our tradition saw in the blessing of God's bright countenance a reference to Torah, for *torah ore,* the Torah is considered light. That is why this blessing is interpreted by the Rabbis as *ya'amid mimkha banim bnei torah,* may the Lord give you children who will be students of Torah (*Tanhuma* [Buber], *Naso* 18). On the second half of the blessing, they offer a comment according to which the word *ve-hunekha* should be translated not as "and God will be gracious unto you," but rather as "*yiten hinkha b'einei ha-beriyot,* God will give you the gift of appearing gracious to others!" (*Sifrei, Naso* 41). This indeed is what has happened: Those of our children who deserve the honorific title of *bnei torah* suddenly appeared in a marvelous and wondrous aura of *hen,* of genuine Jewish graciousness and charm. Would that this unusual but thoroughly proper "image" became usual and natural!

The third point is that what Jews could not accomplish, the Arabs did — they united the Jewish people. The sense of purpose and unity was evident to all. Even in Jerusalem, where opinions are sharp and disagreements strong, religious groups of all types were unified. In New York too, with a few painful exceptions, our people were united. A great spirit of fellowship overtook all Jews of all persuasions. Jews who never admitted to being Jewish — neighbors who, according to the custom of this great and faceless metropolis, never greet each other — suddenly smiled at each other with a new and effusive friendship. The blessing of peace, *shalom*, had overtaken our people.

This, indeed, is the third and greatest blessing: "*yisa Hashem panav elekha*, may the Lord turn His face unto you, *ve-yasem lekha shalom*, and grant you the blessing of peace" (Numbers 6:26). Quite appropriately, the *Yalkut* comments that "*gadol ha-shalom she-afilu be-sha'at milhamah tzerikhin le-shalom*, peace is so great that even in time of war it is necessary to have peace!" (*Yalkut Shimoni, Naso* 711). Apparently what the Rabbis meant by this remark is that war should never be absolute, even when it is necessary. There should always be some pacific residue, some irenic core, some opportunity left for establishing peaceful relationships. Even in the course of war, we must find peace.

However, I should like to express a deeply felt hope based upon a paraphrase of this statement of the Rabbis. I would prefer to read it as *gadol ha-shalom she-afilu be-sha'at shalom tzerikhin le-shalom*, now that we have learned to find peace and unity in time of war, may we, in looking ahead, strive for the blessing of peace even during peacetime! May we learn to cherish this fellowship and oneness even when we are not threatened from without. We must make a new start not for superficial uniformity, but in always asserting the underlying oneness of the people of Israel even while disagreeing and arguing with each other.

Furthermore, our hope for *shalom* must apply to the entire Middle East, as the blessing of peace between Israel and the Arab countries, distant though that seems. A victory can be meaningful only if it results in enduring peace. The Hebrew word for "victory," *nitzahon*, derives from the word *netzah*, which means "eternity." Military victory is meaningful only if it is followed by eternal peace or at least harmony for a long, long time. Our current *nitzahon* will not have been complete unless we can look forward to a *netzah*-type peace which will follow.

Of course, if it does not come, we will survive anyway. The Jewish people has changed part of its character these last twenty years. We will no longer submit to enemies in order to satisfy their whims or interests. In the Biblical era, it appears that our people had to fight every forty years for its survival; nowadays, apparently, the cycle comes every ten years. We can do it if we have to. But this is not our choice. We are not, despite our fantastic military successes, a martial people. Our ambition is always that of *shalom*, that of peace for ourselves and for the entire world, and peace and war cannot long coexist.

So we ask Almighty God on this day for His threefold priestly blessing. We ask Him to bless us and *ve-yishmerekha*, to guard us from all those who would injure us, whether the damaging demons growl black as night or smile bright as dawn. We ask of Him that He cause His countenance to shine upon us, by giving us a generation which will be guided by the light of Torah and which will continue to serve as a source for the special Jewish charm of *hen*; for this is the blessing of *vi-yekhuneka*. And above all else, we ask for *ve-yasem lekha shalom*, unity in our own camp, harmony in the Middle East, peace in the world.

We conclude with the same words with which the priestly blessing concludes: "*ve-samu et shemi al benei Yisrael*, and they shall place My name on the Children of Israel, *va-ani avarkhem*, and I shall bless them" (Numbers 6:27). May the Name of God indeed be placed upon Israel, so that our people will become not only champions in war, but, as the very name Yisrael indicates (as it incorporates His Name in its name), we will become the champions of the Lord; and that shall be our greatest blessing: *va-ani avarkhem*.

O Jerusalem!
(June 15, 1967)

Three localities play roles of importance in the festival of Shavuot: Egypt, because every holiday is *zekher le-yitsiat mitzrayim*, in memory of the exodus from Egypt; Sinai, because this festival commemorates the revelation of the Torah on Mount Sinai; and Jerusalem, because, as one of the three major festivals, Jews throughout Israel and throughout the world would perform the *aliyat ha-reggel*, the pilgrimage to Jerusalem, on Shavuot. It is interesting that all three of these places have taken on added significance in our lifetimes.

Egypt was foremost amongst the Arab countries that attacked Israel at its birth in 1948 and which was soundly defeated. Sinai is the desert in which Israel scored great military successes in 1956; indeed, this was repeated last week, and over Mount Sinai there today flies the blue-and-white flag of the State of Israel. And now, in the past week or two, Jerusalem has risen to prominence: Jerusalem is once again in Jewish hands! After 1,897 years, the ancient Holy City has been reclaimed by her loyal children.

Jerusalem is the symbol *par excellence* of the astounding events of these past two weeks, and I propose to discuss them and to attempt to view them in perspective, using Jerusalem as our symbol. In doing so, I ask you not to allow your vision to be blurred by the details of these past weeks, but to strive for an overview, for a broader horizon and wider perspective. All of us have been reading voraciously this past while; now is the time to put aside all that we have read, to forget our political sophistication, our military knowledge, our amateur *Realpolitik*, our ability to follow the labyrinthine diplomatic twists and turns. Today let us try to see the forest and not only the trees. If we do so, we will realize that a revelation has taken place! Before our very eyes there has unfolded a miracle of a very special kind: a true *giluy shekhinah*, revelation of the Presence of God.

How else can one explain the extraordinary events which we have witnessed? The burden of proof is now on the cynics and the agnostics. It is for them to explain what has happened from the point of view of a naturalistic philosophy and a materialistic view of history. I believe that such explanations as may be offered will be as tortured and as incredible as to make the most far-fetched doctrines of faith sound much more realistic. Hard-boiled Israelis, even supposedly nonreligious ones, have understood the religious dimension and significance of these events better than American Jews, even religious ones. Indeed, it had to be so; they were ready to, and did, give their lives, while we gave support.

And, somehow, faith has closer ties to blood than to cash, no matter how plentiful, how abundant, how generous. No wonder that a radio correspondent told us over the airwaves that, though he was never religious and hardly recognized his Jewishness, when he approached the Western Wall, he rubbed his cheek against it in affection and cried uncontrollably. A visitor, recently returned, told me that the day after the capture of the Wall, Jews who had never in their lives made a blessing stayed three hours in the hot sun in order to be able to pray in *tefillin* at the side of the *kotel ha-maʾaravi*. And the press informed us today that yesterday, the first day of Shavuot, tens of thousands of Jews made the pilgrimage to the Wall. Another visitor informed me several days ago that one of the first Jews to enter the *meʾarat ha-makhpelah*, the burial place of the Patriarchs and Matriarchs (with the exception of Rachel), in some eight hundred or nine hundred years, was General Mosheh Dayan. When he entered, he did not know exactly what to do. But instinctively he straightened up, offered a snappy salute, and said "Shalom" to Abraham, Isaac, and Jacob.

Now, this places a great burden upon us, greater than we realize. Even observant religious people usually possess an element of doubt within their faith. We use this doubt to excuse many of our transgressions, and we excuse the existence of this doubt by saying that had we lived in the age of the prophets or the age of miracles or the age of revelation, we would have been sufficiently persuaded and convinced to be able to live according to the highest precepts of our faith, but that the absence of any such evidence justifies this seed of doubt. Were we exposed to the same wonders as was Israel of old, "and Israel saw the Egyptians dead at the shore of the sea," then we too would react as they did: "and they believed in the Lord and in His servant Moses" (Exodus 14:31).

Such was the justification we offered ourselves for our doubt and our laxity heretofore. Now, we can no longer avail ourselves of that luxury. For we have seen, as did Jews in very special moments of history, *ha-yad ha-gedolah*, the great Hand of the Almighty! Through electronic eyes and ears, each of us has been a personal witness to the great miracle, the great revelation of 1967. How our parents and grandparents and theirs before them, through all the ages, would have thrilled to this singular experience — not only because of the victory that would have given them relief from the humiliation of exile, but because the liberation of Jerusalem in our times is a vindication of their faith throughout all times.

For centuries, they had to put up with an arrogant Christian church that promulgated a cruel doctrine known as "triumphalism," which declares that Christianity must be true because it has triumphed in the world, a church that condemned the Jew as a stiff-necked and obstinate deicide whose sufferings were the result of his refusal to acknowledge the truth of Christianity. The Jew, in an environment of this kind, nevertheless believed — sometimes against his own senses; it was a faith that was often irrational, sometimes even absurd — yet the Jew believed and hoped for the day that his faith would be vindicated against his oppressors, against history itself. That has now come to pass in our time! For indeed the *giluy shekhinah* of the past two weeks is a vindication of ancient promises, the fulfillment of hoary prophecies.

Read carefully all of Isaiah from chapter 40 and on, especially chapter 52. Ponder the words of Zechariah, chapter 8 — and you will see how the past two weeks have fulfilled these old promises.

Just as an example, take the following verses from Isaiah, chapter 52, which for over 2,500 years was just one chapter from the ancient prophetic books — it had not even attained the status and dignity of a Haftorah!

"Awake, awake, show your strength, O Zion;

Put on your beautiful garments, O Jerusalem, the Holy City;

For henceforth there shall no more come into thee the uncircumcised and the unclean" (Isaiah 52:1) — neither Christian nor Moslem can lay claim to Jerusalem, for it is now altogether Jewish, and so it shall remain.

"Shake thyself from the dust; arise and sit down, O Jerusalem; loosen yourself from the chains of your neck, O captive daughter of Zion" (ibid. 2).

"Therefore My people shall know My name; Therefore they shall know in that day that I, even He that spoke" — to Abraham, the promise of redemption — "Behold, here I am. How beautiful upon the mountains are the feet of the messenger of good tidings that announces peace, the harbinger of good tidings that announces salvation; that says to Zion: Your God reigns! Hark, your watchmen" — the prophets of old — "lift up their voice, and together" — with us — "do they sing! For they shall see" — through the centuries — "eye to eye, the Lord returning to Zion. Break forth into joy; sing together, ye waste places of Jerusalem; for the Lord has comforted His people, He has redeemed Jerusalem, The Lord has bared His holy arm" — His might — "in the eyes of all the nations; and all the ends of the earth shall see the salvation of our God" (ibid. 6–10).

"Behold, My servant" — Israel — "shall prosper, He shall be exalted and lifted up, and shall be very high" (ibid. 13). "So shall He startle many nations, kings shall shut their mouths" — in amazement — "because of Him; for that which has not been told them shall they see, and that which they have not heard shall they perceive" (ibid. 15).

"Who would have believed our report? And to whom hath the arm of the Lord been so revealed?" (ibid. 53:1).

"Thus says the Lord: I return unto Zion and will dwell in the midst of Jerusalem; and Jerusalem shall be called the city of truth; and the mountain of the Lord of Hosts the holy mountain. Thus says the Lord of Hosts: There shall yet sit in the broad places of Jerusalem old men and old women. Every man with a staff in his hand for very age. And the broad places of the city shall be full of boys and girls playing therein" (Zechariah 8:3–4).

"Thus says the Lord of Hosts: Behold, I will save My people from the east country and from the west country; and I will bring them, and they shall dwell in the midst of Jerusalem; and they shall be My people, and I will be their God in truth and in righteousness" (ibid. 7).

How wonderfully real and contemporary these words of the ancient prophets sound today! No wonder that upon reading the words of prophecy we make the blessing *ve-davar ehad mi-devarekha ahor lo yashuv rekam,* a rather strangely constructed phrase. It means, as a great sage explained (Rabbi Yehiel Michel Epstein, *Arukh ha-Shulkan*), that not one single word of what was said by the prophets in the past, the *ahor* shall be insignificant for us today, shall return to modern times *rekam,* empty. Instead, every word comes to us from the past full and pregnant with meaning for the present. Indeed, what happened last week has suddenly made new order and new sense out of all the past. The might of the Lord God of Israel has been revealed to us. He has kept His word to us!

How tragically near-sighted and picayune it would be for us to fail to appreciate the larger religious dimensions of these current events. How enormously foolish to see in this Jewish victory nothing more than the brilliant strategy of a Dayan, the wise diplomacy of an Eban, the arrogance of a Nasser, or the cowardice of the Arab soldier. No doubt, these are important elements; but to see only these is to miss the heart of the issue. It is tantamount to explaining love in terms of physiology — heartbeat, pulse rate, breathlessness. It is like a man who describes Einstein's theory of relativity as a matter of his penmanship and handwriting. It makes no more sense than describing the revelation at Mount Sinai by explaining what caused the lightning and the thunder, reducing all of Sinai to a question of atmospheric conditions.

We must be wiser than that, although we are too close to the incident to see it in full perspective. We must appreciate that the God Who revealed Himself to our ancestors at Sinai has now revealed Himself to us in Jerusalem. Indeed, while the revelation at Sinai is always paramount in Jewish life and history, there is one way in which the *giluy shekhinah* of last week has a special significance for us: Whereas at Sinai the lightning and thunder were provided by God, this revelation took place amidst the lightning and thunder provided by the Jews who sped like lightning through the skies and thundered with their tanks and guns through the desert. The difference between Sinai of then and Jerusalem of today is that then God came down on Mount Sinai — "And the Lord descended on Mount Sinai" (Exodus 19:20), whereas in Jerusalem God ascended, and indeed it was Israel that raised its God on high by the power of its faith and its arms, its heart and its blood.

So did our Sages teach us: "From the days that the Temple was destroyed, the Holy One took an oath that He would not go up to the mystical Jerusalem in Heaven until Israel would go up to the Jerusalem on earth" (*Ta'anit* 5a). By the Israeli capture of Jerusalem, we have permitted, as it were, God to rise on high! In this revelation, we were not passive recipients; we went forth toward God and found Him coming toward us.

Is our task done? No, certainly not. Not until the full significance of what has happened has not only been revealed but also understood and digested, not until our eyes and ears and hearts have been opened and our lives and habits radically changed — in a word, not until the Messiah has come. That he has not come is a patent fact. But in our days those who are wise have sensed his approach, those who can hear with the inner ear have heard his footsteps, those who can see with the inner eye have perceived the first rays of his coming. And the Jewish tradition has taught us that we can, by our conduct and our actions, bring on the Messiah before his appointed time.

About young King David, it was said: "Why has not *ben Yishai*, the son of Jesse, come neither yesterday nor today, *gam temol gam ha-yom*?" (I Samuel 20:27). A famed Hasidic rabbi commented on this that *ben Yishai* refers not only to David but to his descendant the Messiah, who will likewise be known as the son of David and the son of Jesse. The verse is then understood as a question and an answer. Why has not the son of Jesse, the Messiah, come yet? The answer is: *gam temol gam ha-yom,* because our today is no different from our yesterday, because our yesterday was no improvement on the day before it, and because in all likelihood our tomorrow will be no better than our today! It is we who have held up the Messiah because of our pitiful lack of understanding, because of our lack of fortitude in doing something with our lives that will make the coming of the Messiah meaningful.

We are, assuredly, on the threshold of a new era. Our response to this revelation must be immediate and profound. None of us dares remain the same after all this. Whoever succumbs to life as usual, whoever permits his *ha-yom* to be nothing but a repetition of his *temol,* has failed the greatest test in the last twenty centuries.

Let me describe this in terms of Jerusalem, our precious symbol. In the Midrash (*Shir ha-Shirim Rabbah* 7), the Rabbis asked what the Jerusalem of the future will be like. They offered two answers. The first one says, Jerusalem will one day spread out until it reaches the very gates of Damascus. The second one avers that Jerusalem will someday rise until it reaches the Throne of Glory, the place of God.

We have seen the first promise come true last week. Jerusalem today reaches the very gates of Damascus! The troops of Israel, of which Jerusalem is the eternal capital, are in striking distance of the capital of Syria. Now our destiny and our challenge is to make the second prediction come true. Now we must attempt to rise upward, to make Jerusalem climb higher and higher until it reaches the very site of the divine Throne of Glory. We have achieved success in expanding Jerusalem horizontally, and now we must expand it vertically. We have stretched forth right and left, now we must rise high upward and dig deep downward into the soul that God has given us.

On this Shavuot, the festival of the revelation at Sinai, we thank Almighty God for His revelation of Jerusalem, for His deliverance of Zion in our day. Let us dedicate ourselves anew to the completion of the tasks that lie ahead of us. Having stretched outward, let us now reach upward .

God has not forgotten us. He has remembered us and He has remembered Jerusalem.

Let us pray, in the words of our special festival petition: Our God and the God of our fathers, *ya'aleh ve-yavo*, may there rise and appear before You the remembrance of we who have experienced the greatest cataclysm in the history of humanity and who now thankfully have experienced great joy; *u-fikdonenu,* may You remember those who are absent from our midst today because they have fallen in battle in defense of Jerusalem and Zion, young and precious souls, sons and husbands and fathers who will never return from the war in which they gave their lives; Remember on this *Yizkor* day parents and grandparents whom we recall with tenderness, and for whom we rejoice vicariously, in the triumph of Israel; *ve-zikhron Mashiah ben David avdekha*, remember also Your Messiah, for whose coming we hope all the more fervently now that we have heard his approach; remember Jerusalem Your Holy City, and never allow it to depart from us again; *ve-zikhron kol amkha bet Yisrael,* and remember, O God, all Your people the House of Israel; on this day of joy for Israel remember those three million Jews behind the Iron Curtain who are not permitted to express their solidarity with us, and the thousands of Jews in Arab countries who live in fear of life and limb as the vengeance of the enemy is wreaked upon them. Remember all this, O Heavenly Father, on this blessed and happy day of Shavuot. Remember us for good, for life, for blessing, and for eternal salvation. Amen.

America, Bless God

A Thanksgiving Day Sermon
Preached at Congregation Shearith Israel
(The Spanish-Portuguese Synagogue)

I am pleased to occupy a pulpit celebrated both because of its historic past and its present distinguished spiritual leadership in a congregation rightfully famous in our city. I am doubly happy because Shearith Israel is not only an illustrious synagogue, but also a good neighbor of my congregation, The Jewish Center. In this context, I prefer to translate the word *she'arit* of "Shearith Israel" not in its primary signification of "remnant," but rather in its secondary meaning, as in the Biblical words *she'er basar* or *sha'arah* — "relative," or "close friend." For indeed both our congregations are part of the larger family of Orthodox Jewry on the West Side of Manhattan.

The Thanksgiving Day Services at the Spanish-Portuguese Synagogue are not only a fine patriotic gesture as loyal American citizens; they are also an authentic expression of Judaism. The source for this judgment is the Sephardi scholar of the late Middle Ages, Abudrahm. Why is it, he asks, that during the repetition of the *Amidah* by the cantor, the congregation joins him for only one blessing, in the course of which it expresses the same sentiments in modified language? Abudrahm was referring to the *Modim* blessing, for while the cantor chants the *Modim*, the congregation recites, in an undertone, the *Modim de-Rabbanan*. The reason for this, says Abudrahm, is that the other blessings consist of petitions for various benefits: We ask God for wisdom, health, prosperity, peace. Such prayers can be delegated to a representative of the congregation, which the cantor, in effect, is — the *shaliah tzibbur*. But when it comes to offering our thanks to the Almighty — and this is the essence of *Modim* — there, no delegation suffices, for the expression of gratitude is too personal, too intimate, too significant for substitutes.

In the same sense, when our fellow Americans repair each to his own house of worship to offer thanks to our Heavenly Father for the blessings of life, freedom, peace, and bounty which we enjoy in our beloved land, we Jews feel quite naturally obliged to turn to God and, in our own way, to thank Him. No real Jew can hear others say *Modim* and remain silent! The very name "Jew" derives from the expression of gratitude to God. The word derives from "Judea," or from "Judah," the fourth son of Jacob and Leah, who was named thus because *ha-pa'am odeh et Hashem*, "this time I will thank the Lord" (Genesis 29:35).

Yet it is not enough merely to approve of Thanksgiving Day. Judaism has, as well, an original approach to the phenomenon of gratitude that is analytic and profound in nature, and in which there is implicit a remarkable spiritual insight. We err if we imagine that the offering of thanks to God is a kind of religious courtesy, a form of spiritual politeness, of good manners to a good God. Thanks may be the sort of good taste that lubricates the machinery of human relations, but certainly God transcends the limits of cultivation and good breeding. The Merciful One desires the heart; God looks to the depths of a man's soul and is unimpressed by ceremonial compliments. Surely the Lord prefers piety over polish, genuineness over gentility, the broken heart over the soft tongue. Obviously our thanks are not made to flatter God. What then does the Torah tradition mean when it emphasizes the importance of thanking Him?

I believe that the true Jewish conception goes to the existential roots of man himself. It addresses itself to the human situation in all its rawness and starkness, and to the human being in his anguished feelings of solitude, terror, and worthlessness. It tells us that an appreciation of God's greatness must be accompanied and enhanced by an awareness and acknowledgment of our pettiness and inadequacy. True thankfulness is coupled with the knowledge that without God we would have nothing and be nothing. When we contemplate God's greatness and beneficence, we realize our own worthlessness; and when we understand our own pettiness and inferiority, we begin to appreciate the divine perfection and the majesty of His loving-kindness. That is why we bow at the *Modim* prayer — in thanking Him for His goodness, we declare our own insufficiency.

The Hebrew language itself reveals this insight. The word *hodayah* means two things: thankfulness — and a confession of guilt. In line with this double meaning, one can give two parallel interpretations to the *Modeh Ani* prayer that we recite every morning. One is the usual translation, in which *modeh* is rendered as "I thank." "I thank Thee, O King, who lives and endures, who has mercifully restored my soul unto me; great is Your faithfulness." The other would follow the second meaning of the word, thus: "I confess, or acknowledge, that as a human being I have no real sovereignty, I am mortal and frail; I keep myself alive only with the greatest difficulty, and often find myself sorely lacking in mercy and compassion; small is my faithfulness."

When man sleeps he is unconscious, close to death, defenseless, prey to the terrors of the night and disease that stalks unseen, a potential victim of nature's cruel whims. *Modeh ani!* In the special prayer of thanksgiving that we are obligated to recite upon deliverance from certain specific occasions of danger, the *Birkhat ha-Gomel*, we explicitly mention this same idea. We thank God *ha-gomel la-hayyavim tovot*, who bestows kindness upon the undeserving. God is good, we are undeserving: both elements are merged in one blessing. Here lies the true significance of thanksgiving in Judaism: the contrast between divine infinity and human finitude; between God's eternity and our transience; His endless might and our helplessness; His all-encompassing wisdom and our pervasive ignorance.

Our gratitude is deepened when we face the fact that we are *hayyavim*, undeserving. For this reason, we American Jews are in a unique position to offer meaningful thanks to the Almighty.

Our *hodayah* consists of both the elements we mentioned. For it has already been pointed out that the Holocaust in Europe has left deep wounds on the collective psyche of American Jewry. We think of the precious individuals, families, and whole communities that perished in the flames that engulfed one-third of our people. What marvelous Jews, what sterling human beings they were! Can we in all honesty say that we are in any way superior to them? Yet, if not, why are we alive and they not? We know ourselves and we knew them. And we know that they were not deserving of their bitter fate, and that we are not deserving of any better destiny than they. It is a feeling of perplexity and also inner worthlessness, a knowledge of being undeserving of being saved, that informs our state of mind. We know that, comparatively, we are *hayyavim* — and therefore how much more grateful ought we to be to Almighty God for having spared us and our families!

So our thanks to our Father in Heaven for this beloved haven called America stem from a unique historical experience and the cumulative vicissitudes of centuries. The distinguishing moral failure of the contemporary world, Jews no less than others, is that we have forgotten both elements: that God is *gomel tovot* and ought to be thanked, and that we humans are *hayyavim*. As a matter of fact, we have all but forgotten Him completely. Modern man contemplates his felicity, his abundance, his surpluses, and he thanks anyone but God except in his speech, and that is but a verbal vestige of ages past. He thanks his stockbroker, labor union, government, the UN, his own shrewdness or luck, or science and medicine, or mankind as such.

And here, speaking as an Ashkenazi rabbi to a Sephardi congregation, is an area where all Jews can benefit from the Sephardi historical experience, Let me explain by referring to a law codified in the *Shulhan Arukh* (*Orah Hayyim* 219). We mentioned before the special thanksgiving prayer, the *Birkhat ha-Gomel*. One of the four occasions when this prayer is mandatory is after one has safely crossed the *midbar*, the desert or wilderness. Here the author of the *Shulhan Arukh* notes a divergence between

Ashkenazi and Sephardi practice: In Germany (Ashkenaz) and France, he writes, the practice is not to recite the blessing when journeying from city to city, for it was intended only for those who travel in the desert, which is frequented by *hayyot ra'ot*, wild beasts, and *listim*, bandits. However, in Spain (Sepharad) the custom is that we do recite the blessing, because all the highways are presumed to be dangerous.

No doubt historians will find good historical reasons for this difference in religious practice. Probably intercity traffic in Spain was far more dangerous than in Germany and France, where highway robbery was less frequent. Yet there is more than a sociological difference between them. The commentators see a halakhic principle in issue. And even more the difference in approach has a larger significance; it is a parable for modern men. For modernity was born in Ashkenaz, in Germany and in France, The whole modern cast of mind, the contemporary celebration of human might and ingenuity and independence from God, the age of humanism — these were sired by the French Revolution and German Enlightenment. Here there took place the collective apotheosis of man, and the dethronement of God. And all too many of us Jews went along with the tide. We hailed the Encyclopedists as our prophets, Goethe as our psalmist, and Marx as our messiah. We all but cried out, "Science is my shepherd, I shall not want ..." We deluded ourselves with that nineteenth-century tranquilizer called "progress." We thought we had conquered the *midbar* and had substituted for it the city, symbol of human achievement. Our journey was from city to city, from one level of culture and civilization to another yet higher. We were making "linear progress" and there was nothing or no one who would or could impede us. With the *midbar* of life and the world vanquished, we were confident that we no longer had any reason to fear the "wild beasts" and "bandits" that once afflicted the human race. Universal peace and justice were, after all, just around the corner — thanks to man's new ways and great knowledge.

We forgot the experience of the Sephardi Jews. We should

have learned from them that you can have a Golden Age and great universities and cultural centers, Barcelonas and Toledos and Cordovas — and yet, so short a time afterwards, expulsions, dispersions, and inquisitions! We should have learned this — but we did not. We ignored the fact that where there is no sense of submission and responsibility to a Higher Power, there are can be no occasion for *gomel*, for there are no *tovot*. And where there is no thankfulness to God, where there is no humility, there man becomes ruthless, he turns into bandits, and all of society abounds in wild beasts.

We of the twentieth century thought that all the world was one "city," one giant, united, cultural human unit. Then suddenly, and to our dismay, we learned that it was really only a *midbar*, a desert, and that the vision of a civilized city was just another mirage in the wide, terrifying desert. We discovered that we were prey to the wild beasts of Hitler and Mussolini, and that decent men and women were being victimized by the international bandits operating out of the Kremlin and Cairo. Oh, how we looked for new ways, new *derakhim*! We tried the "scientific way of life" — and discovered not only penicillin and radio, but also nuclear bombs, fallout, and leukemia. We thought nationalism was the best way and learned that with independence can come new tyrannies undreamed of, and terror more fierce than ever imagined. We tried the way of humanism and found that the ringing declarations soon hung like limp clichés, leaving our youth rootless, psychologically unstable, devoid of ideals or enthusiasm, interested in nothing but themselves — and these selves were morally diminutive.

Kol ha-derakhim be-hezkat sakkanah, as our Sephardi scholars taught: Where there is no Godliness, where man arrogantly asserts his absolute independence, all ways are corrupt and dangerous. Where man fails to acknowledge that he is of the *hayyavim*, where he maintains that he is guiltless and master of his own destiny and need not thank the divine *gomel tovot*, his ways wind through wilderness and wasteland, and he is at the mercy of the bandits and the wild animals. What we learn, therefore, is a marvelous paradox: When man begins with self-assertion and self-confidence, he ends with self-destruction and annihilation; when he begins with self-abnegation and distrust, he ends with a ringing self-affirmation and ennoblement.

It is this thoroughly Jewish idea — the dual nature of *hodayah* and the inexorable failure and mortal danger of human ways without God that should be our specific Jewish contribution to the American experience of Thanksgiving. It is for this reason that, to my mind, Thanksgiving Day is so much more precious than other national holidays. Other patriotic occasions, such as Independence Day, valuable though they are, can easily degenerate into national self-idolatry and collective self-glorification. In order to reestablish the proper harmony we need the kind of corrective of humility inspired by Thanksgiving Day. For if July 4th is Independence Day, then Thanksgiving is our Dependence Day — our dependence upon the Almighty. Let this, then, be our prayer: Almighty God, as we rely upon Thy guidance, recognizing our unutterable debt to Thee as *hayyavim*. You lead us out of the *midbar*, spare us from the *listim* who would unleash unspeakable terror upon all men, and from the *hayyot ra'ot* that lurk unpredictably in the hearts of each of us. May all our *derakhim* (ways) be safe from *sakkanah* (danger), and may they all lead to a greater and better future for all of us, all America, and all mankind.

For all this we thank You, O Lord. And even as during the rest of the year we pray "God, bless America," today we turn to our own hearts and to the soul of our country and declare, "America, bless God."

ABOUT THE EDITOR

The commentary for this book, and the additional *derashot*, were compiled and edited by Dr. Joel B. Wolowelsky, Dean of the Faculty at the Yeshivah of Flatbush. He is associate editor of Tradition and the series MeOtzar HoRav: Selected Writings of Rabbi Joseph B. Soloveitchik. He is a member of the steering committee of the Orthodox Forum and serves as a member of various professional advisory boards, including the Bar Ilan University Lookstein Center for Jewish Education in the Diaspora, the Boston Initiative for Excellence in Jewish Day Schools, the Pardes Educators Program in Jerusalem, and Atid: the Academy for Torah Initiatives and Directions.